MYSTERY READER'S WALKING GUIDE

LONDON

MYSTERY READER'S WALKING GUIDE

LONDON

SECOND EDITION

Barbara Sloan Hendershott
Alzina Stone Dale

Printed on recyclable paper

PASSPORT BOOKS
a division of *NTC Publishing Group*
Lincolnwood, Illinois USA

Library of Congress Cataloging-in-Publication Data

Dale, Alzina Stone, 1931–
Mystery reader's walking guide, London / Alzina Stone Dale, Barbara Sloan Hendershott ; maps by John Babcock and Leslie Zunkel. -- 2nd ed.
p. cm.
Includes bibliographical references and index.
ISBN 0-8442-9610-4
1. Literary landmarks--England--London--Guidebooks. 2. Detective and mystery stories, English--Miscellanea. 3. Walking--England--London--Guidebooks. 4. London (England)--Guidebooks. I. Hendershott, Barbara Sloan. II. Title.
PR110.L6D35 1995
823'.08720932421--dc20 95-39926
CIP

Published by Passport Books, a division of NTC Publishing Group,
4255 West Touhy Avenue, Lincolnwood (Chicago), Illinois 60646-1975 U.S.A.

Manufactured in the United States of America.

5 6 7 8 9 ML 0 9 8 7 6 5 4 3 2 1

Dedication

To the memory of my good friend and fellow traveler, Genevieve Carroll White, 1928–1994.

—B.S.H.

To Ron and Chuck, who have cheerfully assisted us in any way they could, from reading mysteries and manuscripts to seeking out and marking maps, to supplying quantities of much-needed computer expertise. They also accepted gracefully our mental and physical absence while the book was being written.

—A.S.D.

CONTENTS

Maps

Preface

Cities, like all living things, change. London is no exception to this rule. Since the 1985 writing of the first *Mystery Reader's Walking Guide: London*, that city has seen many changes. Piccadilly Circus, which then was in the throes of a major retooling, has emerged functional but irrevocably altered. New buildings have gone up; others have come down. A terrorist bomb has reshaped a small section of the city. Pubs and restaurants have opened and closed.

On the mystery scene, new books have been written, new writers have been launched. The tone and tenor of the times have changed as well. Margaret Thatcher is no longer prime minister, and the fairy tale romances of Charles and Diana and Andrew and Sarah have failed. And we, writers and readers alike, have changed as well.

Keeping all changes that have occurred in mind, it seems fitting that the original guide be revised, updated, and expanded.

Two new walks, one in fashionably trendy Chelsea and the other in the northern "country" villages of Hampstead and Highgate, as well as additional books, have been added to the revised guide.

It would be neither practical nor desirable to attempt to include all or even most of the tales of crime and detection set in London. Following the tradition established in the first edition, the books selected as additions to the second edition are a random, eclectic assortment of crime and mystery fiction that is available on both sides of the Atlantic.

BSH
Elmhurst, Illinois

Acknowledgments

My most profound thanks to everyone who assisted me with the revision of this guide—from the stalwart staff of the Elmhurst Public Library, who never found a request too difficult or too trivial, to my good friends Susan Crowell and Bobi Shields who undertook the walking of walks to make certain everything worked. Special thanks to Mark Burlingame for the loan of *Those Who Hunt the Night*, until I was able to find my own copy; and to Marion McKinney who introduced me to Jack M. Bickham. Thank you to my partner in crime, Alzina Stone Dale, for her suggestions and counsel, and to Anne Perry, Catherine Aird, and Harry Keating for their assistance. Thanks also to Leslie and Dianne Zunkel, first for their friendship, then to Les for his maps of Chelsea and Hampstead/Highgate, and to Dianne for her proofreading skills. Last of all, my thanks to my family—Julia and Paul, Phil, Peach, and Emily, my sisters Donna and Nancy, and most especially, my husband Ronald. Each has given me more than I can ever return.

Acknowledgments from the First Edition

Most authors say their book could not have been written without the aid and comfort of many people, but in our case it is a literal truth. Fortunately for us, devoted detective story readers lurk everywhere, eager to share their special knowledge with others of like mind. Out of many well-wishers, the following people deserve our special thanks. None of them is responsible for our slips and blunders; all of them may take credit for the book as it stands, for they are its mystery godparents.

We would like to thank: Connie Fletcher and Barbara Medcalf for encouraging us to seek publication based on the initial idea; Les Zunkel, Ruth Howell, and Martha Mead for their book suggestions; Mary McDermott Shideler for loaning us her copy of John Buchan's *The Three Hostages*; Julia and Paul Haynie, Carroll and Jack White, and Joyce (Hickey) Fornek for encouragement and support; Martin Fornek for our photograph; Elizabeth Dale for the loan of her Catherine Aird mysteries; Kenneth Dale for dog-sitting; and Phil Hendershott for doing whatever was asked.

Mary Sue Brown and the Adult Services Staff of the Elmhurst Public Library, Mary Goulding of the Suburban Library System, Betty Boyd and Donna Scullion of the York High School Library, Marilyn Roth of the Bridgman Public Library, the entire staff of the Wade Collection (Wheaton College), and the salespeople at Fifty-Seventh Street Books (Chicago) for all their help in finding the facts and books we needed.

Ann Rosenblum Karnovsky, Catherine Kenney, and Lenore Melzer for checking out special London restaurants and hotels for us. Damaris Hendry Day, Sarah Duncan, and Harriet Rylaarsdam for reading the walks in manuscript, and Mindy Ries for her help in indexing.

Two very special helpers were Peter ffrench-Hodges of the British Tourist Authority, who encouraged us and vetted the manuscript as well, and Dr. Margaret Nickson of the British Library, who gave us a special tour behind the scenes.

Among the societies important in the mystery world, the Midwest Chapter of Mystery Writers of America, to which we both belong, provided ongoing support and enthusiasm, as well as introductions to writers at home and abroad. The Chesterton Society provided assistance through the heroic efforts of its chairman Aidan Mackey and his wife Dorene, who checked and rechecked our manuscript, even calling up the Old Bailey. The Dorothy L. Sayers Historical and Literary Society, as always, provided splendid authoritative assistance on a wide variety of details. We owe particular thanks to Chairman Ralph Clarke, who wrote the Society's Sayers Walks which he allowed us to use. The many entertaining *Sidelights on Sayer* by Philip Scowcroft gave us essential clues, while Philip Scowcroft also vetted the entire manuscript for us over one weekend! The former Ruler of the Detection Club, Julian Symons, encouraged us and supplied information on his own mysteries, as did the present Ruler, H. R. F. Keating. Lady Antonia Fraser, then Chairman of the British Crime Writers Association, also provided us with useful information on the real locales of her mysteries and cordial invitations to attend Crime Writers Association meetings of which we availed ourselves.

In London and by correspondence, we have had the fun of becoming acquainted with a number of our favorite writers and have hopes of meeting many more as we work on the succeeding guides. Among those who helped with this particular project were Catherine Aird, Marian Babson, Simon Brett, Amanda Cross, P. D. James, Jessica Mann, Anne Perry, Ellis Peters, and Ian Stuart. We also want to express our gratitude and affection to Robin Rue, our agent, who believed in the idea and sold it for us, and to the people at Passport Books, especially Michael Ross, our editor. Our cover artist and cartographer, John Babcock, also deserves a vote of thanks for the enthusiasm with which he did a great deal of time-consuming work, as does his wife who tracked the walks through the manuscript for him—and us.

We look forward to continuing to fill what seems to be a delightful void in the mystery-travel genre by creating more guides with the help of these devoted Dr. Watsons.

INTRODUCTION

Introduction to the First Edition

London, one of the world's greatest cities, is the center of the thriving English mystery world. Beginning with Charles Dickens and Wilkie Collins, who lived and worked in London, and including Edgar Allan Poe, who attended school there, nearly every mystery writer worth his or her salt has set at least one tale against a London backdrop. Even so American a writer as Robert Parker, in his *The Judas Goat*, took Spenser across the Atlantic to pursue his quarry in London. Because of the richness and of its mystery associations, modern London is a mystery reader's mecca, filled with the real sights and sounds that give the stories their authentic atmosphere.

In the author's note to *Wobble to Death*, Peter Lovesey states that his "characters . . . are fictitious, but the setting is authentic;" this combination is repeated in the works of the many other mystery writers. As a result, turn any London corner, and you will encounter the scene of a fictional crime or discover a haunt of a favorite detective or his creator.

London has always been a tourist's delight, a sprawling metropolis encompassing over 800 square miles; a key is needed to unlock its myriad streets and avenues, passageways and alleys. Many excellent guides have been written for just this purpose. Some focus on specialized areas, such as architecture, history, or literature, but if you want to hunt down the locale of a detective story, you will find these guides deficient. With the exception of the likes of Wilkie Collins, Sir Arthur Conan Doyle, and G. K. Chesterton, little is said about the mystery writers, let alone their detectives. When the author of a detective story is mentioned, he or she is lumped with such writers as Geoffrey Chaucer, Samuel Johnson, and John Donne.

Faced with the knowledge that none of the existing guidebooks provide a mystery reader with a way to see London through the eyes of such characters as Philip Trent, Lady Molly, or Lord Peter Wimsey, we decided to write for ourselves, based on our favorite mystery writers and their works, the guide we would like to be using.

We determined that the guide must be a walking guide, because everyone seems to agree that the only way to see London is on foot. Despite the excellence of public transportation and the availability of taxis, the London we sought was a London available only to those free to duck into a passageway, cut across a square, or poke into a cul-de-sac while chasing an elusive sleuth.

The first thing we had to decide was which books to use for the guide. Our choice had to be personal because the number of mysteries that take place in London runs into the thousands. Our ambition was not to produce an encyclopedia of crime or even a handsome coffee table tome. We wanted something readable, a toteable book that could guide and entertain both our armchair readers and our London walkers.

So, we each sat down and made a list of our favorite authors, being careful to mix types, periods, and sexes. Then we compared lists and kept the names that appeared on both. Next, we consulted such major classics on the detective story as Steinbrunner and Penzler's *The Encyclopedia of Mystery and Detection* and Julian Symons's *Mortal Consequences* to make sure that we had examples from all the tried-and-true mystery types. The resulting list included everything from apple-cheeked spinsters to superspies and ran the gamut from Patricia Wentworth's Miss Silver to Antonia Fraser's Jemima Shore and John Buchan's Richard Hannay. We covered a group of writers who would appeal to an audience of varied reading tastes and, at the same time, satisfy our own.

In planning the guide, we have not followed the established custom of dividing the book into sections on food, shopping, entertainment, museums, and sights. Rather, we divided London geographically into its historic neighborhoods, like Bloomsbury and Soho. Then we cross-indexed our authors (more than forty of them), detectives, and books (over one hundred of them), pulled out the geographic sites mentioned by or in each, and remixed them into these walking tours.

Each of the walks represents a neighborhood. There is a paragraph or two of introductory material about the area of the walk, followed by a list of general points of interest, including all "must-see" spots listed by the British Tourist Authority. Whenever possible, our restaurant suggestions are connected with one of the detective stories.

The walks are area oriented rather than book or author oriented. If you want to follow a particular character or writer or want to know more about an unfamiliar one, look him or her up in the index. A map is included with each walk to make routes following easier.

The starting and ending point for each walk is an underground, or "tube," station. We elected to use the tube because it is quick, efficient, and inexpensive. There are ten principal lines and 275 stations. In addition, many tube stations have lavatory facilities. In case a particular walk becomes too long or your time becomes too short, we have pointed out other tube stations conveniently located on the walk.

We have included many references to points of interest that do not fall into the natural range of the mystery walk but may nevertheless be of interest to the reader. The number of these spots you include in each walk will determine how long the walk will take. If, for example, you choose to go inside the National Portrait Gallery or Westminster Abbey, your walk will take you much longer. The walks are, on the average, about 3.5 miles long.

In preparing the guide, we made a number of discoveries about the authors and their stories. For instance, while each of the writers makes it plain that his or her story takes place in London, just where in London is not always clear. Dick Francis, for example, has his merchant banker Tim Ekaterin work in a new building with a view of St. Paul's "in the City." It might be on

Gresham Street, Old Jewry, or Milk Street—where, north of the cathedral, the bombs of World War II laid waste. Agatha Christie often gives a street address that sounds right but is totally fictitious and then has her characters—Tommy and Tuppence, for instance—eat at a Lyons Corner shop or have tea at the Ritz. On the other hand, she sometimes refers to the Ritz as the Blitz or combines two hotels into one, as is the case with the Ritz-Carlton and Bertram's. On such occasions, since we are walking a real city, we will take you to the Ritz. In still a different way, Margery Allingham, world-famous for her evocative descriptions of London, invents squares and cul-de-sacs, locating them around the corner from real places. In *Black Plumes*, when David Field takes Frances Ivory from Sallet Square to the Cafe Royal for a sundae and walks her to Westminster Bridge by night, we are dealing with the imagined, as well as the real. The railway station in *Tiger in the Smoke* is probably Paddington, but a case can be made for its being Euston or Victoria or even Charing Cross!

We also discovered that many of the writers provided clues in their books to the sections of London in which they lived or had lived or of which they are particularly fond. Dame Ngaio Marsh, for example, had nearly all her characters live and several of her murders take place in Belgravia, near the Brompton Oratory. This is where she always stayed in London and where she and the "real" Charlot Lamprey ran gift shops before the war. Georgette Heyer's first flat after she married was in Earls Court, where her young, ex-convict social secretary, Beulah Birtley, lived in *Duplicate Death*. Dorothy L. Sayers lived and worked in Bloomsbury, as does Harriet Vane, while Jemima Shore lives near Holland Park, as does Lady Antonia Fraser.

We made a number of discoveries that delighted us. While pursuing Graham Greene's colonel in *The Human Factor*, we found Greene's own flat in tiny Pickering Place hidden behind a St. James's Street vitner. Chasing down P. D. James's well-educated Philippa Palfrey, we came upon the Courtauld Institute Galleries, with its magnificent Impressionist collection. Thanks to Agatha Christie, we had tea at the Ritz; we lunched in a pub in Shepherd Market, that maze of old lanes behind rich and modern Park Lane; and we stood on tiptoe to peek in the window of all that remains of bombed-out St. Anne's Soho to see where Dorothy Sayers's ashes are buried. Coming out of Carlton House Terrace, where Christie's Sir James Peel Edgerton lived, we were fascinated to discover the tiny gravestone marking the burial place of a dog that belonged to the German ambassador in 1934.

We hope you will use this guide to tour all of central London, beginning with the oldest part, the City, whose narrow streets still remind us of the medieval days of mysterious Richard III. Then move westward into legal London, reminiscent of Charles Dickens and today's Rumpole of the Bailey. Follow along into "intellectual" Bloomsbury, the foreign restaurants of Soho, and the spacious parks and squares of the true West End.

The time of day you elect to walk will be important. For instance, pub hours are 11:30 A.M. to 3:00 P.M. and 5:30 P.M. to 11:00 P.M. (except in the City, where morning hours do not begin until 11:30 A.M. and in Covent Garden, where they reflect the early hours of the market days). Your feelings about crowds, your shopping plans, and the number of museums that you wish to visit with all affect the time that you set out. (Before 8:30 A.M., London is uncrowded, and walking just about anywhere is a joy.)

If a complete tour is not your aim, use the index of persons, places, and books to chart your tour.

The large map of central London shows you how the geographical sections of London lie in relation to each other, and the sectional maps show the route of each walk, as well as the neighborhood's principal streets and sights.

Our aim has been to give you a guide that is workable, whether you stay at home or sally forth armed with umbrella, camera, and guidebook to track down your favorites for yourselves. For, as G. K. Chesterton, one of the grand masters of detection, said in his "In Defence of Detective Stories," "Modern man has a great need for romance and adventure, which, paradoxically, he can find just around the corner in any ordinary London Street." Or, as Sherlock Holmes observed and we echo, "It is a hobby of mine to have an exact knowledge of London."

1

CITY WALK

BACKGROUND

The first walk begins in the oldest part of London: the square mile known as the City. Here is the financial center of London and one of the most important commercial square miles in the world. Its boundaries extend from the Temple Bar to Aldgate and from Southwark to City Road.

Although there may have been Bronze and Stone Age settlements on the site, the first date in London's long recorded history is AD 43, marking the arrival of the Romans. That first Roman town was sacked by Queen Boudicca (Boadicea) of the Inceni in AD 60, but it was soon rebuilt with walls and a bridge across the Thames. London grew quickly, becoming one of the largest towns in northern Europe.

Today, there is little left of the old Roman city: a bit of mosaic floor uncovered by war damage in All Hallows-by-the-Tower; a larger bit of mosaic under Bucklersbury; a number of smaller relics that can be seen in the London Museum; and, of course, bits and pieces of the wall, such as those near the Tower of London. Although it is built on the site of the old Roman city of Londinium, today's street plan is that of the more recent medieval city. Traces of that medieval city can be found as well in a few churches and the narrow streets with odd names which have survived. The curious street signs—Crutched Friars, Cheapside, Seething Lane, Milk Street, Fish Street Hill, Bread Street, Shoe Lane—delight visitors to the area.

The approximate position of the Roman and medieval walls can be determined by such names as Moorgate, Aldersgate, Bishopsgate, and Newgate.

Although World War II bombs destroyed nearly a third of the City, traces of what once was can still be hunted out. The surviving City churches and other bits of architecture still hold much interest for the visitor, but sadly the City is changing as the old is forced to give way to the new in the name of modernization and traffic flow.

More than half a million people work in the City, but most leave in a rush at the close of the work day, abandoning the narrow streets, alleyways, Wren churches, and pubs to a tiny resident population of 4,500.

LENGTH OF WALK: 3.8 miles

See the map on pages 4 and 12 for the boundaries of this walk and pages 245–46 for a list of the authors, books, and detectives mentioned.

PLACES OF INTEREST

St. Paul's Cathedral, Ludgate Hill. Admission charge.

Bank of England, Threadneedle Street. Tours by appointment only on alternate Saturdays. Free.

Mansion House, Mansion House Street. Tours by appointment. Free.

The Guildhall, Gresham Street. Free.

Tower of London, Tower Hill. Admission Charge.

- ***The Changing of the Guard on Tower Green.*** Daily at 11:30 AM in summer; alternate days in winter.
- ***The Ceremony of the Keys.*** By appointment only; every evening at 10:00 PM. Free.

Barbican Arts Centre, Aldersgate. London's equivalent to New York's Lincoln Center and Paris's Centre Pompidou. Part of a postwar development; home of the Royal Shakespeare Company. Free.

Museum of London, London Wall. Admission charge.

The Monument, Monument Street. Admission charge.

PLACES TO EAT

Note: Eating places and pubs along this walk are open Monday through Friday during lunch hours only.

Sweetings, 39 Queen Victoria Street. London's first fish restaurant, established in 1830. The atmosphere is Edwardian. 071-248-3062.

Bow Wine Vault, 10 Bow Churchyard. This high-ceilinged bar is popular for salads and cheeses. 071-248-1121.

Ye Olde Watling, 29 Watling Street. An archetypal pub occupies the ground floor and features traditional pub food. Upstairs is an intimate restaurant that serves lunch. 071-248-6235.

CITY WALK

Begin the walk at the St. Paul's Underground Station. In H. R. F. Keating's *Inspector Ghote Hunts the Peacock,* Inspector Ghote of Bombay, India, in London for the first time, was on his way to the Wood Street Police Station. He arrived at St. Paul's Underground Station an hour and twenty-seven minutes early, and, with so much time on his hands, he decided to walk to the Tower. (He reversed the route you will follow.)

Business brought Ghote to the City—that is what brings most people there. For example, Graham Bendiz, the husband of the murdered woman in Anthony Berkeley's *The Poisoned Chocolates Case,* had a business appointment in the City.

Business in the City brought the American millionaire

City Walk

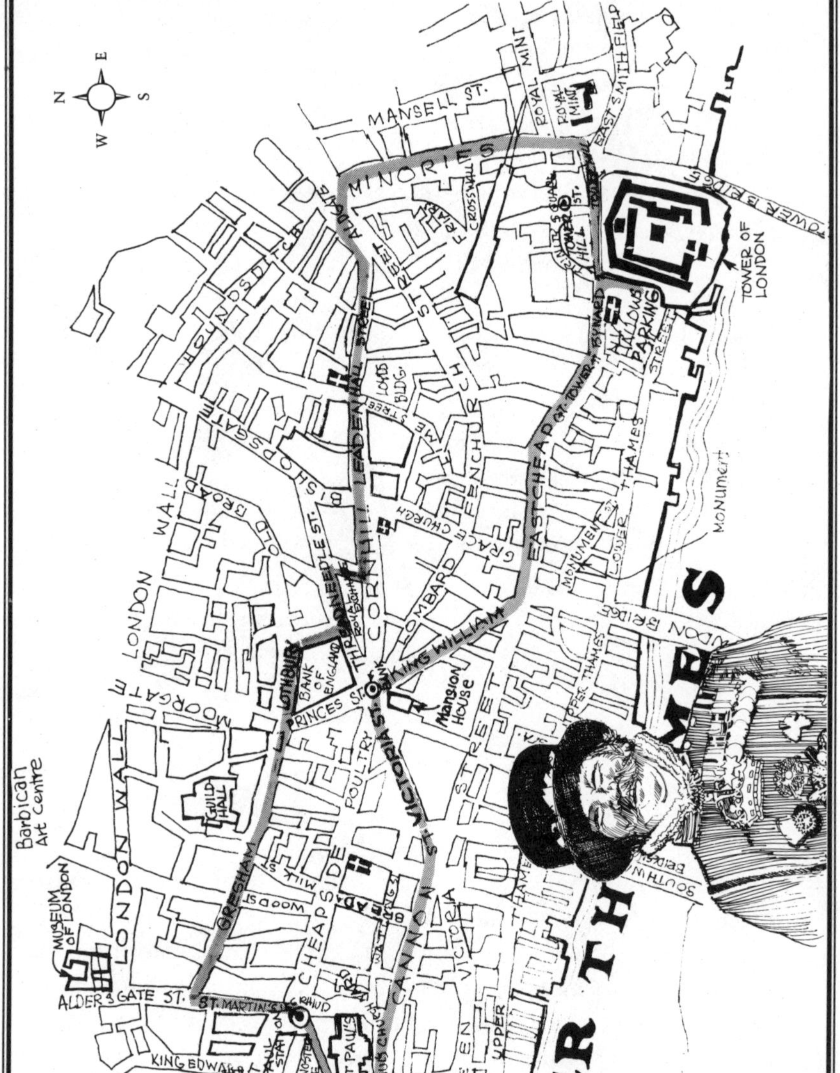

N
E
S
W
Barbican Art Centre
MUSEUM OF LONDON
LONDON WALL
MOORGATE
ALDERSGATE ST.
ST. MARTIN'S
KING EDWARD
NEWGATE ST.
ST. PAUL STATION
PATERNOSTER SQUARE
ST PAUL'S
AMEN COURT
LUDGATE HILL
GRESHAM
CHEAPSIDE
GUILD HALL
LOTHBURY
PRINCES ST.
BANK OF ENGLAND
THREADNEEDLE ST.
POULTRY
BANK
MANSION HOUSE
KING WILLIAM
CORNHILL
LOMBARD
OLD BROAD
BISHOPSGATE
LEADENHALL STREET
LLOYDS BLDG.
FENCHURCH
GRACE CHURCH
EASTCHEAP
ALDGATE
MINORIES
MANSELL ST.
ROYAL MINT
TOWER HILL
TOWER OF LONDON
TOWER BRIDGE
ALL HALLOWS PARKING
MONUMENT
LONDON BRIDGE
CANNON ST.
QUEEN VICTORIA ST.
SOUTHWARK BRIDGE
RIVER THAMES

Rufus Van Aldin to London in *The Mystery of the Blue Train* by Agatha Christie.

In Christie's *The Golden Ball,* when George Dundas quit working for his uncle in the City, he was told that he was not grasping the golden ball of (business) opportunity.

The unpleasant Arnold Vereker, who was found dead in the stocks in Georgette Heyer's *Death in the Stocks,* was a "City man—mining interest" with irregular habits, which meant a series of girlfriends at his riverside cottage.

Detective Inspector C. D. Sloan found it necessary to consult a "City man" for clarification of a matter in a financial dealing in *A Going Concern* by Catherine Aird.

In Mile Ripley's *Angel Touch,* the brokerage firm of Prior, Keen, Baldwin, where Angel's friend Salome worked, was in the City. Angel went undercover there as a building engineer when Salome was accused of insider trading.

Willow King/Cressida Woodruffe also decided to work undercover in her attempt to find the killer of Sarah Allfarthing and exonerate Richard Crescent in Natasha Cooper's *Bloody Roses.* In *A Common Death,* Willow—again in the persona of Cressida Woodruffe—wished that she were more interested in the goings-on of the City or less interested in the lengths to which merchant banker Richard Crescent would go to avoid giving her real information about his work.

Estonia Glassware Company was a front for the conspirators whom Tuppence and Tommy overheard in a Lyon's Corner shop. Tuppence, claiming to be Jane Finn, later showed up at Estonia's City offices and tricked the conspirators out of a £50 advance in Agatha Christie's *The Secret Adversary.*

The City was shaken by the disappearance of Ivor Harbeton of the Harbeton financial empire in Catherine Aird's *In Harm's Way.* There were also financial upheavals when E. C. Bentley's Sigsbee Manderson, a rich American, was killed in *Trent's Last Case,* and when Sir Reuben Levy was murdered in Dorothy L. Sayer's classic tale *Whose Body?*

The City has its own City of London police force. The head office is at 26 Jewry Street. Ray Harrison's Victorian policemen, Detective-Sergeant Bragg and Constable Morton, were part of the City of London force in *Deathwatch*.

In Catherine Aird's *In Harm's Way,* Detective Inspector C. D. Sloan called the City fraud squad to find out about Ivor Harbeton's financial wheelings and dealings.

Leave the underground by the St. Paul's exit and walk southeast along Newgate Street, which becomes Cheapside. Follow the curve to the right into New Change, then turn right again into St. Paul's Churchyard, a curving roadway that flanks the cathedral on the north.

In the middle of the eighteenth century, St. Paul's Churchyard and the surrounding streets were the center of the London book trade. Paternoster Row, which leads off to the right, was an ancient street where strings of prayer beads were made before the Reformation.

In Ngaio Marsh's *A Wreath for Rivera,* Edward Manx wrote highly intellectual theater reviews and the Marquis of Pastern and Baggott wrote a column of advice to the lovelorn for *Harmony,* a monthly magazine located at 5 Materfamilias Lane (Paternoster Row). In 1848, Charlotte and Anne Brontë came to London to see their publisher. They stayed in the Chapter Coffee House, which stood at the entrance of St. Paul's Alley, off St. Paul's Churchyard.

In Mike Ripley's *Angel Touch,* Fitzroy Angel, the jazz-playing, taxi-driving detective left his cab, Armstrong, behind and took a bus to St. Paul's before reporting for his first day of undercover work at Prior, Keen, Baldwin.

St. Paul's Cathedral, which was founded in AD 610, is located on Ludgate Hill; it is the second highest point in the City. The present cathedral is the third on this site. The first burned down in 1087, and its Norman replacement lasted until the Great Fire of 1666. Christopher Wren's masterpiece grew out of the rubble of the fire. An excellent example of English Renaissance architecture, St. Paul's has a Latin cross plan. Its appearance is Neoclassical, although there is much Baroque detailing. The dome is the second largest in the world, after St. Peter's in the Vatican. (Although the dome of St. Paul's appears to be a single structure, it is actually composed of three separate parts: an inner dome, an outer dome, and a central dome.) The bell towers are the cathedral's most Baroque feature. The southwest clock tower houses three old bells. "Great Tom," the hour bell, was recast from Big Ben's predecessor at the Houses of Parliament.

The two scrutineers who had followed Sir John Cranston and Brother Athelstan instructed Athelstan to place a petition in the great statue of Our Lady and the infant Jesus in St. Paul's if he wished to speak with them. The St. Paul's to which they referred was the Norman predecessor of Wren's St. Paul's. *(By Murder's Bright Light* by Paul Harding)

Look to the right down Ludgate Hill from St. Paul's to where Ave Maria Lane is located. There you can find Amen Court. Until World War II, this was the home of Oxford University Press, where Charles Williams worked as an editor. He described his office in the opening chapter of his first mystery, *War in Heaven.* Dorothy L. Sayers would meet him at the Oxford University Press, and they would then go to a nearby wine bar to argue theology.

Turn you attention to St. Paul's Cathedral. Amazingly enough, despite the incessant bombing of the City during World War II and the destruction of the surrounding buildings, St. Paul's survived, a tribute to the efforts of its fire-watching team. Today, the cathedral is an island of classic calm in a sea of skyscrapers.

In Dick Francis's *Banker,* the new glass-and-stone office building of Ekaterin Merchant Bank had a modern fountain on one side, where young Tim Ekaterin found his boss wading one morning. The other side of the building offered a view of the sunlit dome of St. Paul's rising like a "Faberge egg from the white stone lattice of the city."

G. K. Chesterton refers to the cross atop St. Paul's in the title of *The Ball and the Cross.*

Charles Williams, in *All Hallows' Eve,* writes that "the still-lifted cross of St. Paul's" gave hope to Lester, who had died in the crash of a plane on the bank of the Thames, as she scuttled along, sharing an ugly, dwarf body with her friend Evelyn, who had died in the same crash.

Historic associations with St. Paul's are legion. For example, it was at St. Paul's that King John submitted to the Papal Legate and promised to pay tribute to Rome. This is the same King John who later died of a surfeit of lampreys.

Ironically, Frith and Henry (Lamprey) urged Roberta Grey to look at the dome of St. Paul's as they drove past it in Ngaio Marsh's *A Surfeit of Lampreys.*

In Charles Williams's *All Hallows' Eve,* artist Jonathan Drayton had a flat on the top floor of a building near St. Paul's. As one of the official war artists of World War II, he created a painting that showed the light of "co-inherence," or community, of the City, past and present.

If you have time, explore the cathedral, its crypt and towers. St. Paul's is the church of the people of London, just as Westminster Abbey is the church of royalty. It was a departure from tradition when the 1981 wedding of the Prince of Wales and Lady Diana Spencer took place in St. Paul's.

The City is synonymous with Charles Dickens. In the Boz era, however, it was very different from what it is today. Still, many of the place names are the same, and some of the actual places that Dickens knew can still be ferreted out. To find one, turn left to continue on St. Paul's Churchyard and walk around the southern side of the cathedral to Godliman Street; turn right and walk the short distance to Knightrider Street. Here you will find the Horn Tavern, an unspoiled nineteenth-century tavern that was called the Horn Coffee House in the time of jolly Mr. Pickwick, G. K. Chesterton's favorite Dickens character. Return to St. Paul's by walking north along Godliman Street, then go right into Cannon Street.

Walk east along Cannon Street, where Edwards, the cigar-smoking private detective in Julian Symon's *The Blackheath Poisonings,* had a small office.

Continue east along Cannon Street toward the Tower of London. Bread Street (where John Milton was born in 1608) leads off to your left. It was the scene of the sixth in a series of burglaries in Paul Harding's *By Murder's Bright Light.* Cranston and Shawditch made their way through the cold to Bread Street where they stopped "before a tall timber-framed house, well maintained and newly painted." It was the home of Selpot the merchant.

The Mermaid Tavern, where Shakespeare and Ben Jonson met and which Christopher Marlow frequented, was also in Bread Street. It was on this street that bakers would gather to sell their wares.

Sir Thomas More, who was martyred by Henry VIII, was born in a house on Milk Street, farther north, which housed medieval milksellers.

Bread Street runs north into Cheapside, the High Street of the medieval City. Called West Chepe from the Saxon word meaning "to barter," Cheapside was appropriately enough a huge open-air market. The street was also used as the site for great guild pageants, royal tournaments, and other festivities.

As Cranston made his way along Cheapside, he stopped before the stocks where a bagpiper blew shrilly on his pipes, and the petty thieves, their heads and hands locked, took the verbal and physical abuse of passersby. *(By Murder's Bright Light* by Paul Harding)

Continue along Cannon Street past the junction with Bow Lane, once the location of shoemakers' shops. The church of St. Mary-le-Bow stands at the Cheapside end of the lane. The "bows" are the arches upon which the church stands. The bells of St. Mary-le-Bow are the most famous in London. Only those born within the sound of Bow Bells are considered true cockneys.

In the fifteenth century, it was the bells of St. Mary-le-Bow that called Dick Whittington back to the City from Highgate. After his return, Whittington became Lord Mayor four times before his death in 1422.

The bells of St. Mary-le-Bow were shattered in World

War II, but have since been recast. The 217-foot spire is one of Christopher Wren's finest. You may wish to take a side excursion to explore the church.

Brother Athelstan felt self-conscious sitting alone waiting for Sir John to return, so he left the Holy Lamb of God taproom and walked back into Cheapside and into the church of St. Mary-le-Bow where he knelt before the altar and prayed. *(By Murder's Bright Light* by Paul Harding)

Return to Cannon Street, and follow it to the intersection with Queen Victoria Street. Follow Queen Victoria Street to the left to the Mansion House. (On the way, you will pass the temple of the Persian God Mithras, which was uncovered after the area was heavily bombed in World War II.)

The Mansion House stands at the junction of Queen Victoria Street, Poultry, Prince's Street, Threadneedle Street, Lombard Street, Cornhill, and King William Street.

The Mansion House is the official residence of the Lord Mayor of London, who must reside there during his/her one-year term of office. Designed by George Dance the Elder, the Palladian-inspired building was under construction from 1739 until 1753. The Lord Mayor's private apartments are on the top floor. The state rooms, including the ninety-foot-long Egyptian Hall, are elegant examples of eighteenth-century decor.

It was at Mansion House corner that Sir Julian Freke in Dorothy L. Sayers's *Whose Body?* set up the "accidental" meeting with Sir Reuben Levy.

To the left of the Mansion House is Threadneedle Street with its "old lady," the Bank of England. The Bank, founded in 1694, is girded by a massive, blank wall ornamented with mock-Corinthian columns. The wall, which is the work of Sir John Soane, who was appointed architect of the Bank in 1788, gives it the appearance of an elegant penitentiary.

Continuing her commentary despite her frustrations, Kate smiled blandly at Professor Tablor and explained that they were now approaching the "Old Lady of Threadneedle Street," the famous Bank of England. (*Tourists Are for Trapping* by Marion Babson)

Elise Cubitt, in the Sherlock Holmes case of "The Dancing Men," tried to buy off Abe Slaney with £1,000 in Bank of England notes. Plates for counterfeiting Bank of England notes, were found by Sherlock Holmes, and a financial disaster was averted in "The Three Garridebs."

Sax Rohmer's Fu Manchu tried to buy the newly appointed governor of the Bank of England, Sir Bertram Morgan, by offering him Manchu's daughter and a chance to buy gold bullion in *The Trail of Fu Manchu.*

In Mike Ripley's futuristic short mystery "Brotherly Love," jazz-playing detective Fitzroy Maclean Angel worked four nights a week as a meeter and greeter at the Ben Fuji Whiskey and Sushi Bar in Threadneedle Street.

Between Threadneedle Street and Cornhill, across the street from the bank, is the Royal Exchange, with its classical portico. Founded by Thomas Gresham in 1566, the first Royal Exchange was opened for commercial transactions by Elizabeth I, a first step in establishing London's future glory as financial capital of the world. In front of the imposing building stands a statue of the Duke of Wellington. The campanile of the Exchange is topped by an eleven-foot-long golden grasshopper, the crest of Thomas Gresham.

South of the Royal Exchange is Lombard Street, the street of bankers. It was the site of the London office of the Great Milligan railroad and shipping company run by John Milligan. In Dorothy L. Sayers's *Whose Body?* Lord Peter Wimsey visited Milligan there. Wimsey suspected Milligan of having kidnapped Sir Reuben Levy to stop a stock deal.

Mark Culledon, the murder victim in Baroness Orczy's *Lady Molly of Scotland Yard,* had his office in Lombard Street.

In Wilkie Collin's *The Moonstone*, the gem was pledged to a banker in Lombard Street, as well.

In *Odds Against,* Dick Francis located the office run by Bolt, who was helping manipulate shares of race courses, on Charing and King, two fictional streets presumably near Lombard Street. When ex-jockey, now private eye Sid Halley pretended to invest, he met Zanna Martin, Bolt's secretary, and took her to a pub across the road. It was "a warm

THE TOWER OF LONDON

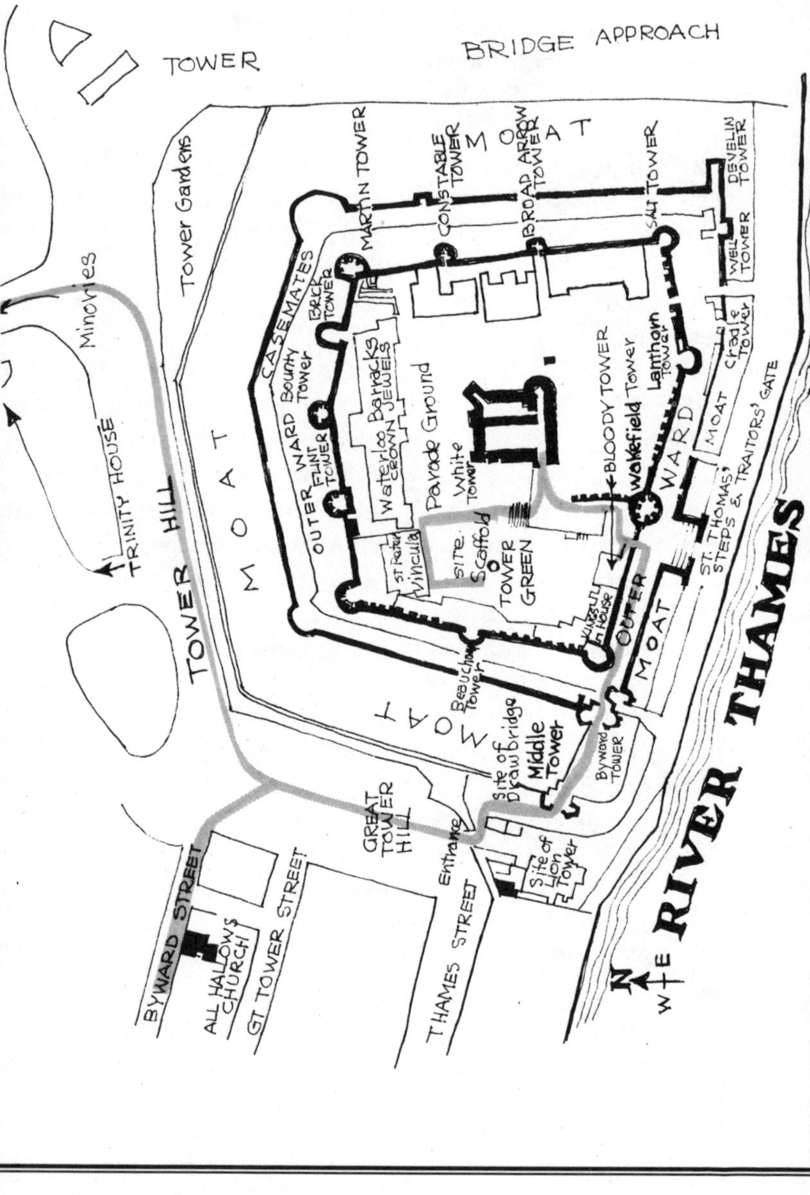

beckoning stop for City gents on their way home." When they left the pub, they walked through the empty City streets toward the Tower and found a quiet little restaurant in which Zanna agreed to have dinner with him. Halley took her home on the underground.

Leave Queen Victoria Street and turn right into King William Street. Follow King William Street to the point where Cannon Street becomes Eastcheap (so named because it was the eastern market in the City). The next point of interest is the Monument, which is located in Monument Street and Fish Street Hill, just beyond this point.

In Natasha Cooper's *Bloody Roses,* Willow King took the Circle line from the Monument tube station back to Sloane Square.

The Monument commemorates the Great London Fire of 1666. The 202-foot-high stone column, designed by Sir Christopher Wren, is the tallest isolated stone column in the world. It is exactly 202 feet from the base of the Monument to the baker's residence in nearby Pudding Lane, where the fire started.

If you feel inclined to climb the 331-step internal spiral staircase to the platform of the Monument, you will find the entrance on Fish Street Hill to the right. The climb is a long one, but the view of London is unequaled.

The walk continues east along Eastcheap, which becomes Great Tower Street and then Byward Street. Before going on to Tower Hill, take time to explore the ancient church of All Hallows-by-the-Tower. (Use the sign posted "pedestrian subways" to cross the streets in this area.)

The first All Hallows was built by the Saxons in the seventh century, but many changes have occurred over time. World War II bombing, which gutted the church, revealed the remains of a wall from the original Saxon church. In the crypt, two Roman tessellated pavements are displayed, along with a detailed model of Roman London. The three Saxon crosses discovered after the Second World War are London's most important Saxon artifacts. The church's most valued possession is its font cover, which was carved by Grinling Gibbons.

In Edgar Wallace's *The Crimson Circle,* St. Agnes on Powder Hill is probably All Hallows-by-the-Tower. It is described as a church that escaped the ravages of the Great Fire of 1666, only to be smothered by the busy city that grew up around it. Entrance to the church was up an alley that led from a side passage. This was the first and only meeting place of all the members of *The Crimson Circle.*

Across the street is the Tower Hill Scaffold Memorial. The chained area marks the location of the scaffold where 125 people were executed between 1347 and 1747. Among them were Sir Thomas More, Thomas Cromwell, and the Duke of Monmouth. The execution site is marked by a stone in the pavement at the west end of Trinity Square gardens.

When you leave All Hallows, you will be on Tower Hill. By following Tower Hill to the left around the north side of the Tower itself, you will come to remnants of the Roman London wall. The wall stands in a sunken garden that marks what was ground level in Roman times.

Because the Tower of London itself takes several hours to explore, you may wish to postpone your visit there for another time. When you do, plan to arrive at the Tower as early as possible, especially in summer, or you will find long lines. (Tour buses tend to begin disgorging their contents around 11:30.)

Characters in crime stories often find their way to the Tower. In H. R. F. Keating's *Inspector Ghote Hunts the Peacock,* Inspector Ghote recognized the Tower immediately. "He had looked at it [the Tower] a thousand times in advertisements, in newspaper articles, on calendars. . . .The grim old building seemed that moment to hold for him in one graspable whole all the past centuries of this noble, sea-girt isle."

In Margaret Yorke's *Cast for Death,* the entreaties of the Greek policeman Manolakis to see the Tower made (don) Patrick Grant admit that he had never been there. "We'll go by boat. . . ," Grant decided. As they approached the Tower, he launched into a fluent description of the young Elizabeth I in the rain, a tale to equal any Greek legend. Grant found himself quite moved as they passed within the huge walls wherein so much pain and tragedy dwelled.

The Tower was originally built within the southeast angle of the City walls, but it was later extended east to cover 18 acres.

The commander of the Tower is an army officer who is called the Constable of the Royal Palace and Fortress of London. His duties are performed by a Major and Resident Governor similar to General Mason in John Dickson Carr's *The Mad Hatter Mystery.*

In Martha Grimes's *The Dirty Duck,* an American tourist, Harry Schoenberg, looked rapturously at Traitor's Gate, the 60-foot watergate from the Thames through which accused traitors, such as Elizabeth I, were brought to the Tower.

The Tower has often served as a backdrop for real intrigue and even murder. The most famous case is that of the "Little Princes"—Edward V and the Duke of York—who were reputedly smothered in the Bloody Tower by order of their uncle, the Duke of Gloucester, later Richard III. Scotland Yard's Allan Grant, hospitalized with time on his hands, investigated this case scientifically. He found many discrepancies in the records and concluded that Richard was not guilty (*The Daughter of Time* by Josephine Tey).

The Tower of London played a central role in John Dickson Carr's classic locked-room tale, *The Mad Hatter Mystery,* about an Edgar Allen Poe manuscript and a prankster who delighted in placing hats in unlikely places. You can explore the Tower by following the action of Carr's plot.

Enter the Tower near the site of the Lion Tower (where the Royal Zoo was kept) and go past the Middle Tower and under the gate of the Byward Tower. This is the way the commandant's secretary, Robert Dalrye, drove General Mason when they returned from Holborn. (General Mason had been attending a luncheon at the Antiquaries Society with Sir Leonard Haldyne, Keeper of the Jewel House.)

Walk along the south side of the Tower in the Outer Ward. To the right are the steps that lead below St. Thomas

Tower to Traitor's Gate. During a dense fog, Phil Driscoll was found here on the areaway steps with a crossbolt in his head. Look down, as Dr. Gideon Fell did; no need to climb to the bottom.

Now head to the left across the Outer Ward to the Wakefield Tower, where Henry VI was murdered in 1471 (by Richard III, according to Thomas More). The Crown Jewels were kept here until they were removed to the Jewel House in Waterloo Barracks. In 1994, the jewels were moved to new quarters, also in Waterloo Barracks.

Because Cromwell either melted down or sold off the original Crown Jewels during the Commonwealth days, the oldest in the collection now is St. Edward's Crown, made for the coronation of Charles II. Of much interest to mystery buffs is the Crown of Queen Elizabeth, made in 1911. It contains the fabulous Koh-i-noor diamond, which was given to Queen Victoria by the Punjabi Army. In Agatha Christie's *The Secret of Chimneys,* Anthony Cade was not impressed to hear that the prime minister of Herzoslovakia knew where the Koh-i-noor was. "We all know that, they keep it in the Tower don't they?"

Across from Wakefield Tower is the Bloody Tower, where the Little Princes are said to have been smothered. It was here that Sir Walter Raleigh spent thirteen years writing *The History of the World* before being executed on Tower Hill by order of King James I.

From Wakefield Tower, you can see the White Tower with its four capped towers. William the Conqueror built it as a fortress. He brought white Caen stone from Normandy to build the walls, which are 12 to 15 feet thick.

The White Tower's Chapel of St. John, the oldest church in London, was the place where Wat Tyler and his peasant mob seized and murdered old Archbishop Sudbury.

The White Tower contains several interesting collections, including one of medieval arms and armor. The murder weapon in Carr's novel purportedly came from this collection.

During the reign of Charles II, bones were found underneath a set of stairs on the south side of the White Tower. These were thought to be those of the Little Princes. They were reverently interred in Westminster Abbey.

In Josephine Tey's *The Daughter of Time,* Inspector Grant sarcastically reflected that history was tainted by the council scene in Shakespeare's *Richard III,* in which Richard denounced his brother's lords as traitors and sent them straight from the White Tower to the block on Tower Green.

In *Watson's Choice,* Gladys Mitchell's redoubtable Dame Beatrice Bradley was amused when, at a Sherlock Holmesian house party given by Sir Bohun, his older nephew refused to wear a black velvet tunic and deep lace collar, declaring that he "wasn't one of the Princes in the Tower."

From the White Tower go left to Tower Green. The Late-Perpendicular Gothic Chapel of St. Peter and Viancula is at the north end and the inner facade of the King's House is at the south. The green is a serene bit of grass, of which the historian Macaulay said there "was no sadder spot on earth." The bodies of a number of Tower victims are buried here under the peaceful green sod.

Only the more illustrious of those executed in the Tower were granted the mercy of a private execution on Tower Green. On a scaffold here—the site is now outlined in granite in the middle of the green—died Anne Boleyn, Lady Jane Grey, Catherine Howard, the Earl of Essex, and others.

In John Dickson Carr's *The Mad Hatter Mystery,* Laura Britten, Phill·Driscoll's mistress, asked one nice old Beefeater if this was where Queen Elizabeth was executed. The guard, shocked by her historical ignorance, answered that "Queen Elizabeth had not the honor. . . .I mean, she died in her bed."

Beyond Tower Green, to the east of St. Peter's, is the former Waterloo Barracks. (In Carr's mystery, this is the building which Sir Leonard Haldyne had in his charge.)

Finish your tour of the Tower by returning to Byward Tower and the exit to Tower Hill. Turn right on Tower Hill and follow it around the walls until you come to the

Minories. (There is a pedestrian underpass that will take you to the Tower Hill Underground Station if you choose to end your walk here.)

If you are continuing the walk, turn left on Minories; you will be walking north. H. R. F. Keating, in *Inspector Ghote Hunts the Peacock,* mentioned that Ghote climbed a slight ascent going along the "oddly-named" Minories. The name came from the Minoresses, who were nuns of the order of St. Clare. In 1293, they founded a convent here just outside the City wall.

Walk up Minories to Aldgate, passing Fenchurch Street Station on your left. Turn left across Aldgate to Leadenhall Street. In an office in Leadenhall Street, Hosmer Angel was supposedly a cashier in Sir Arthur Conan Doyle's Sherlock Holmes Tale "A Case of Identity."

The offices of the Dagger Line were in Leadenhall Street in A. E. W. Mason's *The House in Lordship Lane.*

Walk west along Leadenhall Street among the massive City banks, past St. Andrew's Undershaft (the shaft was a maypole). Note the controversial structure that houses Lloyds of London, the internationally known insurance underwriting firm, to the left at Lime Street. This street figured in Sherlock Holmes's case of "The Mazarin Stone" by Sir Arthur Conan Doyle. It was the street where Van Seddar lived.

Continue on Leadenhall. At the place where Leadenhall Street becomes Cornhill, Bishopsgate leads off to the right. Bishopsgate was the fifteenth-century site of Crosby Hall, where Richard III lived.

The general area to the right was affected when, on April 24, 1993, a massive IRA bomb was exploded in Bishopsgate outside the Hong Kong and Shanghai Bank. A number of buildings were damaged, some virtually destroyed. Following the bombing, the area was sealed off. A year later, the area is still closed to vehicular traffic, but walkers are not affected. The damaged buildings are being repaired and restored. When the restoration and repair work is completed, the vehicular traffic pattern will be somewhat altered.

Now walk down Cornhill past Bishopsgate to tiny Royal

Exchange Building (an alley) where you will turn right to Threadneedle Street.

Slightly to your right and across Threadneedle Street to the north is Old Broad Street, where Lord Peter Wimsey found the tobacconist's shop called Cummings, not Smith. It was the place Tallboys mailed this alphabet letter to his stockbroker each week using letters from Pym's Nutrax and in Dorothy L. Sayers's *Murder Must Advertise.*

Turn right off Threadneedle Street into Bartholomew Lane. Follow it north to Lothbury and turn left. Follow Lothbury west; it will become Gresham Street.

In *Angel Touch,* when Mike Ripley's Fitzroy Angel reported for work at Prior, Keen, Baldwin, he took the bus to St. Paul's and "walked round to Gresham St."

Cross Old Jewry Street and Ironmonger Lane and keep walking along Gresham Street until you come to Guildhall Yard. The Guildhall is to your right.

Purvis, the surly security man for Prior, Keen, Baldwin, took Angel to a pub near the Guildhall. (*Angel Touch*)

The Guildhall, the City's most important secular building, has stood on or near its present site since the eleventh century. The banners and coats of arms of the important City Guilds that once met here are displayed on the gatehouse.

The City is administered from here by the Court of Common Council, which developed from the ancient Court of Hustings.

The Guildhall is associated with a string of Lord Mayors, among them Sir Richard (Dick) Whittington (the one with the cat).

In Catherine Aird's *In Harm's Way,* George and Tom Mellot agreed to divide their family's farm in Kent. George was to run the farm while Tom "went off to do a Dick Whittington." Aird's Detective Inspector C. D. Sloan thought it was funny that only one Lord Mayor got into the history books, but concluded that perhaps it was because he also got into a nursery rhyme.

Sir John Cranston, the portly, wine-loving Coroner of the City in Paul Harding's *By Murder's Bright Light,* had his office in the Guildhall. It was in his office that he and Brother Athelstan convened the gathering of truculent-faced individuals connected to the disappearance of three sailors from the ship, *God's Bright Light.* The courtroom where Sir John heard such cases as the accusations of witchcraft brought against widow Eleanor Raggleweek by Alice Frogmore and her husband was also in the Guildhall.

Come out of Guildhall Yard and continue west (to your right) on Gresham Street to Wood Street. To the right along Wood Street at Love Lane is the Wood Street Police station where Inspector Ghote arrived early for the international conference on drugs in Keating's tale, *Inspector Ghote Hunts the Peacock.*

End your walk by continuing on Gresham Street to St. Martin's le Grand; turn left. Follow St. Martin's le Grand back to the St. Paul's Underground Station where this walk began.

2

INNS OF COURT/ FLEET STREET WALK

BACKGROUND

This walk combines legal and journalistic London, or the Inns of Court and Fleet Street. They coexist in the ancient no-man's-land between the City of London, which ends in the west at Ludgate, and Temple Bar, where Westminster begins.

The Inns of Court are located on a north–south axis that runs along Gray's Inn Road and Chancery Lane, crosses Fleet Street, and ends at the Thames River Embankment. Fleet Street, a part of London's main east–west axis, is an extension of the Strand, which stretches from Temple Bar to Ludgate. Located on the Fleet River, which rises in Hampstead Heath and flows into the Thames at Blackfriars Bridge, Ludgate was the western gate of the medieval City. Both the law and the press consider themselves a class apart, standing between the government and the governed, and, in London, their geographic placement reflects this.

By the time of the first Elizabeth, legal London, with its four major Inns of Court, was known as the third English University. It was where young barristers lived, studied, and worked. Many of the buildings here are quite old. They are set in handsome squares and tiny courtyards that are unsuspected by the passing tourist unless he/she catches a glimpse of a black-robed, bewigged barrister rushing along.

Fleet Street is the name given to the whole area east of the Strand. Spreading into the small, winding alleyways and cul-de-sacs, and until the present day, it is where London's newspapers have been published since the time of Charles I. The local taverns (City pubs) have been inhabited by a mixture of lawyers and journalists since the time of Fleet Street's famous son, Dr. Samuel Johnson. G. K. Chesterton, a journalist by profession, liked to work in a wine bar and then wander amiably down the center of Fleet Street or take a cab 200 feet to drop off his copy. Edgar Wallace and E. C. Bentley, detective story writers who were also journalists, worked in Fleet Street.

LENGTH OF WALK: 5 miles

This walk can be covered in two parts, each about 2½ miles long. One comprises the Inns of Court; the other, Fleet Street and the Old Bailey. The entire walk can be covered in a morning and an afternoon or on two separate days, but both parts should be done on a weekday, if possible, because the Courts and most restaurants and taverns are closed on weekends. Although the major British legal holidays are in August and September, cases are tried at the Old Bailey and the Royal Courts all year round.

See the map on page 24 for the boundaries of this walk and page 247–49 for a list of the authors, books, and detectives mentioned.

PLACES OF INTEREST

Inns of Court. Closed weekends.

Gray's Inn.

Lincoln's Inn.

Inner Temple.

Middle Temple Royal Courts of Justice, The Strand.

Temple Bar, Fleet Street/The Strand.

Staple Inn, High Holborn.

Public Record Office Museum, Chancery Lane.

St. Clement Dane's Church, The Strand.

The Old Bailey (Central Criminal Court).

Sir John Soane's Museum, Lincoln's Inn Fields. Closed in August. Free, but donation requested.

Courtauld Institute Galleries, Somerset House, The Strand. Admission charge.

Places to Eat

Ye Olde Cheshire Cheese, 145 Fleet Street. A favorite with Dr. Johnson, you'll need reservations here. 071-583-4562.

The Devereux Pub, Devereux Court. G. K. Chesterton's Distributists met here. 071-583-4562.

Edgar Wallace Pub, 40 Essex Street. 071-353-3120.

The Royal Courts of Justice Cafe, The Strand.

The Central Criminal Courts Canteen, Old Bailey.

– INNS OF COURT/FLEET STREET WALK –

THE INNS OF COURT

Begin this walk at the Holborn Underground Station. Use the Southampton Row exit and turn left to walk up Southampton Row. Turn right at Fisher Street and follow it to Red Lion Square. Cross the square to Princeton Street; continue along Princeton to Bedford Row where you will turn right.

In Dorothy L. Sayers's *Strong Poison,* Joan Murchison, who had been planted in the law office of Norman Urquhart to look for suspicious goings-on, walked around Red Lion Square after the office closed. She wanted to kill time before going back to burgle the office safe.

As you walk along Bedford Row, note the dark-red–brick

Inns of Court
Fleet Street

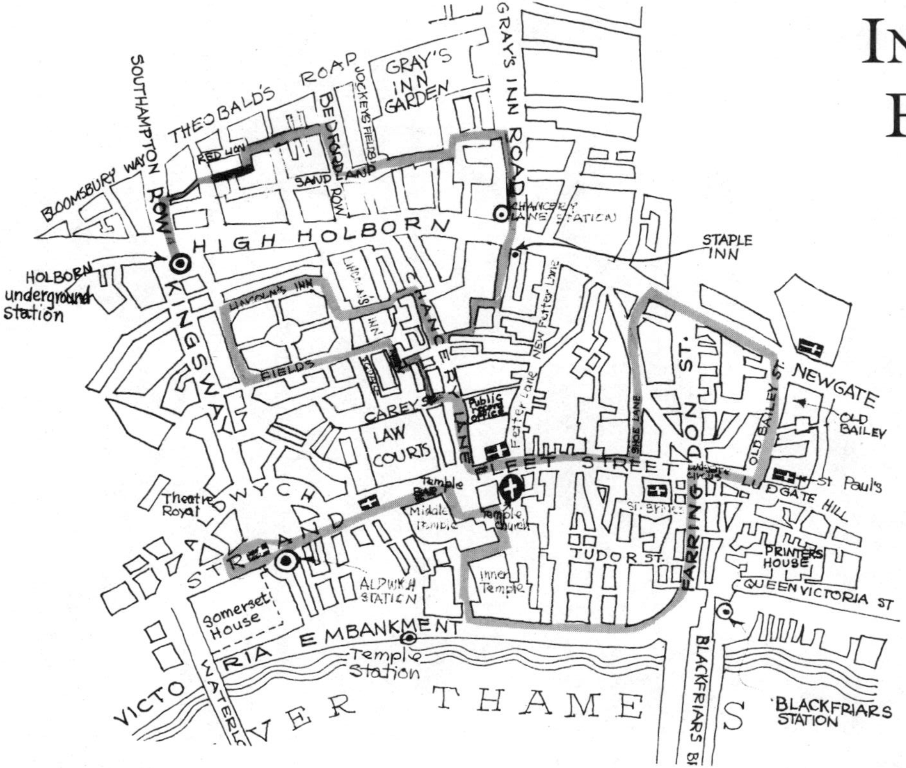

houses dating from the 1700s. Today, most of these bear brass plates listing barristers' or solicitors' names.

(The difference between a solicitor and a barrister is quite distinct. The solicitor does everyday legal work; he or she prepares the case and instructs or briefs the barrister, who then goes into court to plead the case. It is the barrister who wears the black gown and wig; John Mortimer's flamboyant Rumpole of the Bailey is a barrister, whereas Dorothy L. Sayers's precise little Mr. Murbles is a solicitor.)

Norman Urquart had his office in Bedford Row. He was the solicitor cousin of Philip Boyes, the poisoning victim in Sayers's *Strong Poison.* Sayers must have associated this street with lawyers, for it is also the place where, in *Unnatural Death,* Inspector Charles Parker found Mr. Tripp, the lawyer whom Mary Whitaker consulted about the new inheritance law.

At the end of Bedford Row, turn left into Sandland Street and walk past Jockey's Fields, where Margery Allingham placed the Queen Anne house with the offices of the ancient publishing firm of Barnabas & Company "at the Sign of the Golden Quiver" in *Flowers for the Judge.*

Go through the open gateway into Gray's Inn Gardens and turn right. Here both Pepys and Addison walked and Charles Lamb declared it to be the best of the Inns of Court gardens. A stern sign warns that you are here only on sufferance and that each Inn of Court is an independent organization run by its Benchers (Masters of the Bench who are judges and senior barristers) and an elected Treasurer.

Walk through the Field Court where an ancient catalpa tree is associated with the memory of Gray's most famous son, the Lord Chancellor Francis Bacon, who was Gray's Treasurer. (At the height of his political career, Bacon was accused of taking bribes, tried by the House of Lords, found guilty, stripped of his honors, and banished to his country estate.)

Follow the signs into Gray's Inn Square, which was rebuilt after sustaining heavy bomb damage during World War II. You can still see the medieval chapel, library, and hall where, in 1594, Shakespeare's *Comedy of Errors* was first performed.

Matthew Bouff, the solicitor in Wilkie Collins's *The Moon-*

stone, had his offices in Gray's Inn Square. Another more recent luminary of Gray's Inn was F. E. Smith, Lord Birkenhead, who helped prosecute G. K. Chesterton's brother Cecil for libel in the 1913 Marconi Trial.

It was in Gray's Inn that Sayers's Mr. Towkington, a barrister friend of Mr. Murbles, had his chambers. He invited Parker, Wimsey, and Murbles to try his port and get the definitive word on the new inheritance statute in *Unnatural Death.*

Leave Gray's Inn by the ancient stone gateway that leads into Gray's Inn Road. Solicitor Reginald Colby had his offices in Gray's Inn Road. There he denied that he had ordered a hired car to meet Mrs. Benson at the airport in Patricia Moyes's *Who Is Simon Warwick?*

Now turn right and walk south to High Holborn. Inspector Stanislaus Oates, newly promoted to the Big Five, was being followed down High Holborn by a short, squat, shabby man in Margery Allingham's *Police at the Funeral.*

Hillary, Selena, Ragwort, and Cantrip planned to meet in the Corkscrew, a wine bar on the north side of High Holborn, whose proximity made it popular with the members of Lincoln's Inn. (*Thus Was Adonis Murdered* by Sarah Caudwell)

At the intersection of Gray's Inn Road and High Holborn, you will see, across the roadway, the marvelous black-and-white timber and plaster Tudor facade of Staple Inn. This point marks another boundary of the ancient City of London. It is marked with two stone obelisks called the Holborn Bars. The Staple Inn was originally used by the Wool Trade's Merchants of the Staple. Its overhanging facade, although much restored, is a survivor from the Elizabethan era. Dr. Johnson lived here when he wrote *Rasselas.* It took him only a week to do so, because he needed money to pay for his mother's funeral.

Old Todd, the last cabby in the rank before Staple Inn, made a note of the spectacle of Inspector Oates being followed. (*Police at the Funeral* by Margery Allingham)

Cross Holborn and walk through the gateway marked Staple Inn. You are now in the quiet eighteenth-century courtyard where Wimsey's solicitor, Mr. Murbles, had his chambers. In *Clouds of Witness,* Murbles had Wimsey, Sir Impey Biggs, and

Lady Mary to lunch in a "delightful old set of rooms with windows looking out upon the formal garden with its odd little flower beds and tinkling fountain."

Go through the court past the little fountain on the right; turn right past the Southampton Buildings and follow the passageway that leads to Chancery Lane.

According to Hillary Tamar in Sarah Caudwell's *Thus Was Adonis Murdered,* his colleagues could be found any morning at eleven o'clock in the nearest coffee house down Chancery Lane.

Cross Chancery Lane and go through the Stone Buildings' gate into Lincoln's Inn, the second great Inn of Court. Its records begin in 1422, and its most famous sons were Sir Thomas More and Prime Minister William Pitt the Younger, whose politics, with the help of the Duke of Wellington, finally finished off Napoleon.

Mr. Pritchard, Ann Dorland's lawyer in Sayers's *The Unpleasantness at the Bellona Club,* had his office in Lincoln's Inn.

The very distinguished and very expensive barrister hired to defend Isabel Mortimer in Julian Symons's *A Three Pipe Problem* also had his chambers here.

This Inn may be where the charming young oboist, Charlotte Rossignol, came to see her uncle's solicitor in Ellis Peters's *City of Gold and Shadows.*

Another firm of solicitors with a Lincoln's Inn address was Gammon & Hanbury. It was from their offices that the Honorable Richard Rollison, DSO, MC, MBE, received word of a strange and sinister legacy in John Creasey's *Leave It to the Toff.*

The Old Square is on the left as you come into Lincoln's Inn. The ancient chapel was bombed in World War II as was the red-brick Old Hall, where the High Court of Chancery met. The Hall was the scene of the famous trial of *Jarndyce v. Jarndyce* in Charles Dickens's *Bleak House.*

Cross the open area and turn left before the red-brick, Victorian New Hall and go to your right through the gateway into Lincoln's Inn Fields. This is the largest square in central London. It was laid out in 1618 by Inigo Jones, who also may have built some of the houses on the south and west sides of the square. Most of the original houses are gone today; however, the Lindsey House (Nos. 59–60) is attributed to Jones.

In the middle of the north side of the Square, No. 13, one of the square's fine homes, survives as Sir John Soane's Museum. (Soane was the architect of the Bank of England.)

The Soane Museum is unique in that Soane stipulated in his will that his collections not be augmented or disturbed. As a result, the museum retains the air and flavor of a private home. The sense of spaciousness is achieved by a clever use of mirrors. Among the miscellany, some of it priceless, that the museum contains are the painting of William Hogarth and the sarcophagus of Seti I.

Charles Dickens's friend and biographer John Forster lived at No. 58 Lincoln's Inn Fields. Dickens described the house in *Bleak House,* making it the home of the sinister lawyer Tulkinghorn.

Complete your walk around Lincoln's Inn Fields and exit through the main gate to Lincoln's Inn. On the right is New Square, where Michael Gilbert had his office and where he placed the offices of the firm Horniman, Birley, and Craine in *Smallbone Deceased.*

In Sarah Caudwell's *Thus Was Adonis Murdered,* Julia Larwood was a member of the small set of Revenue Chambers in 63 New Square.

Continue straight ahead to the northeast corner of New Square. Go through New Square to Star Yard, turn right and go through Star Yard to the ancient archway. Go under the archway toward Carey Street. Set into the archway between two sets of stairs is Wildy & Sons Legal Bookstore, which was established in 1830. The wonderfully old-fashioned interior is jam-packed with prints and books including the paperbacks of John Mortimer's Rumpole series.

Coming out of Wildy's, turn left on Carey Street and walk on to Chancery Lane. Across the street (at Chancery Lane) is the Public Record Office, a large, gray building that stretches one block east to Fetter Lane.

Only serious researchers are allowed to work here. This is where, for thirty years, Muriel St. Clare Byrne read, collated, and edited her lifework, *The Lisle Letters.* Byrne was Dorothy

L. Sayers's friend from Somerville College days. With Sayers, Byrne co-authored the play *Busman's Honeymoon*.

The Public Record Office Museum is open to the general public. The museum has among its exhibits a copy of Shakespeare's signature; a copy of the *Domesday Book* of William the Conqueror; the signed confession of Guy Fawkes, whose effigy is burned in bonfires throughout England every November 5; and the gaol (jail) book from "Hanging" Judge Jeffrey's Bloody Assizes, which followed the rebellion of the Duke of Monmouth.

When you leave the Public Record Office note that almost opposite are the offices of the Law Society, which controls the education, admission, and discipline of the solicitors' branch of the legal profession.

At this point, you have walked approximately 2.5 miles. To end the walk here, turn left along Chancery Lane to High Holborn, then turn right to the Chancery Lane Underground Station near Staple Inn.

If you wish to continue, the next part of the walk will take you along Fleet Street. Turn right and follow Chancery Lane to Fleet Street, then turn left. This brings you to the area known as the Temple. (You are near the junction of the Strand and Fleet Street, which is marked by Temple Bar to your right.)

In *Bitter Herbs* by Natasha Cooper, Willow King met Richard Crescent and Sebastian Borden in Borden's chambers in the Temple.

If, at this point, you are ready for break, there are many taverns clustered about Temple Bar or, having booked a table in advance, you can continue along Fleet Street to 145, **the Cheshire Cheese**, and lunch here.

As the tourist bus came to an abrupt halt on Fleet Street, Kate directed everyone to cross the street for lunch at the "famous Cheshire Cheese, Dr. Johnson's pub." (*Tourists Are for Trapping* by Marion Babson)

FLEET STREET

The Temple Bar marks the point where the Strand ends and Fleet Street and the City begin. The memorial here was erected in 1880 to replace a gateway that had been erected in 1672 by Christopher Wren. Wren's Temple Bar replaced an earlier wooden marker that was destroyed in the Great Fire of 1666. Wren's seventeenth-century stone gate is now the entrance to Theobald's Park near Waltham Cross in Hertfordshire.

The reigning monarch must stop at Temple Bar before entering the City. There, in a colorful ceremony that reflects the ancient freedom of the City, the Lord Mayor presents the monarch with the Sword of London and grants him/her the freedom to enter the City.

The original Anodyne Necklace pub once stood near the Temple Bar. The painted pub sign displayed a chain of beads representing an anodyne necklace. The necklace could cure such ailments as teething, fits, and convulsions. Martha Grimes called one of the early books in her string of pub mysteries *The Anodyne Necklace,* but she moved the pub to London's East End.

"There's Fleet Street," said Henry Lamprey to Roberta Grey in Ngaio Marsh's *A Surfeit of Lampreys*. "Do you remember 'up the hill of Ludgate, down the Hill of Fleet'?"

Many characters in crime and mystery fiction were members of Fleet Street's journalistic fraternity. For example, Paul Mortimer, in Julian Symons's *The Blackheath Poisonings,* aspired to be a Fleet Street reporter, but his merchant family felt journalism was not a genteel enough profession.

Lambert, after writing his "highly amusing" piece for *The Mail,* tried to convince Cassie that he was not the sort of journalist that was interested in the "cut and thrust of Fleet Street." (*Death Takes a Hand* by Susan Moody)

Writers of detective fiction have journalistic associations as well, many being or having been journalists. Mike Ripley, creator of the award-winning series featuring the street-smart, jazz-playing taxi driver Fitzroy Maclean Angel, is crime critic for the Sunday *Telegraph*. Alan Scholefield, creator of Macrae and Silver, started out as a journalist but turned to crime in the 1960s. Both Robert Richardson and H. R. F. Keating are former journalists, and among the past masters of detective fiction are Edgar Wallace, G. K. Chesterton, Anthony Berkeley, Graham Greene, and E. C. Bentley, all of whom were working journalists. Others, such as Dick Francis, worked for the media for a time. He wrote a racing column for the *Sunday Express;* Dorothy L. Sayers wrote guest editorials and did reviews of crime fiction for *The Sunday Times.*

The Fleet Street scene plays a role in any number of mysteries. For example, in Dorothy L. Sayers's *Murder Must Advertise,* the indefatigable young reporter Hector Puncheon worked for the *Morning Star,* the paper that ran the Pym's Publicity Nutrax ads. Look for a Fleet Street cafe like the one where, after covering a warehouse fire and an heroic cat, young Puncheon ate a 3:00 AM breakfast of grilled sausages before strolling past the Griffin at Temple Bar, the Royal Law Courts, and St. Clement Danes's.

In E. C. Bentley's *Trent's Last Case,* artist Philip Trent wrote freelance articles about murders that baffled the police for *Record* editor-in-chief Sir James Molloy. The *Record* was across Fleet Street from its sister evening paper, *The Sun.*

In G. K. Chesterton's Father Brown story "The Purple Wig," a spineless editor for the *Daily Reformer* altered his own copy on orders from his publisher. Chesterton had a similar experience, but he resigned from the *Daily News* rather than be edited by its owners, the Cadbury (chocolate) family.

Walk east on Fleet Street, which, like the Fleet Prison, takes its name from the Fleet River (one of London's underground rivers). As you follow Fleet Street, take notice of the many places of interest along the way. Directly across from the Temple Bar is 1 Fleet Street where Child's Bank has stood since 1673.

At No. 22 is Ye Olde Cock Tavern, the street's oldest tavern, dating from Elizabethan times, with a sign featuring a gilded cock. The tavern has long been popular with members of the literary establishment, among them such notables as Dr. Samuel Johnson and Charles Dickens.

It was at the Cock Tavern that Hector Puncheon, who had gone there for a well-deserved beefsteak after a long day's work, realized that the packet of white powder he had been given might not be soda. He dashed out to a chemist's to have it analyzed. (*Murder Must Advertise* by Dorothy L. Sayers)

At No. 47 (on the south side of Fleet Street) is El Vino, a wine bar once patronized by G. K. Chesterton. It is very like

Pommeroy's Wine Bar where John Mortimer's Rumpole likes to drink his claret (Chateau Fleet Street).

In *Bitter Herbs* by Natasha Cooper, after Willow King met Richard Crescent and Sebastian Borden in Borden's chambers, they went from there to the El Vino for a drink.

Continuing along Fleet Street, you will pass St. Dunstan's in the West (the last church within the City). The Great Fire of 1666 was contained just yards east of the church, which is mentioned by Samuel Pepys in his diaries. John Donne was once its vicar and Isaak Walton its vestryman. In 1830, the church was demolished by a widening of Fleet Street. The present church, an early example of London Gothic revival, was built in 1829–33 by John Shaw.

Inside the church are figures of the legendary King Lud and his two sons. The statues can be seen just inside the doorway to the east of the main church entrance. They came to the church when the Ludgate (one of the old City gates) was demolished in 1760. The statue of Queen Elizabeth I above the small east porch is from the Ludgate's west side. Carved by Kerwin in 1586, it is the oldest public statue of an English monarch. The fine clock with its 'striking Jacks' was made for the old church as a thanksgiving for escaping the 1666 fire. It was the first public clock in London to include a minute hand.

Across the street from St. Dunstan's No. 135 was The Falstaff, where Lord Peter Wimsey, Charles Parker, and reporter Salcombe Hardy lunched in *The Unpleasantness at the Bellona Club* by Dorothy L. Sayers.

Continue walking along Fleet Street. Soon you will come to Fetter Lane where you will pass the site of Clifford's Inn, the oldest inn in Chancery.

Follow Fleet Street to Johnson Court. Turn left and follow Johnson Court until it turns into Gough Square. This will bring you to Dr. Samuel Johnson's four-story brick house, which is now a small museum. It was in the attic here that Johnson, one of the most remarkable men of his age, worked for eight years compiling the first comprehensive English dictionary. The dictionary was completed in 1755. In addition to being a lexicographer, Dr. Johnson was a scholar, poet, essayist, conversationalist, dramatist, and literary critic.

Return to Fleet Street from Gough Square and go one short block to the left to Wine Office Court; turn left again into Wine Office Court. On the right is the Cheshire Cheese, the most famous of all Fleet Street taverns. It was beloved by Dr. Johnson and a favorite of G. K. Chesterton. It still has sawdust on the floor and the plastered ceilings are low-raftered. The menu is traditional old English pub food including roast beef, steak and kidney pie, and Welsh rarebit (Chesterton's favorite).

Return to Fleet Street from the Cheshire Cheese. Along this stretch of Fleet were located the offices of the *Daily Telegraph,* where for many years E. C. Bentley (*Trent's Last Case*) was an editorial writer. Next door is the black-tile and chromium building where, in the 1930s, Lord Beaverbrook published his *Daily Express.*

The Daily News, where G. K. Chesterton, Hilaire Belloc, and E. C. Bentley all worked before the first world war, was located across Fleet Street to the south of Whitefriars Street.

In Ian Stuart's *A Growing Concern,* bank inspector David Grierson met a reporter named Carlton who let him use the morgue of an unidentified Fleet Street paper. Note Reuters, the international news association, located at No. 85 Fleet Street.

Continue east on Fleet Street until you reach Shoe Lane; turn left and walk north. Shoe Lane is a street redolent with history. In the seventeenth century, it was known for its sign-writers, designers of broadsheets, and its cockpit. Samuel Pepys came to cockfights in 1663 when the spectators included Members of Parliament, as well as merchants and shopkeepers.

In 1657, Richard Lovelace, Cavalier poet and supporter of the king, died in wretched lodgings in Gunpowder Alley between Shoe Lane and Fetter Lane.

At the Windmill Tavern in Shoe Lane, John Felton, after reading the Parliamentary Remonstrance against the Duke of Buckingham, made up his mind to assassinate the Duke.

Follow Shoe Lane north past St. Andrew's, another of Wren's churches. It is across from the City Temple, the "cathedral'' of the Free Churches. Here, take Plumtree Court to your right. This will bring you to the Victorian iron bridge that connects Holborn with Holborn Viaduct. If you go to the left, you will find a stairway which will take you onto the viaduct.

Margery Allingham and her husband, Pip Youngman Carter, lived near the London Wall before and during World War II. The area is very much like the one portrayed in her fictional St. Peter's Square in *Tiger in the Smoke,* but the vague landmarks Allington gives seem to transport it to Paddington Station and Marylebone.

Turn right and follow the viaduct over the top of Farringdon Street past the Holborn Viaduct Railway Station. On the left is the Crusaders' Church of St. Sepulchre without Newgate, with its restored fifteenth-century tower. Captain John Smith, governor of Virginia and a principle in the Pocahontas legend, is buried in the churchyard. He died in 1631.

Known as ''the musicians' church,'' it contains windows dedicated to the singer Dame Nellie Melba. The ashes of Sir Henry Wood, founder of the Promenade concerts, are interred here.

The church also has more sinister associations. In 1792, a watchhouse was built to help deal with the body snatchers—students from nearby St. Bartholomew's Hospital, who were intent on robbing the graves in the churchyard.

Inside the church is the Execution Bell, preserved in a glass case. The small hand bell was rung outside condemned prisoners' cells at Newgate Prison to rouse them to their prayers—in the event that they had dozed off on the eve of their execution. The great bell from St. Sepulchre is also here. It tolled as the condemned prisoners passed by on the way from Newgate to the gallows of Tyburn Hill (now Marble Arch). The prisoners were housed across the road from the church in Newgate Prison. It was on what is now the site of the Central Criminal Courts, or the Old Bailey. The historic and fictional connections with the Old Bailey are legion.

From St. Sepulchre's you can see the Old Bailey's famous copper dome topped by a statue of Justice that, contrary to tradition, is not blindfolded. As the tour bus passed the Old Bailey, Jim slowed the bus to give the passengers a glimpse of the statue. (*Tourists Are for Trapping* by Marion Babson).

Sir John Cranston explained to Shawditch, the sheriff, that Trumington and Beadle and the tiler thief were now in Newgate awaiting trial for the murder of the young maid (*By Murder's Bright Light* by Paul Harding).

From the church, cross to Old Bailey Street, which was widened here to allow room for the crowds who came to watch the hangings. You are near a pub called The Magpie and The Stump. The aristocracy, which had the same blood tastes as the masses, would rent rooms here in order to watch the executions in comfort. It was at The Magpie and The Stump that Caroline Ross, in John Dickson Carr's *The Bride of Newgate,* waited to see if she were both a bride and a widow.

According to John Mortimer, Rex's Cafe was in the same area as The Magpie and The Stump. Rumpole got the best scrambled eggs in London at Rex's. It has now been replaced by an Indian restaurant, and "even Rumpole [couldn't] stomach tandoori chicken for breakfast." As a result, he was forced to patronize the Public Canteen in the Old Bailey itself.

In 1539, the first Old Bailey Sessions House was built beside Newgate Prison. It was replaced by a new building in 1774. The name Old Bailey is that of the street that passes nearby. These sessions, which had exercised criminal jurisdiction over the London area since time immemorial, were superseded by the Central Criminal Court in 1834.

The present Sessions House, designed by E. W. Mountford, stands on the site of Newgate Prison. It was opened by King Edward VII in 1907 and had four courtrooms and offices. The building was severely damaged by enemy action in 1941. In 1972, an extension modernized the facilities and extended the number of courtrooms to nineteen. In 1973, it was attacked by IRA terrorists. Among famous trials held in the Old Bailey were those of Oscar Wilde (1895); Dr. H. H. Crippen (1910); George Joseph Smith, the "Brides in the Bath" murderer (1915); and Peter Sutcliffe, "the Yorkshire Ripper" (1981).

The Old Bailey serves as the setting for a variety of detective stories. Many of John Mortimer's Rumpole tales take place here.

In *The Blackheath Poisonings* by Julian Symons, the Old Bailey trial of Isabel Mortimer for the poison murders of both her lover and her mother-in-law is described in detail.

In Margery Allingham's *Flowers for the Judge,* Mike Wedgewood was tried at Old Bailey, and, in *Fog of Doubt* by Christianna Brand, Doctor "Tedward" was tried for murder in Court No. 1.

In Dorothy L. Sayers's *Strong Poison,* Lord Peter Wimsey first saw Harriet Vane in the dock at the Old Bailey; she was on trial for poisoning her lover. "There were crimson roses on the bench; they looked like splashes of blood. The judge was an old man. . . .His scarlet robe clashed harshly with the crimson of the roses."

Beulah Birtley, in *Duplicate Death* by Georgette Heyer, was convicted of criminal fraud because her fiance, "Terrible Timothy" Harte, wasn't "an Old Bailey chaser" (a term for the lawyers Rumpole called "Old Bailey hacks").

In Cyril Hare's *Tragedy at Law,* Justice Barber was murdered just outside the Central Criminal Court.

If you wish to see the court in action, simply go to the Public Gallery entrance and join the others awaiting admission. Court sessions begin at 9:15 AM and 1:45 PM. Leave your camera at home; you will not be allowed to take it into the courtroom. (A posted notice suggests leaving cameras at one of the nearby pubs—a somewhat unnerving idea.)

Trials are often well attended. Some of the crowd will be anxious friends and relatives of the accused; some will be retirees with time on their hands; there will be school groups who have come to see justice done; and, of course, there will be tourists. An introduction from a barrister or solicitor can get you a seat in the court itself. On most days, the crowd may be very like the amusing bunch described in the opening chapter of Michael Gilbert's *Death Has Deep Roots.*

When you have soaked up enough courtroom atmosphere, leave the Old Bailey and turn left to walk along Old Bailey

Street. At Ludgate Hill, turn right and go past Lime Burner Lane (Old Seacoal Lane), where the Fleet Prison once stood. This is where Mr. Pickwick was incarcerated after refusing to pay his fine. (*The Pickwick Papers* by Charles Dickens)

During the hearing to determine if Eleanor Raggleweed were a witch, the highly irritated Sir John Cranston threatened his laughing scrivener, Osbert, with a week in "Fleet prison" if he did not sit up. Later in the same book, Sir John ordered that the two responsible for the murder of Captain Roffel be taken to "the Fleet." (*By Murder's Bright Light* by Paul Harding)

Continue along the north side of Ludgate Hill to Ludgate Circus. In the days of Sherlock Holmes, the King Lud Pub, located here, was renowned for its Welsh rarebit, which was available from morning to late evening on its free lunch counter.

In *Forfeit* by Dick Francis, the reporter, Tyrone, walked a drunken sportswriter called Bert down Fleet Street to Ludgate Circus. Later, Tyrone found Bert dead on the pavement below his newspaper office.

An impressive memorial tablet dedicated to Edgar Wallace is on the northwest side of Ludgate Circus. Although a successful writer of both crime novels and screenplays, Wallace regarded himself, first and foremost, a journalist.

After looking at the Wallace plaque, cross Ludgate Circus to go south on New Bridge Street and follow it to Bride's Lane. Bridewell Prison was located here. Turn right and follow Bride's Lane to the steps into St. Bride's Passage. This will take you into Salisbury Square; turn right again to St. Bride's Church. The original St. Bride's Church was destroyed in the Great Fire. The present church, which is often called the "Cathedral of Fleet Street," was built by Christopher Wren. The church features a many-tiered "wedding cake" spire, Wren's tallest. The diarist Samuel Pepys was baptized in St. Bride's, and Cavalier poet Richard Lovelace is buried there.

The tiny area where St. Bride's is located is similar to the fictional Pie Crust Court off Pie Crust Passage that was created by P. D. James in *Unnatural Causes.* She describes the alley as being so narrow that one man would have difficulty getting through it. When Adam Dalgleish came there to interrogate

Justin Bryce about the murder of mystery writer Maurice Seeton, Dalgleish found himself in an eighteenth-century courtyard so carefully preserved that it looked artificial.

Return to New Bridge Street and turn right to walk toward Blackfriars Bridge. The entrance to Printing House Square is across the wide roadway to the left, just north of Queen Victoria Street. The *Times,* queen of the London papers, was published here until 1974.

In the fifteenth century, Wynkyn de Worde, a pupil of William Caxton, set up a printing shop in Printing House Square. In 1627, King Charles I authorized the first official *London Gazette,* and, in 1785, the *Times* began publication.

The *Times* seems to be the paper of choice for characters in detective novels. In Sayers's *Whose Body?,* Lord Peter placed an ad in the *Times* concerning the pince-nez found on the body in the Thipps's bath in Battersea. Like many other Londoners, Lord Peter routinely "took" the *Times* and the *Times Literary Supplement.*

The general area around Blackfriars Bridge often pops up as background in crime stories. In Ngaio Marsh's *Killer Dolphin* the warehouse flat of Jeremy Jones and Peregrine Jay was located east of Blackfriars Bridge and south of Queen Victoria Street. By Dame Ngaio's last book, *Light Thickens,* the flat had been converted into a family residence for Jay, his wife Emily, and their three sons. At the end of the tale, the Jays entertained Superintendent Alleyn there. From their patio, they watched the tour boats going back and forth between Westminster and the Tower.

Dickens's David Copperfield spent a miserable time in the vicinity of Blackfriars, washing and labeling bottles in Murdstone and Grimby's warehouse.

Not far downriver from Blackfriars and Puddle Dock is the Queenhithe Dock, which was one of the four original City deep-water harbors. This is where Superintendent Adam Dalgleish had his flat. (*Unnatural Causes* by P. D. James)

In *The Skull Beneath the Skin,* Cordelia Gray moved nearby to a City "warehouse flat off Thames Street."

In *By Murder's Bright Light* by Paul Harding, the cog *God's Bright Light* was berthed in the Thames opposite Queenhithe.

The entrance to the Blackfriars Underground Station is at the end of New Bridge Street where it branches off to the left near the Blackfriars Bridge. To the right is the Victoria Embankment.

In Sayers's *Murder Must Advertise,* knowing he was being followed, Lord Peter Wimsey daydreamed about luring his assassins into some such secluded spot as the Blackfriars subway or the steps beneath Cleopatra's Needle, then facing them and killing them with his bare hands.

Follow the Victoria Embankment to the right, crossing John Carpenter Street, Carmelite Street, and Temple Avenue, which is an extension of Bouverie Street. Young E. C. Bentley, down from Oxford and reading for the Bar at the Temple, moonlighted at the *Daily News.* He walked up Bouverie Street by night to help put the paper to bed and then walked home. In this way, he kept up his habit of long walks at night. G. K. Chesterton writes of his walks with Bentley in the dedication (to Bentley) of *The Man Who Was Thursday.* After Bentley moved to Hampstead, he composed *Trent's Last Case* as he walked from his home into London.

To your right is the beautiful Inner Temple Garden, which, unfortunately, is closed to visitors.

The two Inns of Court, known as the Inner Temple and the Middle Temple, were formed from the property of the military order of the Knights Templar. Their task was to guard the pilgrims who were en route to the Holy Land during the Crusades. The order grew to great size and wealth and became very powerful. So much so, in fact, that in 1312 the King of France conspired with the Pope to destroy the order and seize its wealth. The land then was granted to another order of knights, the Knights Hospitalers of St. John of Jerusalem. When that order, too, was closed down, lawyers began to lease the land and organized themselves into two legal societies. They were granted the freehold of the land by James I in 1608.

Turn right when you reach Middle Temple Lane. (This is

the boundary between the Inner Temple—nearer the City— and the Middle Temple.) This is where Timothy Shepherd in Sarah Caudwell's *Thus Was Adonis Murdered* had his flat.

Follow Middle Temple Lane past the doorways with staircases similar to those of an Oxford college. There will be rows of names by each. Among them you will find that of John Mortimer, creator of Rumpole. Mortimer himself is a QC, or Queen's Counsel, one of the most august of senior barristers. When the Rumpole episodes are being filmed, Mortimer's name is covered with that of Rumpole to give authenticity to the shot.

To the left is the Middle Temple Library and, at the southern edge of Fountain Court, Middle Temple Hall. Law clerk Charles Dickens described Fountain Court as an oasis in the dry, dusty channels of the law.

Middle Temple Hall was bombed in the blitz but has since been restored to much of its former grandeur, which includes paneled walls and a spectacular double hammerbeam roof, beneath which Shakespeare's own company of actors is said to have performed *Twelfth Night* in 1602.

Turn right into Crown Office Row. On the right are the Inner Temple Gardens. The fountain figure of a child is in memory of essayist Charles Lamb who was born in 1775 in Crown Office Row.

The white and red roses that became badges of the Houses of York and Lancaster were plucked in one of the Temple Gardens. (*Henry VI, Part I,* ii)

In "Rumpole and the Man of God," Mortimer's Rumpole walked through the Temple Gardens to his chambers one late-September morning and then set out for the Old Bailey.

You are now in the Inner Temple where you will pass the Inner Temple Hall. It was also rebuilt after the blitz. Beyond Crown Office Row is an open space called King's Bench Walk. In King's Bench Walk at Staircase No. 9, there once lived a young barrister named Montague Druitt who committed suicide by drowning himself in the Thames. After his death, Druitt was suspected of having been Jack the Ripper.

Austin Freeman's detective, Dr. Thorndyke, had his chambers at 5A King's Bench Walk.

In Ngaio Marsh's *Black As He's Painted,* the African ruler known as the Boomer had eaten his dinners at the Temple as a law student, and both E. C. Bentley and his friend Lucian Oldershaw (Chesterton's brother-in-law) read law at the Temple but followed careers in journalism.

Just beyond King's Bench Walk are the Paper Buildings. In Georgette Heyer's *Duplicate Death* this is where the young barrister "Terrible Timothy" Harte lived while wooing Beulah Birtley, the social secretary to Mrs. Haddington whose murder brought Beulah under suspicion. Giles Carrington, another Heyer lawyer, had his own flat in the Temple. There he entertained Superintendent Hannasyde in a comfortable, book-lined sitting room in *Death in the Stocks.* Heyer's lawyer husband, Ronald Rougier, also had his chambers here.

Turn left on Inner Temple Land and go past Tanfield Court. Continue walking until you see the beautifully restored Temple Church. Like so many other buildings in the area, it was severely damaged by World War II bombs. It is one of five surviving circular churches in England. These churches were built on the plan of the Holy Sepulchre in Jerusalem.

Inside the church there are battered stone effigies of the Templars and, in the churchyard, several discernible graves. The poet Oliver Goldsmith is said to be buried just north of the church where the porch has sunk into the hillside.

Follow Inner Temple Lane under the seventeenth-century arch into Fleet Street. Turn left to walk west to Devereux Court, where the Devereux Pub was located.

In *Forfeit* by Dick Francis, the Devereux was the place where newsmen from the *Sunday Blaze* went for a lunch of cold meat and pickled onions. The Devereux was also the site of Distributist League meetings and "sing-alongs" when G. K. Chesterton was chairman and editor of *G. K.'s Weekly,* which was located a few steps away in Essex Street.

Also in Essex Street is another pub worth a visit: the Edgar Wallace Pub, at No. 40. It is dedicated to the memory of the prolific journalist-cum-detective story writer.

Return from Devereux Court to Fleet Street and turn left; here Fleet Street becomes the Strand. Across the street are the Royal Courts of Justice, or Law Courts, where civil law is practiced. These courts once met in Westminster, but more space was needed; in 1882, this huge Gothic building with its enormous central mosaic floor and courts was built.

As you enter under the porch you will see bewigged and gowned lawyers and their clients, often followed by members of the media. This is where, in Court No. 5, Ambrose Quince, the lawyer in Patricia Moyes's *Who Is Simon Warwick?* was located by Scotland Yard's Henry Tibbett. Marion Babson also featured these courts in *The Lord Mayor of Death*.

You may choose to sit in on a case in a courtroom, visit the small legal museum, to go for a cup of tea in the Royal Courts of Justice cafeteria, or to skip the whole legal thing and hurry past to where Christohpher Wren's Church of St. Clement Dane stands in the middle of the road where the Strand separates into Aldwych to the right and continues as the Strand to the left.

(Aldwych is the location of the Waldorf, where Loretta Lawson met Veronica Puddephat for an "Agatha Christie" type tea after Veronica had been questioned by a representative of the French police in Joan Smith's *A Masculine Ending*.)

St. Clement was the parish church of Dr. Johnson, whose statue is in the yard. The church's bells were immortalized in the rhyme, "Oranges and lemons say the bells of St. Clements."

It was from the now-gone Clements Inn to the north that Walter Harkright began his long evening hike to his mother's cottage in Hampstead in Wilkie Collins's *The Woman in White*.

To the right, just beyond Aldwych, is the London School of Economics, where, in Georgette Heyer's *Duplicated Death*, the boorish peer, Lance, was an instructor.

Continue west along the Strand past St. Mary-le-Strand, the small Baroque church designed by Gibbs, and past King's College on the south side of the street. Soon you will come to the open courtyard of Somerset House. It is on the site of the first Renaissance palace in England, built in 1547–50 for Lord Protector Somerset, the uncle of King Edward VI. Later it became the headquarters of the Parliamentary Party. It was here that Oliver Cromwell lay in state.

The house was demolished in 1775 and its site allocated for government offices, the first large block ever built. The Royal Academy was here from 1771 to 1836, The Royal Society from 1780 to 1857, and the Society of Antiquaries from 1781 to 1857. From 1836 until 1973, the offices of the General Register of Births, Deaths, and Marriages were also here, along with the Inland Revenue. Today Somerset House contains the national archives of wills, which you may consult for a fee.

Since 1990, Somerset House has housed the superb collection of Impressionist and Post-Impressionist paintings that were collected by Samuel Courtauld and left to the University of London.

In many detective novels, Somerset House has furnished sleuths with sinister facts and valuable clues. P. D. James's Cordelia Gray, in *An Unsuitable Job for a Woman,* went to Somerset House to trace Mark Callender's parentage and ended up reading his grandfather's will.

Lord Peter Wimsey consulted the archives in *The Unpleasantness at the Bellona Club* and in "The Piscatorial Farce of the Stolen Stomach." In *Unnatural Death,* Wimsey sent Miss Climpson to Somerset to hunt out the personae in the Dawson murder.

It is where Sherlock Holmes examined the will of the Stoner sisters' mother in the case of "The Speckled Band."

In *Those Who Hunt the Night,* Barbara Hambly's thriller about the murder of vampires in Victorian England, Lydia was to search public records for information about the vampire victims. Asher suggested that she begin with Somerset House.

We will end our walk here by returning to the Strand and going to the left to the Charing Cross Underground Station near Trafalgar Square.

3

COVENT GARDEN/ THE STRAND WALK

BACKGROUND

This walk covers the heart of London's performing arts world. It contains a heady mix of hotels, restaurants, and theaters. Lying between the financial City and the government at Westminster, Covent (convent) Garden was built on the site of the Westminster Abbey gardens, which were seized by Henry VIII, then sold to the Russells, Dukes of Bedford. They, in turn, used Covent Garden to create the first planned urban development in London. Until 1974, Covent Garden was the central produce market for London, excitingly alive in the wee hours when everyone else slept.

Before Charing Cross Road was opened in 1887, rambling St. Martin's Lane was the route used to go from Covent Garden to the Strand. The Strand itself has been the major land route between London and Westminster since Roman times. It was as full of traffic centuries ago as you will find it today.

When the Covent Garden area began to develop, the Thames River's shoreline was lined with the palaces of the Tudor aristocracy—Somerset House, Durham House, Savoy House, and Northumberland House. The once-fabulous palaces now have given way to hotels, shops, and restaurants.

The streets in and around Covent Garden have been celebrated in detective fiction since the time of Sherlock Holmes.

LENGTH OF WALK: 4 miles (3 miles if ended at the Covent Garden Underground Station)

See the map on page 47 for the boundaries of this walk and pages 249–51 for a list of the authors, books, and detectives mentioned.

PLACES OF INTEREST

St. Martin's-in-the-Fields, St. Martin's Place. Often features noon concerts.

Covent Garden

- ***St. Paul's Church.*** Closed Sunday.
- ***London Transport Museum.*** Open daily, admission charge.
- ***The Royal Opera House.***

Bow Street Police Court, Bow Street.

Cleopatra's Needle, Victoria Embankment.

The Theatre Royal, Drury Lane.

Queen's Chapel of the Savoy, Savoy Hill.

St. Martin's Theatre, West Street. Ongoing production of Agatha Christie's *The Mousetrap.*

PLACES TO EAT

Covent Garden. There are a variety of restaurants and snack shops within the confines of Covent Garden.

- ***Tutton's Brasserie,*** 11–12 Russell Street, Covent Garden. This inexpensive restaurant cafe, built in old Potato Market, has tables on the sidewalk in summer and serves international dishes. 071-836-1167.

Rule's, 35 Maiden Lane. Rule's is a "clubby" restaurant, very English in atmosphere, with Victorian decor and good traditional fare. Prices are expensive: there's a cover charge, and no credit cards are accepted. Reservations are needed. 071-836-5341.

Simpson's-in-the-Strand, 100 Strand. This English institution is famous for its roasts. Reservations are needed. 071-836-9112.

The Salisbury, 90 St. Martin's Lane. A theatrical pub opposite the Coliseum. The Salisbury has gorgeous etched glass, paneling, bronze nymphs, and red velvet alcove seating. 071-836-5863.

— COVENT GARDEN/THE STRAND — WALK

Begin this walk at the Charing Cross Underground Station. Take the St. Martin's-in-the-Fields exit. It will bring you to the east side of Trafalgar Square, in front of South Africa House.

In *Missing Joseph* by Elizabeth George, Deborah St. James fought her way to the door of the crowded bus as it inched its way toward Trafalgar Square.

Rose Mills, Tansy's sister, had heard Nell Bray speak in Trafalgar Square (*Sister Beneath the Sheet* by Gillian Linscott).

Douglas Perkins of Perkins and Tate Detective Agency was also on a bus passing Trafalgar Square when he felt homesick for his office and the lure of something constructive to do. (*Tourists Are for Trapping* by Marian Babson).

Turn left and walk north across the east side of the square to Duncannon Street. Cross Duncannon Street and you will find yourself in front of the colonnaded, classical church of St. Martin's-in-the-Fields. The present church was built by James Gibbs in 1722–24, but there has been a church on this site since the reign of Henry II.

A rich assortment of luminaries are buried at St. Martin's, including Nicholas Hilliard, the miniature painter (1619); Nell Gwynne, actress and mistress of King Charles II (1687); Jack Sheppard, the highwayman (1724); William Hogarth (1762); and Sir Joshua Reynolds (1762).

St. Martin's is the parish church of both the Admiralty and Buckingham Palace. Francis Bacon and Charles II were

Covent Garden
The Strand

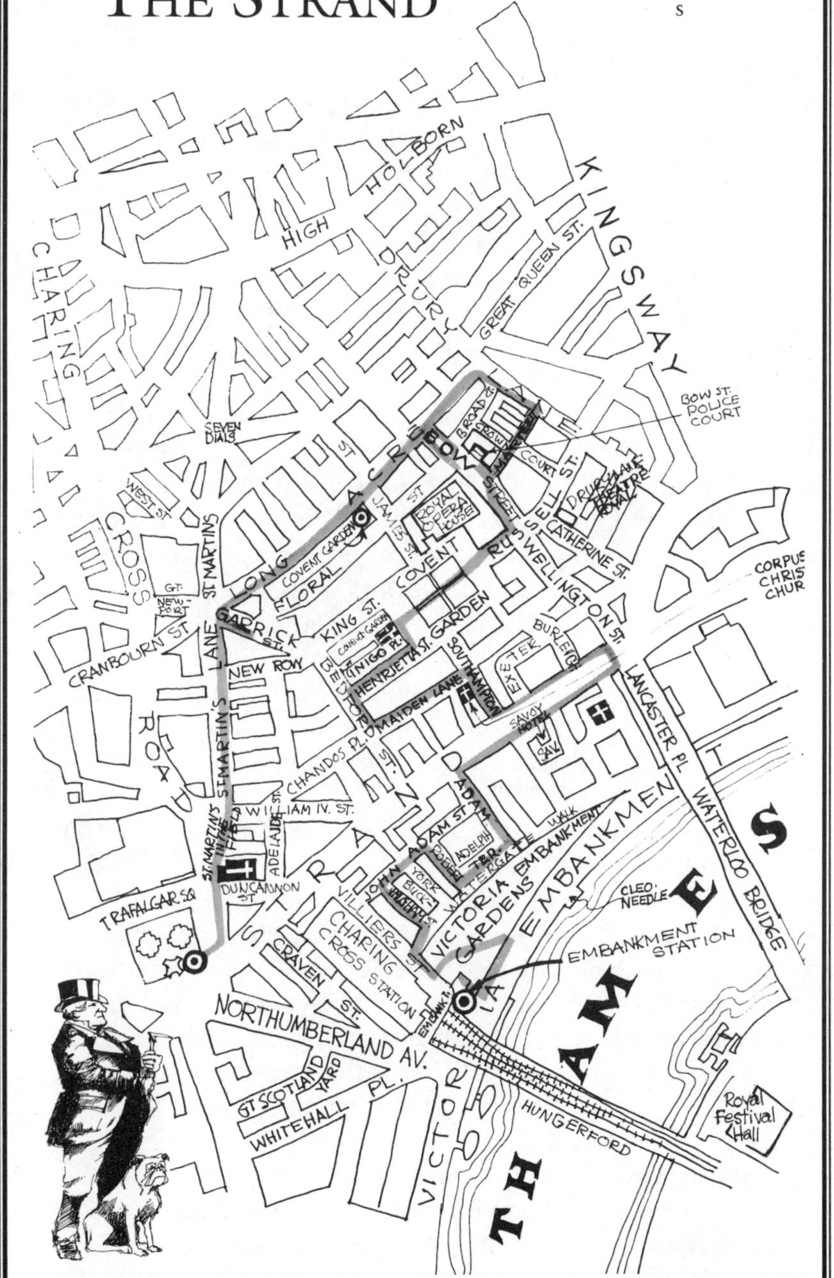

christened here, and George I was its first church warden. Today it is famous for its choir.

In Robert Lee Hall's *Benjamin Franklin and a Case of Christmas Murder,* Benjamin Franklin, along with his landlady Mrs. Stevenson, her daughter, Polly, and little Nick, attended Christmas Eve services at St. Martin's. Franklin, however, was still puzzling over the Fairbrass Ghost.

Go up the wide steps to St. Martin's and pause to look down Duncannon Street toward the Strand. Across the Strand, you will see the high sandstone facade of the Charing Cross Railway Station and Hotel. It is built over the site of Warren's Blacking Factory, where the young Charles Dickens was sent to work when his father was in Marshalsea Prison for debt.

Dentist Endicott Zayle had to meet his wife at Charing Cross Station, knowing that she was expecting the murdered Tyler Meredity (in *The Teeth of Adversity* by Marian Babson).

In *Sister Beneath the Sheet* by Gillian Linscott, at 10 o'clock on Monday morning, Nell Bray caught a train from Charing Cross Station. At 7:27 Tuesday morning, she stepped onto the sunlit platform of Biarritz Station after traveling all night from Paris.

In the Sherlock Holmes story, "A Scandal in Bohemia," Irene Adler and her future husband, Godfrey Norton, escaping from the King of Bohemia, left London from Charing Cross Station.

In Agatha Christie's *The Secret Adversary,* Tuppence Cowley took the train from Charing Cross to chase after the villains who had kidnapped an American, Jane Finn.

In the station yard is the gray stone monument called the Charing Cross. It commemorates one of the "Eleanor crosses" that Edward I erected wherever the coffin of his queen, Eleanor of Castile, rested on its final journey from Lincoln to Westminster Abbey. Until the Civil War in the seventeenth century, the original cross was at the head of Whitehall, where the statue of King Charles I is today.

Charing Cross in one of London's most popular landmarks. The Lampreys dutifully pointed it out to New Zealander Roberta Grey in Ngaio Marsh's *A Surfeit of Lampreys.*

Sherlock Holmes, in Sir Arthur Conan Doyle's "The Adventure of the Bruce-Partington Plans," set up the capture of Hugo Oberstein and the recovery of the Bruce-Partington Plans in a room above the station in the Charing Cross Hotel.

Leave the steps of St. Martin's and walk in front of the church to the right on St. Martin's Place. Cross William IV Street to St. Martin's Lane, taking note of the area to the right. In Julian Symons's *The Blackheath Poisonings,* it was here, in the area of Adelaide Street, where Isabel Mortimer walked after leaving Charing Cross Station. She finally stopped at a tall, narrow house.

St. Martin's Place becomes St. Martin's Lane when you cross William IV Street. St. Martin's Lane was the original way north from Charing Cross but was superseded as a major traffic route when Charing Cross Road to the west was carved out in 1887.

The east side of St. Martin's Lane is lined with eighteenth- and nineteenth-century buildings. A host of theaters are also located in the general area, making it almost the center of the theater district.

Theaters often serve as settings for detective novels because they are inhabited by people who act out their emotions dramatically, and because theaters classically embody the kind of "locked room," or controlled environment, so loved by mystery writers. Many writers, among them Dame Ngaio Marsh and Josephine Tey, were passionately fond of the theater.

In Dorothy L. Sayers's *Whose Body?,* Lord Peter airily suggested to Charles Parker that they quit work, go home and lunch, and then go to the Coliseum, where the shows were not taxing to the mind. The Coliseum, with its vertical black sign, is the first theater you will pass as you walk north; it is on the west side of St. Martin's Lane.

Built in 1902 to rival Drury Lane, the Coliseum has a three-piece revolving stage, three tearooms, and a roof garden. Until 1968 it was the home of the Sadler's Wells Ballet; it is currently dedicated to opera.

As you walk north on St. Martin's Lane, keep to the east side past the tiny alleyways of Brydges Place, Mays Court, and

Goodwin's Court. Stop here to peek at the tiny row of narrow eighteenth-century houses with their bow windows, where Chippendale had his workshops.

In *Bleak House,* Charles Dickens called this area a slum.

Continue past the Friends' Meeting House. Across the street is the Salisbury Pub where actors like to congregate, and beyond it, the Duke of York's Theatre. The tiny, gaslit street next to the Duke of York's is called Cecil Court. It runs west from St. Martin's Lane. Although its shops do not include a theatrical flea market, Cecil Court makes an excellent candidate for Memory Lane, an alleyway in the heart of London's theaterland where Jemima Shore and the elderly Prideaux brothers went to Tony Jerrold's "Stage Whispers" in Antonia Fraser's *A Splash of Red.*

Cross New Row and continue along St. Martin's Lane past the Albery Theatre to the junction with Cranbourne Street and Great Newport Street to the west, and Garrick Street and Long Acre to the east.

The Arts Theatre Club, known for its avant-garde productions, is to the left in Great Newport Street. A group of Mark Callender's Cambridge friends were attending a play there while Mark was being murdered near Cambridge (*An Unsuitable Job for a Woman* by P. D. James).

At West Street, just before St. Martin's Lane becomes Monmouth Street, are the twin theaters of St. Martin's and the Ambassadors. Agatha Christie's record-setting *The Mousetrap* has been running at St. Martin's since 1974. The play opened at the Ambassadors in 1952 and ran there for twenty-two years before being moved to St. Martin's.

The Mousetrap began life as a twenty-two–minute radio play written for the BBC for the eightieth birthday of Queen Mary. Because the Queen was pleased and because the radio presentation was well received, Dame Agatha decided to turn it into a full-length play. She gave the earnings from the play to her only grandchild, Mathew Prichard, as a birthday gift.

In 1958 *The Mousetrap* became the longest-running play of any kind in the history of British theater. In 1961, when Mathew was captain of the Eton cricket team, the play was still going strong. The family took the entire team to see a performance. Throughout the sixties, seventies, eighties, and now into the nineties, the play's run has now turned *The Mousetrap* from a record-setter into a theatrical phenomena.

The Phoenix Theatre, where actress Marta Hallard was performing while Inspector Grant was in hospital, is just north of here on Charing Cross Road. In Josephine Tey's classic *The Daughter of Time,* when Grant's landlady visited him, he asked her to go around by St. Martin's Lane to the Phoenix Theatre and give old Saxon at the stage door a note for Hallard.

At the corner of Garrick and Long Acre is the Garrick Wine Bar. Turn to the right and go a short distance along Garrick Street, which is named for the famous eighteenth-century actor David Garrick. No. 15, the tall, gray stone building with ironwork trim, on the south side of the street, is the Garrick Club.

The Garrick Club is primarily an actors' or theatrical club. This made it an appropriate place for Ngaio Marsh's leading actor, Sir Dougal, to be feted after the opening night tour de force production of *Macbeth* in *Light Thickens.*

The Garrick was the club of Brigadier Sir James White, head of British Intelligence, in Evelyn Anthony's series of thriller featuring superspy Davina Graham. In *The Defector*, White had Graham bring Sasanov, the defecting Russian, to lunch at the Garrick. Sasanov admired the bronze busts and marble inscriptions, the portraits and scenes from famous plays, and the glass cases of mementos of past celebrities, but he could not imagine a setting less appropriate for the head of British Intelligence than this flamboyant eighteenth-century club.

A rebellious Jeremiah "Jorrocks" Atkins remembered when Plum's was a club for gentlemen who understood "about foxes and hunting; [now] anyone would think it was the Garrick, [with] the kind of actor fellows they were letting in." (*Murder at Plum's* by Amy Meyers)

Leave the Garrick Club and turn left. Return to the intersection of St. Martin's Lane and Garrick Street. Turn right and walk along Long Acre, one of the older Covent Garden Streets. It was once the home of the wholesalers who supplied the markets. In *Frequent Hearses,* Mr. Snerd, Edmund Crispin's private eye, had his office in Long Acre. When Snerd sold a letter that he had stolen from the Cranes to the news media, the CID came to Long Acre searching for him.

Long Acre, with its vintage lampposts, has an old-fashioned charm about it. There are a variety of shops along the way, featuring art, apparel, books, and even food.

As you approach the shopping area that has been created out of old Covent Garden, you will cross a succession of small alleys and courtyards: Rose Street, Conduit Court, Langley Court, and James Street, and finally, the Covent Garden Underground Station.

Beyond James Street is tiny Hanover Place. The crowds will thicken as you enter the Covent Garden area. It is a fabulous place for all kinds and conditions of tourists and shoppers to loiter, linger, and window-shop. The next cross street is Bow Street, where you will be turning right.

At the corner of Long Acre and Bow is the cream and red-brick facade of the *International Herald Tribune.*

Bow Street is rich in murder and mystery associations. It was here that the famous Bow Street runners originated and received their name.

Walk south to Floral Street, where you will see the Royal Opera House with its facade of gigantic columns and its classical pediment. The Opera House occupies the northeast corner of Covent Garden.

In *Swan Song* by Edmund Crispin, Elizabeth, an attractive writer, watched tenor Adam Langley rehearsing *Der Rosenkavalier* as she sat in "the large, rococo splendor of the opera house, where tier upon gilded tier of boxes and galleries, radiating on either side from the royal box, towered into the upper darkness and callipygic cherubs and putti held the pillars in a passionate embrace."

When Philip Trent came back from Europe to haunt the opera in hopes of seeing Mabel Manderson, he finally met her at a performance of Wagner's *Tristan and Isolde* and fell in love all over again. (*Trent's Last Case* by E. C. Bentley)

In Robert Barnard's *A Scandal in Belgravia,* Peter Procter

was having dinner with a political "wannabe" called Veronica at the long-gone Les Truiterie restaurant, when Timothy Wycliffe and Derek Wicklow turned up. They had been trying to get in to see Maria Callas in a performance of *Norm* at the Opera House.

Walk back from the Opera House to the corner of Long Acre and Bow Street. Cross Bow Street and continue down Long Acre to Drury Lane. The northern part of Drury Lane is old and narrow. It is lined with coffee bars and pubs. It is easy to imagine the spot as the lodging place of actress Nell Gwynne, mistress of Charles II and mother of several of his ducal sons.

In Dorothy L. Sayers's *Murder Must Advertise,* Lord Peter and a contingent of men from Scotland Yard caught the drug dealers they had been chasing in a fictional Drury Lane pub called the Stag at Bay.

In *Time of Hope* by Susan B. Kelly, Alison Hope, trying to sort out her relationship with Detective Inspector Nick Trevellyan, arranged to meet her old fried Ralph Squires for lunch in a pricey Covent Garden restaurant "just around the corner. . .in Drury Lane." After a long lunch, Alison left the restaurant and hurried off toward the solicitor's office in Long Acre.

Across Drury Lane, Long Acre takes a jog and becomes Great Queen Street, which is named for Henrietta Maria, wife of Charles I. In *Murder Must Advertise,* reporter Hector Puncheon went into the White Swan, a pub on Great Queen Street, where he accidentally gave the drug gang's code word and was passed cocaine by a man in evening dress.

The Connaught Rooms at 61 Great Queen Street were the site of a luncheon for a distinguished airman that Puncheon was sent to cover. The Freemasons Hall is further along Great Queens Street.

The West London Methodist Mission, formerly Kingsway Hall, is on the left at the corner of Great Queen Street and Kingsway. It is where Hector Puncheon covered a political meeting. It also may easily stand in for the sinister Simon's Hall in Holborn, where Simon the Clerk hypnotized his followers in Charles Williams's *All Hallows' Eve*.

Dorothy L. Sayers worked as a copywriter at Bensons at 75 Kingsway. The iron spiral staircase at Bensons was recreated in *Murder Must Advertise*. In recognition, the Bensons' staircase was later marked with a plaque to Sayers.

Instead of walking all the way to Kingsway, turn right off Great Queen Street into Drury Lane and go past Broad Court to Martlett Court. Turn right again and return to Bow Street. At Bow Street, turn right once more and look for the Bow Street Police Court, which opened here in 1740. In 1748, the playwright and novelist Sir Henry Fielding and his half-brother, Sir John Fielding, became the presiding magistrates. The Court can be distinguished by an iron railing along the sidewalk.

It was from this court that the pre-Scotland Yard detectives, the Bow Street Runners (or Robin Redbreasts as they were sometimes called because of their red waistcoats) were sent out to improve on the work of the inefficient Watch.

Mr. Jeremiah Dimm, a Bow Street Runner who suspected Marisol Denning of the murder of her tyrannical husband, took pride in his red vest, his badge of office in Barbara Metzger's *A Suspicious Affair*. The Runners were the chief detectives in London until the Home Secretary, Sir Robert Peel, formed the uniformed Metropolitan Police, or Bobbies, in 1829. By doing so, law and order was brought to society, and writers were given a new kind of hero to write about. A point noted by both G. K. Chesterton, in his essay "In Defence of Detective Stories," and Dorothy L. Sayers, in her introduction to Gollancz's first collection of detective stories.

John Creasey, in his novel *The Masters of Bow Street,* wrote of the development of the London police beginning with the Bow Street Days.

In *Murder Must Advertise,* Lord Peter Wimsey, in his role as Death Bredon, was seen entering the Bow Street Court dressed in a dark suit.

Lord Worth's brother, Captain Audley, promised to personally escort Judith Tavener to Bow Street in order to put the Runners on the trail of her missing brother, in Georgette Heyer's *Regency Buck*.

Kevin John Athlone, the lover of Jemima Shore's friend

Chloe, was arraigned for Chloe's murder at the Bow Street Court in Antonia Fraser's *A Splash of Red*.

Sherlock Holmes appeared at the Bow Street Court with Dr. Watson in the case of "The Man with the Twisted Lip," and Gideon, J. J. Marric's (John Creasey's) Scotland Yard detective, witnessed a brassy-haired woman being brought up before the Bow Street magistrate in *Gideon's Wrath*.

G. K. Chesterton's brother, Cecil, was arraigned at Bow Street on charges of libel in 1913.

Like so many others, Inspector Thomas Pitt, Anne Perry's inimitable detective, worked out of Bow Street Police Station.

Turn left at the Bow Street Police Court and walk back along Bow Street to the corner of Russell Street, where Bow Street becomes Wellington Street. One short block to your left, up Russell Street, is the Theatre Royal, Drury Lane, on Catherine Street. It is across from the Nell of Old Drury pub at No. 29. The pub is named for Charles II's mistress, actress Nell Gwynne. A definite plus, it serves real ale.

The Theatre Royal, Drury Lane, which was begun by royal charter under Charles II, retains some of its original Georgian features. The present building is the fourth on this site and comes with its own ghost. The spectre, which has been seen by any number of witnesses, is a slim figure of a young man dressed in grey. He has a white wig, carries a tricorn hat, and wears riding boots. A sword hangs from his waist. Who he is or why he haunts the building is not clear, but theater historian W. J. Macqueen Pope suggests that in the eighteenth century, the young man had a girlfriend in the theater. For whatever reason, the management of the theater did not want him about and ordered him out; a fight followed and the young man was killed. His body was hastily walled up in the little passage along which he had walked every night to meet his sweetheart. This theory is based on a discovery in mid-Victorian days that took place during renovation work at the theater. A skeleton was found in an area that had been walled off. The skeleton had a Cromwellian-style dagger embedded in its ribs (*Haunted London* by Peter Underwood).

In John Dickson Carr's Regency thriller *The Bride of Newgate*, Dick Derwent knew the actors at Drury Lane well, for his mistress Dolly was one of them.

Adjoining the Theatre Royal on the corner of Russell Street was the Rose Tavern where, in 1712, a duel between Lord Mohun and the Duke of Hamilton ended with both men dead.

Turn left on Russell Street, known in the seventeenth and eighteenth centuries for its many "literary" coffee houses. Boswell first met Dr. Johnson in 1763 in Tom's Coffee House, which was located over a bookshop at No. 8 Russell Street.

Follow Russell Street into Covent Garden. The London Transport Museum is to the left as you come into the area. This exhibit of stagecoaches, buses, and trains is housed in the old flower market. Tutton's Brasserie, a cafe on the site of an old potato market, is to your right, facing the Central Market.

Originally, Covent Garden was the convent garden of Westminster Abbey. The garden was seized by Henry VIII in 1552 and sold to the first Earl of Bedford, who built himself a house facing the Strand. Later, the fourth earl hired Inigo Jones to lay out a residential quarter to the north, stretching to the Bedford House Gardens on the south. In 1661, the then Duke of Bedford established a small market here. It grew to become London's principal fruit, vegetable, and flower market until it was relocated in 1974.

The old Covent Garden was then converted into an attractive, high-ceilinged, two-level pedestrian mall, with shops and sidewalk cafes. It has become a haunt for tourists from everywhere. A performance by street entertainers of some kind is often underway in the open area at the end of the covered arcades of the Central Market.

It was before Covent Garden's transformation that Dorothy L. Sayers's reporter Hector Puncheon walked into Covent Garden after a night spent covering a warehouse fire. The market was filled with vans and lorries laden with fruit and flowers; porters were unloading stout crates and barrels filled with a variety of produce. Puncheon had come to Covent Garden because its pubs had early opening times to accommodate the market's men.

Sheila Wexford explained to her father that she had bought a pair of wire cutters in a DIY place in Covent Garden before going to Northhamptonshire with PANDA—Players Anti-Nuclear Direct Action—in *The Veiled One* by Ruth Rendell.

In *The Killing of Ellis Martin* by Lucretia Grindle, the type of scarf that had Ellis's blood on it was sold only in two places, one of them a trendy little boutique off Covent Garden.

Walk through the Central Market with its blue arches and red stalls into the open area, where you will see the red-brick back of St. Paul's Church, Covent Garden, often called the "actors' church."

In Jack M. Bickham's *Breakfast at Wimbledon,* Brad Smith was operating on the rule of "minus two" as he made a call from a telephone kiosk. This left him plenty of time to catch a taxi for Covent Garden. By the time he got there, people were milling about everywhere. They flocked to the open-air pavilion in the center, where the stands of arts and crafts were. Some of the street players had started up near the church. Smith stood and waited.

When the Duke of Bedford asked for an inexpensive building, Inigo Jones designed for him what is called "the handsomest barn in Europe." The present St. Paul's retains Inigo Jones's Tuscan-arched eastern portico. It served as a backdrop in *My Fair Lady* and was the church Alfred Doolittle was insistent that his friends get him to on time. the portico also provides the setting for the opening scene of Shaw's play *Pygmalion*. Pedestrians run under it to escape the "torrents of heavy summer rain." *My Fair Lady,* is of course, based upon Shaw's play.

The church entrance is on the far side, at Inigo Place, which runs into Bedford Street. The churchyard, between King Street and Henrietta Street and joined by Bedford Street, is still lit by gaslights decorated with a ducal coronet in honor of the Dukes of Bedford.

Inside the church are many memorials to actors. There are said to be more famous people buried here than in any other London church except St. Paul's Cathedral and Westminster Abbey. Among the illustrious buried here are Samuel Butler, Grinling Gibbons, Thomas Rowlandson, and Ellen Terry. Legend has it, although no record supports it, that the highwayman Claude Duval was buried here after being hanged at Tyburn. A stone marks the place where he is said to be interred. It is inscribed: "Here lies DuVall: Reader if male thou art/Look to thy purse; if female to they heart."

G. K. Chesterton preached a series of lay sermons here, and in 1978 the Dorothy L. Sayers Historical and Literary Society held a Thanksgiving service here in her memory.

You may end the walk here by turning right at King Street at the northern edge of Covent Garden and then go left to James Street and Long Acre for the Covent Garden Underground Station.

To continue the walk, turn left behind St. Paul's into tiny Henrietta Street. At No. 14 Henrietta Street, you will see the display windows of Victor Gollancz, whose yellow-jacketed, hardbacked, crime thriller series featured the works of Dorothy L. Sayers, together with many other mystery writers.

Jane Austen, whose *Northanger Abbey* is one of the classic spoofs of the gothic genre, often visited her brother Henry in London and, in 1813, stayed with him at No. 10 Henrietta Street. At the end of the street, turn left and go one short block on Bedford Street to Maiden Lane. Turn left again and walk up Maiden Lane toward Southampton Street. Near Bedford Street, you will pass the stage door of the Adelphi Theatre, which fronts on the Strand. In the nineteenth century, an actor was stabbed to death here in a dispute over a part.

When Ginger Joe was collecting alibis for Lord Peter in *Murder Must Advertise,* he discovered that Mr. Haagedorn of Pym's Publicity had a leave of absence to attend his aunt's funeral on the day Victor Dean was killed on the agency staircase, but that Haagedorn was actually seen leaving a matinee at the Adelphi Theatre.

Halfway up Maiden Lane on the north side of the street, at No. 35, is a creamy yellow building with a red awning. This is Rule's, a world-famous restaurant known for choice vintage wines and high-quality food. With its richly comfortable Victorian furnishings and excellent English fare, Rule's was a favorite eating spot of Charles Dickens and the Prince of Wales, who became King Edward VII. Both had private alcoves in which to dine. One of Dickens's *Sketches by Boz* was called "Covent Garden."

Rule's is still popular with royalty and other VIPs, but its main clientele, who tend to treat it like a private club, come from many walks of life.

Rule's is popular with writers of detective fiction, and has had mention in numerous works. Dorothy L. Sayers and her college friend, Muriel St. Clare Byrne, met at Rule's to plot their play, *Busman's Honeymoon.*

Lord Peter Wimsey in *Strong Poison* took various guests to Rule's; among them was Cattery staffer Joan Murchison after she had successfully burgled Norman Urquhart's office safe.

In Patricia Moyes's *Who is Simon Warwick?,* Sir Percy Crumble was seen eating at Rule's with lawyer Ambrose Quince and Bertie Hamstone. All of them were implicated in the murder of one claimant to the Charlton fortune.

On the south side of Maiden Lane, a blue historical plaque marks the place where the French writer Voltaire once lived, and toward the end of the block is the tall, dark bulk of Corpus Christi Roman Catholic Church.

Walk to the corner of Maiden Lane and Southampton Street, where you turn right. In Anthony Berkeley's *The Poisoned Chocolates Case,* a forged letter was mailed by night from the Southamptom Street Post Office, which was directly across from the Hotel Cecil, where Crimes Circle member (and suspect) Sir Charles Wildman had been attending his old school's reunion dinner.

Continue south on Southampton until you reach the Strand, and turn left to walk along the north side of the street. Called the noisiest street in all London, the Strand is jammed with traffic, as befits the oldest route by land from the City of London to Westminster. Once lined with noble palaces, it is now filled with hotels, restaurants, and a variety of shops.

Robert B. Parker's American PI, Spenser, walked up the Strand in *The Judas Goat* and passed a London cop walking along with his hands behind his back, a walkie-talkie in his hip pocket, and a nightstick concealed in a deep pocket. Spenser felt an excited, tight feeling in his stomach knowing that he was "in the old country, the ancestral home for people who spoke English and could read it."

In Josephine Tey's *The Man in the Queue,* Inspector Grant walked up the Strand at dusk. It was "as brilliant as day and crowded, the ebb of the late home-goers meeting the current of the early pleasure seekers and causing a fret that filled both footpath and roadway." He walked up "the gaudy pavement . . .in and out of the changing light from the shop windows: rose light, gold light, diamond light, shoe shop, clothes shop, jewellers. Presently the crowd thinned and men and women became individual beings instead of the corpuscles of a mob."

A figure lurking in the shadows watched Gaylord Erskine stroll along the Strand on his way to Plum's in Amy Meyers's *Murder at Plum's.*

In Julian Symons's *The Blackheath Poisonings,* the Mortimer family business was in the Strand. In *Death in Ecstasy* by Ngaio Marsh, Inspector Alleyn went down the Strand to a little street where the victim's solicitor had his office. The place looked like a memorial to Charles Dickens, with its dingy entry smelling of cobwebs and old varnish. A dark staircase led to a landing where a frosted glass skylight let in enough light to show the name on the door. The atmosphere was made up of dust, leather, varnish, dry sherry, and age.

Harriet Vane's publishers, Grimsby and Cole, had their offices in the Strand. Lord Peter Wimsey went there to interview them in Dorothy L. Sayers's *Strong Poison.*

Walk past Exeter and Burleigh Streets to Wellington Street. North of here on Wellington Street is the former Lyceum Theatre where, in *The Sign of Four,* Sherlock Holmes, Dr. Watson, and Mary Morstan began an adventure that led to Watson and Mary's marriage. The theater is now a dance hall.

Cross the Strand to the south side and turn right. Soon you will see a brass marquee marking that "London institution" called Simpson's-in-the-Strand. It is a restaurant that has the aura of a gentlemen's club, although women are now allowed. Reservations are a must.

On a weekday in August, the dining room was not particularly crowded, so it was difficult to imagine Willis wiggling about unnoticed as he jealously tried to spy on Lord Peter Wimsey and Pamela Dean while they were at Simpson's for lunch in *Murder Must Advertise*.

Sherlock Holmes and Dr. Watson were great patrons of Simpson's, once remarking that "something nutritious at Simpson's would not be out of place."

In Parker's *The Judas Goat,* Spenser was taken to Simpson's by a London representative of the rich American who had hired him to wipe out the Liberty gang. The Englishman had told Spenser that Simpson's was rather a London institution, so Spenser watched with a sardonic eye as he was served the native cuisine.

In E. C. Bentley's *Trent's Last Case,* Trent celebrated his engagement to Mabel by taking her uncle, Burton Cupples, to Sheppard's (undoubtedly, Simpson's). Cupples ordered milk and soda water, appalling both Trent and the wine waiter.

After Simpson's, go left for a short distance to Savoy Court, the only place in London where taxis are allowed to drive on the right-hand side of the street. Across the court is a shining, silver-colored marquee topped by a Roman soldier.

Walk to the back of the courtyard and go into the lobby of the Savoy Hotel. It is a pleasant place to sit for a few minutes, admiring the gold and marble columns. It is also a pleasant spot for an afternoon or after-dinner drink, although prices tend to be steep.

The original Savoy was a handsome palace that belonged to John of Gaunt. It was burned down in the Peasant's Revolt under Wat Tyler at the time of Gaunt's nephew, Richard II, was king.

A new hotel was built in the grand manner in 1889 by Richard D'Oyly Carte. One revolutionary feature was the inclusion of a bathroom for every bedroom.

The newly refurbished Savoy Theatre is on the site of an earlier theater where D'Oyly Carte staged the Gilbert and Sullivan operettas.

In Anne Perry's *Resurrection Row,* Charlotte Pitt and her husband, Police Inspector Thomas Pitt, had attended a performance of *The Mikado* at the Savoy. As they were leaving the theater the body of a man was discovered in a hansom cab outside the theater.

The Savoy Chapel, built in 1864 on the site of (and as a replica of) the earlier medieval one, is the chapel of the Royal Victorian Order. It is often the scene of grand weddings, with the receptions held next door in the hotel.

Savoy Hill, to the south of the chapel, was the location of the first offices of the BBC.

The Savoy Hotel is mentioned in a variety of detective stories, including the spy novels of E. Phillips Oppenheim, in which his heroes seem to lunch regularly at the Savoy Grill.

In Edmund Crispin's *Frequent Hearses,* one of the Crane film family tried to impress a secretary by taking her to dine at the Savoy. And in *The Unpleasantness at Bellona Club,* Lord Peter Wimsey took heiress Ann Dorland there.

In John Buchan's *The Thirty-Nine Steps,* Richard Hannay, using up time before the trap was to be sprung on the Black Stone conspiracy, had a very good lunch at the Savoy, then smoked the best cigar they had to offer.

Deborah St. James, in Elizabeth George's *Missing Joseph,* went to the Savoy to show her portfolio to an up-and-coming producer called Richie Rica. After a definite rebuff, she drank cappuccino in the stylish Upstairs, the hotel's upscale coffee shop.

The Savoy Hotel is most definitely Christie territory. In *The Mystery of the Blue Train,* American millionaire Rufus Van Aldin always stayed at the Savoy when in London.

Hercule Poirot sent Hastings to the Savoy to work as a secretary for another rich American in *The Big Four.*

In *The Secret Adversary,* Tommy Beresford told Tuppence Cowley that it was perfectly sickening during the war (World War I) how those brass hats drove from the War Office, to the Savoy and the Savoy to the War Office. Nevertheless, Tommy seemed to enjoy Julius Hersheimer's private supper party in a private Savoy dining room.

Agatha Christie's publishers threw several large parties in her honor at the Savoy, and, in 1954, she hosted one for over 100 people to celebrate the opening of her mystery play, *Witness for the Prosecution*.

Leave the precincts of the Savoy and walk westward along the Strand to Adam Street. When she left the Savoy, Deborah St. James hurried out into one of those wind-fierce, misty London days. As she thought about walking home, she heard the roar of traffic in the Strand and fancied a walk along the Embankment instead. (Elizabeth George, *Missing Joseph*)

Before ending this walk at Embankment Underground Station, take time to explore the Adelphi, as the area south of the Strand is called. (*Adelphi* in Greek means brothers.) This section was developed by the Adam brothers on the site of the townhouse of the bishops of Durham. The Adams built terraces of houses raised on arches above the Thames, but many of them no longer survive.

Turn left and walk down Adam Street where, at Nos. 7, 8, and 9, you can see how the Adelphi was meant to look, with rows of tall, plain houses built of dark brick. Looking down toward the Embankment and the Thames, you can see how high the whole development was built above the river. You are standing on the "steep streets of Adelphi looking towards the sunset-covered river," described by G. K. Chesterton in his Father Brown story "The Man in the Passage." In that tale, a murder occurred in a dark alley off the fictional Apollo Theatre on the Strand.

In Nicholas Blake's *End of Chapter,* the publishing firm of Wenham and Geraldine, where Nigel Strangeways investigated a mystery, had its office on fictional Angel Street, Adelphi Terrace, for which Adam Street makes the best substitute. According to Blake (aka C. Day Lewis), Wenham and Geraldine, Publishers, occupied the last house on Angel Street. Its front faced the street, and its rear overlooked the [Embankment] Gardens. Angel Street was a "distinguished backwater," where the Strand traffic roared softly. Nigel Strangeways thought it would be nice to live in a top-floor flat in one of these tall, elegantly uniform houses. The firm's main door, flanked by two display windows, was set in the facade of brick. The exquisite molding and fanlight of the doorway created an impression of solidity and grace when Victorian grandees went up the shallow steps to take a glass of Madeira.

In Georgette Heyer's *Death in the Stocks,* the law firm of Carrington, Radclyffe and Carrington had its offices on the first floor of a house at the bottom of Adam Street, facing the Adelphi Terrace. The head of the firm, Giles Carrington's father, worked in a big, untidy room with a view of the Thames River through a gap between nearby buildings.

Now walk to the end of Adam Street and turn right into the Adelphi Terrace. This is the place where John Dickson Carr's G. K. Chesterton look-alike detective, Dr. Gideon Fell, lived at No. 1, handy to Scotland Yard consultations.

Follow Adelphi Terrace to Robert Street. Turn left and look for the steps down into Lower Robert Street. Lower Robert Street will give you a glimpse of one of the original Adam arches. This "basement" area was where young thieves like Dickens's Oliver Twist plied their trade.

Now return to ground level and take Robert Street to John Adam Street and turn left. The elegant building at No. 8 houses the Royal Society of Arts. A short distance ahead is Buckingham Street (the street names indicate that this area once belonged to the Villiers, Dukes of Buckingham). At Buckingham Street turn left toward the river. This street is filled with small houses with old-fashioned door hoods and iron snuffers for linkboys' torches. No. 15 stands on the spot where Charles Dickens lived when he was a young journalist. He used the house that was there as a setting in *David Copperfield.*

At the end of Buckingham Street is the Watergate, a huge arch that marked the entrance to the Villiers palace from the Thames. Go through the arch and turn right on Watergate Walk. Take Watergate Walk to Villiers Street, where, at No. 47, you will find Gordon's Wine Bar.

Gordon's is very popular with the bureaucrats from Whitehall. It is very likely the model for the pub frequented by Blake's Nigel Strangeways.

At Watergate Walk and Villiers Street is the Players Club, which is open only to members. Dorothy L. Sayers corresponded with the secretary of the club about a production of her comedy, *Love All,* but World War II made casting it impossible.

Turn left into the Embankment Gardens, which stretch along the Embankment and afford a striking view of the Thames. From the gardens, you have a good view of Cleopatra's Needle, which was given to Queen Victoria by the viceroy of Egypt in 1819. It was set up here in 1878; its twin stands in Central Park in New York City. Under the cover of darkness, the anarchist, Thursday, was landed near the needle by a river tug in G. K. Chesterton's *The Man Who Was Thursday.*

From the gardens, you will also have an excellent view of the South Bank across the Thames. Since World War II, many changes have occurred in this area, including the building of the Royal Festival Hall, across the Hungerford Bridge footpath, and, farther east by Waterloo Bridge, the National Theatre. Oxford don Patrick Grant in Margaret Yorke's *Cast for Death* took the Hungerford footpath across the river to the Players' Theatre (a fictional mix of the National Theatre and Festival Hall). This was near the place where the body of his actor friend was found in the river.

When you are ready to end this walk, return to the bottom of Villiers Street and the Embankment Underground Station.

4

BLOOMSBURY WALK

BACKGROUND

This walk take you into Bloomsbury, the heart of intellectual London. Both the British Museum and London University are here, together with publishing houses, bookstores, art galleries, small museums, and thousands of students.

Bloomsbury is a corruption of the word *Blemonde,* so called because, in the eleventh century, William the Conqueror gave the land here to his vassal, Baron Blemonde. Today's Bloomsbury had its beginning in 1660, when the Earl of Southampton decided to lay out a square south of his house. The Duke of Montague then built a lavish mansion on the site of the present British Museum. To the west, the Duke of Bedford and other great landowning families established their residences. Their family names—Russell, Tavistock, Bedford, and Woburn—are still prominent in the area.

In the eighteenth and nineteenth centuries, this was an elegant neighborhood of handsome row houses and attractive squares. Gradually it became less desirable, although it has always remained respectable. Eventually, the mansions became flats, boardinghouses, and small hotels, places where students, artists, and other intellectuals could afford to live.

Perhaps it was in this area that Anne Perry located the newly built home of Charlotte and Thomas Pitt in *Traitors Gate.*

The well-known Bloomsbury Group, which was formed in the early part of the twentieth century, lived in and around Gordon Square located in the heart of the London University buildings. The group included Virginia Woolf; her husband, Leonard; her sister Vanessa; and Vanessa's husband Clive Bell; in addition, it included Lytton Strachey, E. M. Forster, and others from the world of arts and letters, who met "for human intercourse and the enjoyment of beautiful objects." Allusions to this group abound. For example, as the second Mrs. Machin talked of her husband and his writing in Robert Barnard's *Posthumous Papers,* her words carried "a heady whiff of Bloomsbury in the twenties. . . ."

LENGTH OF WALK: 3.2 miles

See the map on page 69 for the boundaries of this walk and pages 251–53 for a list of the authors, books, and detectives mentioned.

PLACES OF INTEREST

University of London, University College, Gower Street. The central range. The Petrie Museum of Egyptology. Free.

British Museum, Great Russell Street. World's greatest collection of antiquities. Free. Scholar's pass needed to use the library.

Percival David Foundation of Chinese Art, Gordon Square. Chinese ceramics from AD 960. Free.

Jewish Museum, Adolph Tuck Hall, Woburn House, Tavistock Square (site of Tavistock House, where Dickens wrote *Bleak House*). Free.

Dickens House, 48 Doughty Street. Dicken's home from 1837 to 1839. Only surviving Dickens residence in London. Admission charge.

PLACES TO EAT

The Lamb, 94 Lamb's Conduit Street. A favored spot of Charles Dickens, this is an excellent example of authentic Victorian architecture and decoration. It has Rowlandson engravings, plus hundreds of photographs of early theatrical personalities. 071-405-0713.

Pizza Express, 30 Coptic Street. This reliable chain has a wine license. 071-636-3232.

Museum Tavern, 49 Great Russell Street. Across from the British Museum, Karl Marx drank here. Echoes of the Bloomsbury Group can be heard among stained glass and velvet draperies. 071-242-8987.

BLOOMSBURY WALK

Begin the walk at the Euston Square Underground Station. Leave the station and take Melton Street to Euston Road. Cross Euston Road and go right to Gower Street. Parallel with Gower Street, a couple of streets off to the right, is Tottenham Court Road, which has several mystery associations worth mentioning.

In Patricia Wentworth's *The Case is Closed,* a model called Celia refused to show a "ghastly pink rag" because it was not her style, and "she wouldn't be seen dead in it in Tottenham Court Road."

In the stage directions of *Busman's Honeymoon,* Dorothy L. Sayers referred to the bargains in cheap furniture for which Tottenham Court Road is known.

Sherlock Holmes bought his Stradivarius violin from a pawnbroker in Tottenham Court Road.

The Knightsbridge School of English had been in business for 12 years. Before setting it up, Ned Nurse had been employed by a series of schools around Tottenham Court Road (*English School Murder* by Ruth Dudley Edwards).

Gervase Fen checked up on the alibi of the suspect, novelist Evan George, in a Tottenham Court Road pub in Edmund Crispin's *Frequent Hearses.*

Lovejoy, Lydia, Lorane, and Max the hung-over writer made up a moody quartet at the Tottenham Court Road Tube Station as they met and began a day of filmmaking in Jonathan Gash's *The Very Last Gambado.*

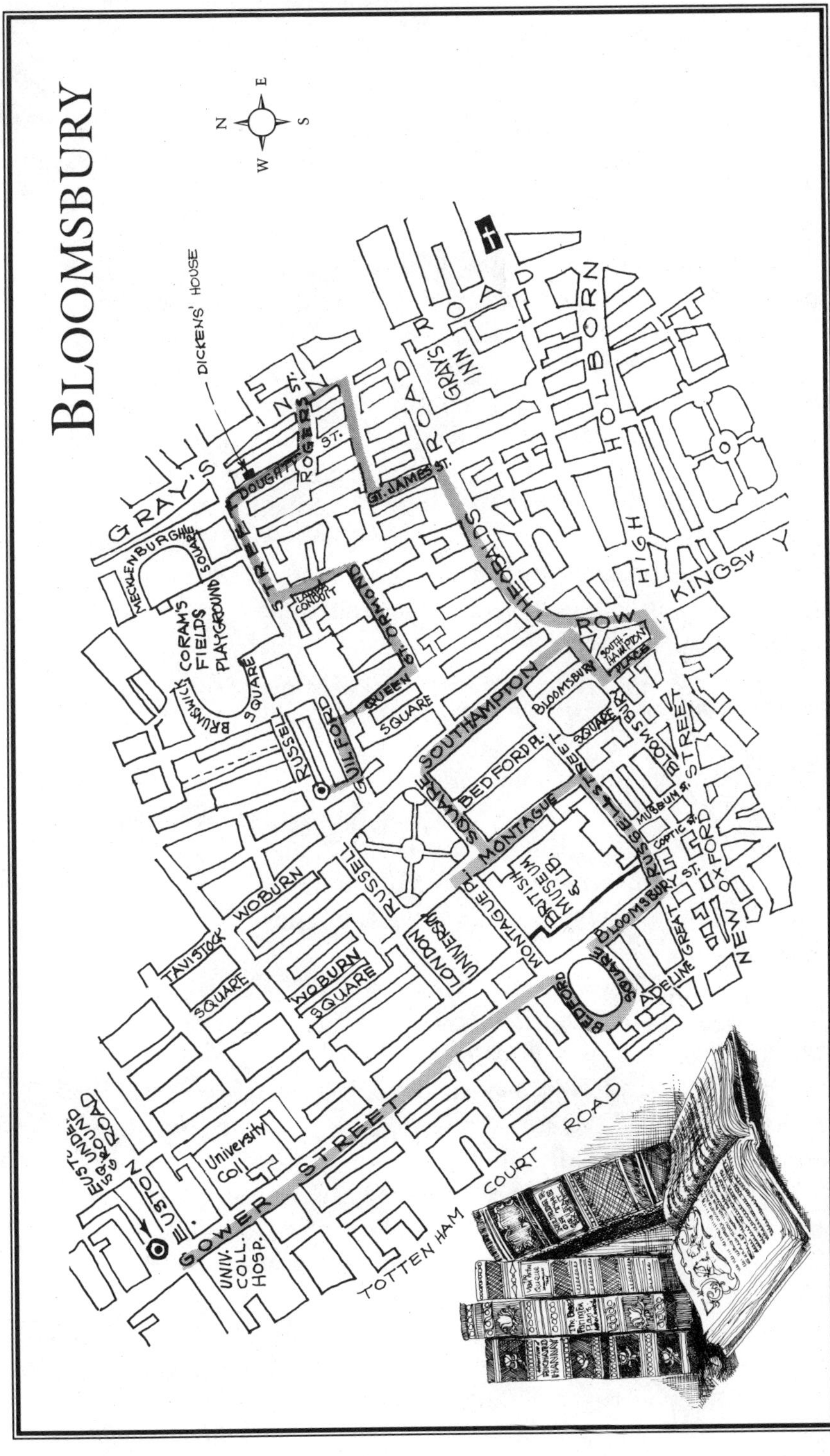
BLOOMSBURY
N
E
S
W
DICKENS' HOUSE
GRAY'S INN ROAD
GRAYS INN
HOLBORN
HIGH HOLBORN
KINGSWAY
DOUGHTY ST.
ROGERS ST.
ST. JAMES ST.
THEOBALDS ROAD
MECKLENBURGH SQUARE
CORAM'S FIELDS PLAYGROUND
BRUNSWICK SQUARE
LAMBS CONDUIT
GT. ORMOND
QUEEN SQUARE
GUILFORD
RUSSEL
SOUTHAMPTON ROW
SOUTHAMPTON PLACE
BLOOMSBURY
BLOOMSBURY SQUARE
BEDFORD PL.
RUSSELL SQUARE
MONTAGUE
MONTAGUE PL.
BRITISH MUSEUM & LIB.
MUSEUM ST.
COPTIC ST.
BLOOMSBURY ST.
GREAT RUSSELL STREET
BEDFORD SQUARE
ADELINE
NEW OXFORD STREET
WOBURN
WOBURN SQUARE
TAVISTOCK SQUARE
LONDON UNIVERSITY
EUSTON UNDERGROUND
EUSTON ROAD
University Coll
UNIV. COLL. HOSP.
GOWER STREET
TOTTENHAM COURT ROAD

Jemima Shore was confronted in the Tottenham Court Road Underground Station by the querulous old stepfather of the girl Chloe who was murdered in Antonia Fraser's *A Splash of Red*.

On the night a body was put into his bathtub, Mr. Thipps and his friend went to a nightclub near Tottenham Court Road and Oxford Street. While they were there, the club was raided (*Whose Body?* by Dorothy L. Sayers).

Go south along the left-hand side of Gower Street. Gower Street is the main thoroughfare of London University. You will pass the entrance to University College, with its neoclassic portico, high steps, and dome. It was described by G. K. Chesterton in his essay, "The Diabolist." Chesterton attended the Slade School of Art, which used to be in the north wing of the main university building. While there he decided to be a writer rather than an artist.

In Robert Barnard's *A Scandal in Belgravia,* Marjorie Knopfmeyer, sister of murder victim Timothy Wycliffe, began her art studies in 1956 at the Slade.

In Antonia Fraser's *A Splash of Red,* the Queen Mother was seen at University College. A witness thought she was there to "open" Sir Richard Lionnel's Adelaide Square.

Thriller writer Helen MacInnes attended University College before marrying classics professor and World War II secret agent, Gilbert Highet.

In *Funeral Sites,* Professor Thea Crawford of University College had taught Jessica Mann's sleuth, Tamara Hoyland, archeology when she was a student.

Agatha Christie's second husband, Max Mallowan, was the first professor of Western Asiatic archeology at the Institute of Archeology of London University.

According to Janet Morgan in *Agatha Christie,* Christie worked as a volunteer dispenser in University College Hospital during both world wars. (Her hospital work was the source of much of her knowledge of medicines and poisons.)

In Ruth Rendell's chilling *From Doom with Death,* the Prewetts' alibi was that they were at University College Hospital with Mrs. Prewett's sick mother.

Dr. Watson attended medical school at University College in the years before he met Sherlock Holmes.

The west side of Gower Street, from University College south, is lined with one of London's longest unbroken stretches of late Georgian houses.

In *Those Who Hunt the Night* by Barbara Hambly, James Asher, trying to lose anyone or anything that was following him, walked down Gower Street, scanning the stream of traffic that passed the long line of Georgian shops.

Just past Gower Mews, turn right into Bedford Square. On the way, you will pass the Royal Academy of Dramatic Art, where Sayers's friend, Muriel St. Clare Byrne, lectured.

Bedford Square is the only complete Georgian Square left in Bloomsbury. It was built in 1775–1780. Until 1893 the square was sealed off by gates; tradesmen were required to deliver goods in person.

The offices of the Jonathan Cape publishing firm, as well as those of publisher William Heinemann, are located in Bedford Square. In *A Splash of Red,* Antonia Fraser located the offices of the fictional publishing firm Brighthelmet next to the offices of Jonathan Cape.

Bedford Square is replete with blue historical markers, making it great fun to walk around and see who lived where. There are plaques to reformers, doctors, scientists, and literary people. Sir Anthony Hope, the author of the romantic thriller *The Prisoner of Zenda,* lived at No. 40 with his beautiful, red-haired wife.

Adelaide Square is sandwiched between Bedford Square and Tottenham Court Road. It is the fictional location where Jemima Shore spent an incognito vacation in the penthouse of her college friend, Chloe Fontaine, in order to work in the British Museum. (*A Splash of Red* by Antonia Fraser)

In the same book, there were two amusing American women professors, who were also sisters, staying in a small hotel in Adelaide Square. They discovered the body of Brighton in the British Museum Reading Room.

From her window in Adelaide Square, Jemima could look across the trees to the elegant eighteenth-century houses on the opposite side of the square. Her building, designed by developer Sir Richard Lionel, was a concrete, balconied block, in a style somewhere between the Mappin Terrace at Regent's Park Zoo and the National Theatre.

Look west beyond Bedford Square, and you will see an ugly modern building looming before you. It is an example of the architecture that Prince Charles has referred to as "stumps."

Antonia Fraser, like P. D. James and others, often comments on the aesthetics of London's buildings in her mysteries.

Leave Bedford Square at the southeast corner and turn right into Bloomsbury Street. Walk south to Great Russell Street and turn left. At the end of Bloomsbury Street on the right-hand side is the Kenilworth Hotel. The Redgauntlet Hotel in Dorothy L. Sayers's *The Documents in the Case* very likely was modeled after the Kenilworth, as was the Peveril Hotel in *Unnatural Death*. Both names are taken from the writings of Sir Walter Scott. Sayers's Paul Harrison stayed in the Redgauntlet while he tried to discover who had murdered his father.

After turning left at Great Russell Street, head east along the left-hand side of the street toward the main entrance to the British Museum.

In Barbara Hambly's eerie tale of London vampires, *Those Who Hunt the Night,* Asher, back in London from Oxford, hunted for lodging for himself and his wife Lydia. He settled on two lodging houses in Bloomsbury not far from the museum. The lodging houses faced different streets but backed on the same alley, and he could see the window of Lydia's suite at 109 Burton Place from his own at 6 Prince of Wales Colonnade.

In Antonia Fraser's *A Splash of Red,* artist Kevin John Athlone was seen in a Great Russell Street pub by a waitress from a local cafe.

The young Sherlock Holmes consulted in the library of the Pharmaceutical Society in the offices at No. 40 Great Russell Street.

Lark's friend Ann explained that she had seen Milos's friend coming out of a door and called to him, but he was already in Great Russell Street by the time she reached the square. (*Skylark* by Sheila Simonson)

Pick out a seedy-looking tobacco shop near the museum, where the classics scholar, Meredith, could have ventured to buy tobacco while working on the Duke of Nesfield's medieval manuscript of Juvenal in Michael Innes's *From London Far.*

Jemima Shore, en route to the Reading Room of the British Museum, had the perfect scholar's lunch of pizza, salad, and one glass of white wine at the Piazza Perfecta. (Try Pizza Express at 30 Coptic Street as a stand-in.

The shop at No. 46 Great Russell Street specializing in books of the Orient has been doing so since 1740.

Turn left to the British Museum.

Directly across the street from the museum is the place where Randolph Caldecott, the artist and book illustrator, once lived. He gave his name to the Caldecott Medal, which is annually awarded to an outstanding children's picture book.

Now walk through the great iron gates into the forecourt of the British Museum. Note the imposing classical frontage with intricately sculpted prediment and portico above massive pillars.

In Margaret Truman's *Murder in the Smithsonian,* Heather McBean, in London in pursuit of information in the murder of her fiancé, Dr. Lewis Tunney, walked from her hotel in Mayfair to Bloomsbury and the British Museum: "She stood in front of the neoclassical facade [of] Britain's vast and most celebrated storehouse of past cultures and peoples, millions of items consecrated to the benefit of millions of yearly visitors."

The British Museum houses the world's most extensive collection of antiquities in a series of vast halls. It is easily worthy of a full day's exploration.

The museum has certainly not been ignored by the creators of mystery fiction.

In G. K. Chesterton's *The Man Who Was Thursday,* Gabriel Syme thought that Sunday looked like the British Museum's great Mask of Memnon.

Jemima Shore, upon arriving at the Reading Room, was tempted to abandon her plans to research a book on Edwardian women philanthropists in favor of the cooler halls of the museum itself, "presided over by huge, wide-mouthed, slat-eyed Egyptian monarches and eagle-headed Assyrian deities."

In Margaret Yorke's *Cast for Death,* Oxford don Patrick Grant knew that his friend, the Greek policeman Manolakis, would want to make a sentimental trip to see the Elgin Marbles, so he met him outside the museum after Manolakis had kept a tryst with the fragments of the Parthenon. (The government of Greece is still trying to get Britain to return these sculptures, which were brought to London by Lord Elgin in 1802.)

In *Skylark* by Sheila Simonson, Ann, Lark's friend and traveling companion, set her alarm for an early start. She planned to spend the day in and around the British Museum.

In *The Judas Goat,* Spenser, Robert Parker's visiting American private eye, went to the British Museum to look at the Elgin Marbles and the Reading Room's enormous, high-domed ceiling. There was a grand and august quality about it. He could imagine Karl Marx writing the *Communist Manifesto* there.

In Sayers's *Murder Must Advertise,* Ginger Joe discovered that during Victor Dean's murder, Mr. Barrow of Pym's Publicity was in the British Museum studying Greek vases with a view to an advertising display for Klassika Corsets.

Alan Grant, while hospitalized in Josephine Tey's *The Daughter of Time,* asked his actress friend, Marta Hallard, if she knew anyone at the British Museum who would help with his research of Richard III.

There is a lovely case of haunting associated with the mummy case of a high priestess of the Temple of Amen-Ra. From the time the mummy case passed into the possession of an Englishman in Egypt in about 1860, a series of fatalities followed its journey. Even after it came to reside in the Mummy Room at the British Museum, sudden death followed those who handled the 3,500-year-old relic. Eventually, the mummy case was removed from public exhibition and sent to a museum in New York. It disappeared when the Titanic sank on her maiden voyage across the Atlantic. (*Haunted London* by Peter Underwood)

In *Unnatural Death,* Lord Peter Wimsey told a taxi driver to take him to the British Museum because he was going to collate a twelfth-century manuscript of *Tristan.*

In *A Splash of Red,* Jemima Shore saw the Reading Room, with the sun beating on the great glass dome, as a humid temple in the midst of the sprawling castle of the museum.

George Bernard Shaw worked in the museum Reading Room when he was a poor, young music critic.

This is also where John Munting, the biographer in Sayers's *The Documents in the Case,* did his research.

There is an actual mystery connected with the British Museum. Henry Symons, a sometime deputy superintendent of the Reading Room, allegedly shot himself in the Cracheroda Room. According to the story, his superior's first comment on hearing the news was, "Did he damage the book bindings?"

There is also a mystery surrounding the officially licensed copy of Dorothy L. Sayers's play *Love All.* The censored copy (it was wartime) had been sent to the British Library from the Lord Chamberlain's office. The copy was somehow "lost" until it was discovered after the 1940 performance that a license had not been obtained. The play was "found" thanks to the efforts of Dr. Margaret Nickson, the Assistant Keeper of the Department of Manuscripts of the British Library's Reference Division.

During our visit, Dr. Nickson treated us to a behind-the-scenes tour of the library which was extremely informative. Through doors camouflaged to look like the rows of books circling the room high above the floor, we entered the vast, domed Reading Room where we looked down upon the scholars working diligently below, despite the late August heat. Then, closely following Dr. Nickson, we wove our way through a maze of mysteriously arranged stacks and arrived back in the public area of the museum.

When you are ready, leave the British Museum and walk east on Great Russell Street to Montague Street. Turn left and follow Montague Street to Russell Square. It was at No. 24 Montague Street, just around the corner from the British Museum, that the young Sherlock Holmes took rooms when he first came down from Oxford. The building, a four-story, late-Georgian house, is still standing.

But before you contemplate Russell Square itself, note some of the mystery associations and places of interest that lie just beyond the boundaries of this walk.

Arthur Conan Doyle, lived just down the Square at No. 23 Montague Place when he first arrived in London and hung out his shingle to practice medicine.

Anne Perry's Victorian mystery *Callander Square* is set in nearby Tavistock Square. Workmen, planting shrubs in Callander (Tavistock) Square dug up the bodies of two babies. Charlotte Pitt, who lived only a carriage ride away, was intent on sleuthing despite her husband's warnings. She came upon a full-grown body among the roots of the previous year's Michaelmas daisies.

Up Southampton Row at 34 Tavistock Chambers, Tavistock Square, Phil Driscoll, the murder victim in John Dickson Carr's *The Mad Hatter Mystery* had his flat. Driscoll's mistress went there to burn her love letters and, in the process, accidently burned the manuscript of an unknown story by Edgar Allen Poe.

Like Tavistock Square, Woburn Square lies north of Russell Square. Today, it has been partly torn down because of the expanding London University. It was in Woburn Square that Philip Boyes stayed with his cousin, lawyer Norman Urquhart, in Dorothy L. Sayers's *Strong Poison.*

The Courtauld Institute Gallery, which since 1990 has been located in Somerset House, was previously housed in Woburn Square. In *Innocent Blood,* P. D. James's Philippa Palfrey took her mother to the Courtauld to see the Impressionist paintings.

Now, return your attention to Russell Square. It was laid out in 1800 by Humphrey Repton and took its name from the Russells, dukes of Bedford; it is one of London's largest squares. Russell Square was once an exclusive residential area, but today it is a collection of offices serving the university as well as the British Museum.

Walk around the square to Southampton Row. As you do so, notice the garden in the center, which is large, lovely, and open to the public; also note the many blue plaques on the surrounding buildings marking places of historical interest. In addition, note the addresses with mystery and other literary associations.

No. 24 Russell Square was the address given to the cabbie by Sir Julian Freke when he tried to share a cab with Charles Parker in Dorothy L. Sayers's *Whose Body?*

The American philosopher and poet, Ralph Waldo Emerson, stayed at No. 63 Russell Square when he visited England in 1833.

In Kate Ross's *A Broken Vessel,* the woman who wrote the mysterious letter that Sally gave to Julian Kestrel lived at No. 9 Stark Street, "a fairly respectable neighborhood, near Russell Square."

Leave Russell Square at Southampton Row and head south to Vernon Place, where you will turn right.

Lord Peter Wimsey worked as a copywriter for Pym's Publicity in Southampton Row in Sayers's *Murder Must Advertise.*

The offices of Hughes Massie, the literary agents for both Ngaio Marsh and Agatha Christie, are at No. 31 Southamptom Row.

In Sayers's *Strong Poison,* Harriet Vane bought arsenic in the Southamptom Row chemist shop to show that it could be obtained easily. Later, she was accused of poisoning her lover, Philip Boyes.

Turn right into Vernon Place. Bloomsbury Square, on your right, was laid out in 1600 for Thomas Wriothesley, fourth Earl of Southamptom. The "little towne" became one of London's most sought-after neighborhoods. In its early days, it was so fashionable that foreign princes were carried to see it as one of the wonders of England; however by the late nineteenth century, the square was no longer fashionable, although it has always remained respectable.

Many people of historical note have lived in Bloomsbury Square. To point out a few: Sir Hans Sloane, physician and benefactor of the British Museum, lived near the northeast corner of the square in Bloomsbury Place. At No. 45 is the townhouse belonging to the Earls of Chesterfield. Dr. Johnson's *Lord Chesterfield* undoubtedly stayed in the place, but this was not his major London home.

Lord Chief Justice Mansfield's house on the east side of

the square was sacked and burned by Gordon Rioters in 1780. Two of the ringleaders, Charles King and John Gray, were later hanged.

Eliza Polidori, aunt of the literary Rossettis, lived at No. 12, where poet Christina Rossetti often stayed for long periods of time.

The American writer Gertrude Stein lodged with her brother at No. 20.

Fictional associations are also part of the square's heritage. In *Skylark* by Sheila Simonson, the headquarters of the Henning Institute was located near Bloomsbury Square.

Bloomsbury Square seems a likely location for the office where P. D. James placed Maurice Palfrey in *Innocent Blood.*

Portions of the Michael Caine film *Half Moon Street* were filmed in Bloomsbury Square.

Now, turn left off Vernon Place into Southampton Place. Here, next to the National Westminster Bank, is where Stamford introduced Watson to Holmes. Dr. Watson had his surgery for several years at No. 6 Southampton Street (now Place).

Follow Southampton Place to High Holborn. Turn left and, after a short distance, turn left again into Southampton Row. Follow Southampton Row to Theobald's (pronounced Tibbald's) Road and turn right; you will be walking east.

In *End of Chapter* by Nicholas Blake, the senior editor for Wenham and Geraldine, Stephen Prothero, had Nigel Strangeways to tea in his Holborn flat. The gym where interior designer Denton Westburys, the son of Lord Charlton, studied karate was located on High Holborn in Patricia Moyes's *Who Is Simon Warwick?*

Continue walking east along Theobald's Road. In Sayers's *Strong Poison,* Philip Boyes stood about in Theobald's Road for some time looking for a stray taxi after his last visit with Harriet Vane.

Follow Theobald's Road to Great James Street and turn left. Dorothy L. Sayers and her husband Atherton Fleming lived in a neat, two-story, yellow-brick maisonette at No. 24.

Great James Street was "the mean street" in the Lord Peter

Wimsey story, "The Vindictive Story of the Footsteps That Ran."

Turn right off Great James Street into Northington Street. Follow Northington Street to Gray's Inn Road. In *Strong Poison,* Philip Boyes staggered into the fictitious Nine Rings Pub in Gray's Inn Road after his final visit with Harriet Vane.

Go left to Gray's Inn Road to Roger Street, turn left. Reginald Colby, a lawyer in *Who Is Simon Warwick?* had his offices here on the northern edge of legal London.

Tyrone, the reporter in *Forfeit* by Dick Francis, lived with his handicapped wife Elizabeth in a mews off Gray's Inn Road, perhaps King's Mews.

Jemima Shore, in Antonia Fraser's *Quiet as a Nun,* saw the photo of her lover, MP Tom Amyas on the front page of the *London Times.* The *Times* had its editorial offices in New Printing House Square on Gray's Inn Road. (The offices were moved to the East End at Wapping in 1986.)

Author Nicholas Freeling, creator of Inspector Van der Valk, was born in Gray's Inn Road. It is also home ground to crime novelist Marian Babson.

Turn right off Roger Street into Doughty Street. The house where Charles Dickens lived early in his married life and where he wrote *The Pickwick Papers* and *Oliver Twist* is here at No. 48. It is one of a long row of dark brick houses with bright blue doors. It is the only one of Dicken's London residences still standing. Today, it is the site of a Dickens museum that is well worth a visit.

Originally, Harriet Vane had a flat at 100 Doughty Street. (Hers was a bogus number; No. 29, 30, or 31 would make a fair substitute.) She moved from Doughty Street to a new flat that overlooked the tennis court in Mecklenburgh Square (directly ahead). There, in *Gaudy Night,* she sat at a writing table and looked out onto the square. She watched a group of tennis players for a while, then turned her attention to the invitation to attend the Gaudy of her old Oxford college, Shrewsbury. Suddenly, she decided to go. Before she could change her mind, she quickly ran out to drop her acceptance in the pillar box.

In *Strong Poison,* the police hunted in Mecklenburgh Square for a small white packet of arsenic that Harriet's lover, Philip Boyes, might have lost there.

Sayers herself lived in a flat at 44 Mecklenburgh Square, next to Coram Fields where Thomas Coram set up a Foundling Hospital in 1739.

Turn left at the end of Doughty Street and walk along the south side of Mecklenburgh Square, past Mecklenburgh Place, turn right on Guilford Street. Continue along Guilford Street until you come to Guilford Place where you will turn left into Lamb's Conduit Street. The Lamb, a late Victorian pub complete with settles, cast-iron tables, and boxed-in bar, is at No. 94.

Mecklenburgh and Brunswick Squares (at either end of Coram's Fields) are the two remaining squares that were built for the prosperous bourgeois. They are the best places to imagine the large and tomblike house of Mrs. Manderson's Uncle Cupples, a retired banker, where E. C. Bentley's Philip Trent listened to the conversation of a retired Egyptologist while gazing at Mabel Manderson in *Trent's Last Case.*

The flat where Margery Allingham lived over the studio of artist George du Maurier—father of actor Gerald du Maurier and grandfather of author Daphne du Maurier—was in this area.

In Julian Symons's *The Blackheath Poisoning,* Paul Mortimer had a flat in Guilford Street.

Follow Lamb's Conduit Street to Great Ormond Street; turn right. The Hospital for Sick Children on the north side of Great Ormond Street was combined with the Foundling Hospital in Patricia Moyes's *Who Is Simon Warwick?* The infant Simon was taken there when his parents were killed by a World War II buzz bomb.

Charles and Lady Mary Parker lived at 12A Great Ormond Street, as did Lord Peter Wimsey when he as masquerading as Death Bredon, in *Murder Must Advertise.*

Follow Great Ormond Street to Queen Square (now Hospital Square), on your right behind the hospital. It was laid out in the days of good Queen Anne. At the north end of the square is a garden with a statue, not of Anne, but of George III's queen,

Charlotte. Queen Square offers another choice for Callander Square, where Charlotte Pitt investigated the deaths of two babies. Today, instead of upper-class homes, Queen Square is the site of hospital buildings and offices.

Walk to your right through Queen Square to Queen Anne's Walk. Turn left and take Guilford Street to Herbrand Street, where you will find the Russell Square Underground Station. In Robert Parker's *The Judas Goat,* Spenser took the tube from Russell Square to Regent's Park Zoo. You may wish to follow his example; otherwise, end the walk here.

5

SOHO WALK

BACKGROUND

The unusual name Soho probably came from the hunting call "so-hoe." It was used as a battle cry by the Protestant followers of the Duke of Monmouth, the ill-fated, illegitimate son of Charles II, who once lived in the area. Soho became London's chief foreign quarter in 1685, when the French king Louis XIV revoked the Edict of Nantes, sending thousands of Huguenots fleeing across the Channel. Soho is still known for its foreign shops and restaurants, as well as for the cosmopolitan, if rather seedy, atmosphere found in its narrow streets.

Soho encompasses London's Chinatown, but other nationalities—French, Italian, and Swiss—are present as well. Soho is a great place to go in search of foreign food after an evening of theater in the West End. The western curve of the theater district is Soho's Shaftesbury Avenue.

Soho is London's red-light district, as well as being an area of petty crime, vice, and viciousness. This atmosphere of the underbelly of London life is faithfully duplicated in detective fiction. Although caution should be exercised, it is a safe area to walk, especially during daylight hours.

LENGTH OF WALK: 3 miles

See the map on page 84 for the boundaries of this walk and pages 253–55 for a list of the authors, books, and detectives mentioned.

PLACES OF INTEREST

Statue of Eros, Piccadilly Circus.

Leicester Square, Movie houses, half-price ticket kiosk.

National Gallery, Trafalgar Square. Free. Restaurants and a shop.

National Portrait Gallery, St. Martin's Place. Free. Fine shop.

Carnaby Street, Site of sixties fashion revolution.

Shaftesbury Avenue Theaters.

Palladium Music Hall, 8 Argyll.

House of St. Barnabas, 1 Greek Street, Soho Square. Eighteenth-century mansion. Open by written appointment.

The Trocadero Centre, Coventry Street.

PLACES TO EAT

Au Jardin des Gourmets, 5 Greek Street. This French restaurant is famous for its wine cellar. Reservations are needed. 071-437-4839.

Red Lion (pub), 14 Kingly Street. 071-734-4985.

Loon Fung, 37 Gerrard Street. 071-437-0540.

SOHO WALK

Begin this walk at the Shaftesbury Avenue exit from the Piccadilly Circus Underground Station. (This is a station with many exits; be careful to select the correct one.) As you come up into Piccadilly Circus, you should see a Boots chemist store. According to Julian Symons in *Mortal Consequences,* it was lending libraries located in the Boots chain that helped fan the fire of public demand for detective stories. Unfortunately, the libraries no longer exist.

Tessa Crichton was about to set off on an expedition to Soho (probably by underground to Piccadilly Circus) when Lorraine's cable from Washington arrived in *The Men in Her Death* by Anne Morice.

Here in Piccadilly Circus you are at the hub of London,

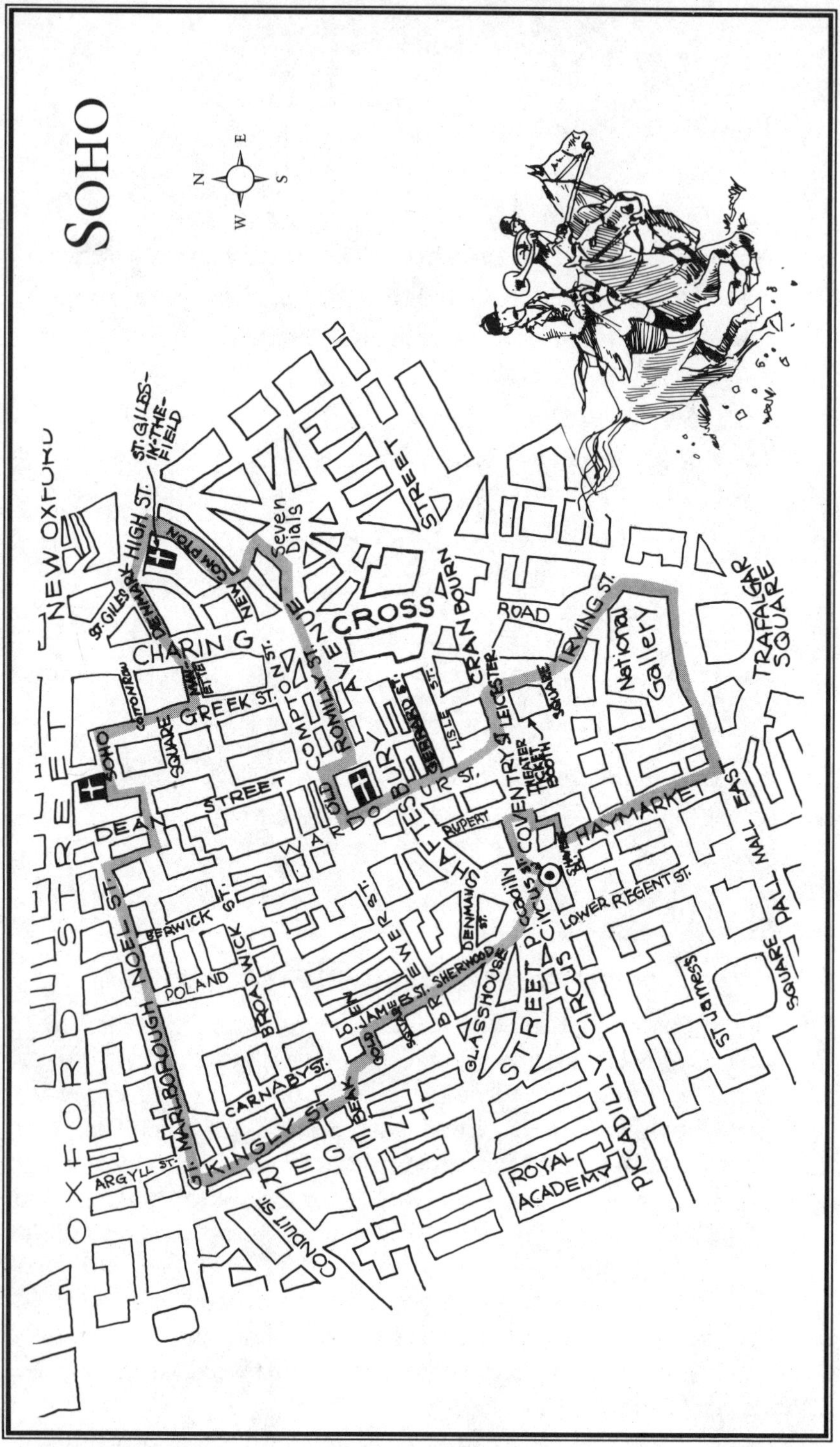

SOHO
N
E
S
W
NEW OXFORD
OXFORD STREET
ST. GILES-IN-THE-FIELD
HIGH ST.
ST. GILES
DENMARK ST.
COMPTON
CHARING CROSS ROAD
NEW
Seven Dials
SHAFTESBURY AVENUE
CRANBOURN
IRVING ST.
National Gallery
TRAFALGAR SQUARE
LEICESTER SQUARE
LISLE
GERRARD ST.
ROMILLY ST.
OLD COMPTON ST.
GREEK ST.
SOHO SQUARE
DEAN STREET
WARDOUR ST.
RUPERT
COVENTRY ST.
THEATER TICKET BOOTH
HAYMARKET
PALL MALL EAST
LOWER REGENT ST.
Piccadilly CIRCUS
DENMAN ST.
GLASSHOUSE
SHERWOOD
BREWER
GOLDEN SQUARE
BEAK
KINGLY ST.
CARNABY ST.
GT. MARLBOROUGH
NOEL ST.
BERWICK ST.
BROADWICK ST.
POLAND
ARGYLL ST.
REGENT STREET
CONDUIT ST.
ROYAL ACADEMY
PICCADILLY
St James's SQUARE

and the very name of this spot, according to New Zealander Ngaio Marsh, brings a lump to the throat of someone from the Antipodes. It is a place where people love to congregate or perhaps to rendezvous. Central to the circus is the memorial to philanthropist Lord Shaftesbury. It is a tiny Art Nouveau statue made of aluminum and fashioned in the form of Eros, the Angel of Christian Charity.

In Ngaio Marsh's *A Surfeit of Lampreys,* Roberta Grey knew that to British colonials, the symbol of London was a "small figure perched slantwise above a traffic roundabout, an elegant Victorian god with a Grecian name." The traffic configuration in Piccadilly Circus has changed since Marsh wrote those words, but Eros still keeps a watchful eye over all.

John Nash created Piccadilly Circus from existing streets and alleyways in order to make a grand sweep from the Prince Regent's Carlton House to Regent's Park.

In Martha Grimes's *The Dirty Duck,* Superintendent Jury, deploring the traffic mess, thought the green lights never changed in Piccadilly Circus.

Piccadilly Circus, near the Shaftesbury exit, was where, in Simon Brett's *Not Dead, Only Resting,* Charles Paris met "Henry," the aristocratic ingenue he promised to take to a musical audition.

In Agatha Christie's *The Secret Adversary,* after meeting for the first time since the war with shouts of "Tuppence, old thing," and "Tommy, old bean," Tommy told Tuppence, "What an awful place Piccadilly Circus is, there's a huge bus bearing down on us."

In Barbara Hambly's *Those Who Hunt the Night,* Asher, reasoning that there would be no one stirring in Ernchester House until dark, turned his steps westward. He dodged tangles of traffic in Piccadilly and noted that lights were beginning to go up around the wrought-iron palisade of the public lavatories in Piccadilly Circus.

Dorothy L. Sayers's Lord Peter Wimsey entered detective fiction in *Whose Body?* sitting in a taxi in Piccadilly Circus and saying to his infuriated driver, "Oh damn, d'you mind putting back to where we came from?"

Robert B. Parker's private eye, Spenser, exploring London in *The Judas Goat,* found Piccadilly Circus "implacably ordinary with movie theaters and fast foods," but in *Frequent Hearses,* Edmund Crispin's Oxford don, Gervase Fen, recognized its centrality when he said that, by taking Piccadilly Circus as your center, you could draw a circle with an eighteen-mile radius and include all the major British film studios. Things have changed since Crispin made that statement; major British film studios seem to have become things of the past.

Piccadilly Circus's garish charm is probably best seen at night, when gigantic electric billboards glitter and the crowds swell to great proportions. It is a time to mind your wallet and handbag, for along with the good people of London and the tourists, the pickpockets and purse snatchers find the pickings here ripe.

Willow King was passing the statue of Eros in Piccadilly, when she realized that the previous day she had had a marvelous opportunity to find out about the Gripper and had wasted it. (*A Common Death* by Natasha Cooper)

In Helen MacInnes's *Cloak of Darkness,* secret agent, Robert Renwick, commented that, like New York's Times Square, Piccadilly was just as bright by day as by night.

The famous Criterion Long Bar used to be in the Criterion Theatre Building, which you can see on Lower Regent Street, across Piccadilly Circus. The Criterion Bar was the site of the meeting between Dr. Watson and young Stamford, in Conan Doyle's *A Study in Scarlet;* their meeting led later to Watson's introduction to Sherlock Holmes.

Turn left and walk east, as Tommy and Tuppence did. Leave Piccadilly Circus on Piccadilly. It will quickly become Coventry Street as it crosses the Haymarket.

Despite the fact that it was early May, Gaylord Erskin, wearing a top hat and a light overcoat, strode along the Haymarket to Piccadilly on his way to Plum's in Amy Meyers's *Murder at Plum's.*

It is easy to become confused and follow the wrong street at this point in the walk, so note that Shaftesbury Avenue is on your left and Lower Regent Street is on your far right. On the left, you will pass the Trocadero Centre, with bookstores, record and clothing shops, the three-dimensional Guinness World of Records Museum, and much, much more. This complex is on the site of three restaurants: the old Trocadero, Scotts, and the original Lyons Corner House, toward which Tommy and Tuppence were heading for tea in *The Secret Adversary*.

In Georgette Heyer's *Death in the Stocks,* Roger Vereker, the family black sheep, who appeared to claim his murdered brother's money, had dined at the Trocadero the night Arnold Vereker was murdered and his body placed in the stocks.

The old Lyons Corner House was where the Canadian, Mr. Cropper, ate his breakfast and fell in love with one of the Dawson maids in *Unnatural Death* by Dorothy L. Sayers.

One day, Dorothy L. Sayers left her friend Muriel St. Clare Byrne and went to the Lyons Corner House for supper. While idling over her food, Sayers worked out the method of murder that she would use in the play *Busman's Honeymoon,* which she was writing with Byrne.

In *The Man in the Queue,* Josephine Tey notes that Jerry Lamont and his boss, bookie Bert Sorrell, who was later murdered, had lunched in the Coventry Street Lyons.

Two of Pym's Publicity's secretaries were coming out of Lyons Corner House when they met Death Bredon in evening dress, then saw him apparently being arrested in front of the Criterion Bar in Dorothy L. Sayers's *Murder Must Advertise.*

Cross Conventry Street at Rupert Street and turn right to walk back along Coventry Street to Shavers Place. It is a tiny, angular alleyway leading to the Haymarket. It is the nearest thing in the vicinity to the cul-de-sac where Ngaio Marsh's detective, Roderick Alleyn, lived before his marriage to Agatha Troy. In his flat, he had Troy's painting of Suva Harbor—which she had been painting on shipboard when they first met in *Artists in Crime.*

Walk through Shavers Place into the Haymarket and turn left to go south toward Trafalgar Square. As its name suggests, the Haymarket was the site of London's market for hay and straw. It is also associated with the theater world. Her Majesty's Theatre (which changed from Her to His with a change in sovereign) and the Haymarket Theatre are both located here. Her Majesty's stands where the Haymarket Opera House once stood.

During Victorian times, the Haymarket was a center of prostitution, as young Paul Mortimer discovered in Julian Symons's *The Bleackheath Poisoning.*

In Anne Perry's *The Devil's Acre,* the fastidious upper-class young blades preferred Haymarket prostitutes to those in Devil's Acre.

According to Kate Ross in *A Broken Vessel,* accommodation houses were very common around the Haymarket, where girls like Sally were "as numerous as the paving-stones they trod each night."

Murder suspect Jerry Lamont, in Josephine Tey's *The Man in the Queue,* went to a movie house and then meant to duck into the Haymarket to hide, but he saw Inspector Grant shadowing him and ran (all the way to Scotland).

In Natasha Cooper's *Poison Flowers,* Willow King had lunch with Michael Rodenhurst in a fish restaurant just off Piccadilly. After lunch she walked down the Haymarket toward Trafalgar Square.

You will pass Panton Street on your left as your walk south on the Haymarket to the corner of Pall Mall. Turn left into the northern end of Trafalgar Square where you will find yourself standing in front of the National Gallery. Opened in 1824, it is built high above Trafalgar Square with a spectacular view down Whitehall to Parliament. The Gallery has a Grecian portico that incorporates marble columns from the Prince Regent's Carlton House. On July 10, 1991, the new Sainsbury Wing, built by Robert Venturi and Denise Scott-Brown Associates, was opened by Queen Elizabeth II. The National Gallery houses a major collection of paintings covering the thirteenth to the twentieth centuries.

After being questioned by Inspector Thorne, Lark and Ann put in some time at the National Gallery, where Ann was awed by everything but Van Gogh's *Sunflowers*, which she found too brown. They had a quick lunch in the gallery cafeteria then went on to the National Portrait Gallery next door. (*Skylark* by Sheila Simonson)

After failing to find a taxi in Queen Anne's Gate, Willow King walked across the park past Admirality Arch and into Trafalgar Square with its assortment of litter, pigeon droppings, and foreign school children who surged past her to the National Gallery and went up the steps. She hurried on, crossing the road in front of St. Martin's-in-the-Field and resisting the temptation to buy a bag of roasted chestnuts from an old man tending a brazier. (*Bitter Herbs* by Natasha Cooper)

In *A Surfeit of Lampreys* by Ngaio Marsh, when Henry and Frith Lamprey were pointing out London sights to New Zealander Roberta Grey, Frith pointed to the National Gallery, "That's the Tate," she said. Henry quickly corrected her.

Cordelia Gray, depressed by the suicide of her partner, left their Kingly Street office and walked to Trafalgar Square. There she sought consolation in the National Gallery. (*An Unsuitable Job for a Woman* by P. D. James)

Promptly at ten o'clock, Tuppence met Tommy in the National Gallery. It was their first business meeting as Young Adventurers. While she waited, Tuppence settled herself comfortably on a red velvet seat and gazed at the Turners with an unseeing eye.

Walk past the National Gallery to St. Martin's Place and turn left. There, tucked behind the National Gallery, is the National Portrait Gallery, which was the source for the copy of the Richard III portrait actress Marta Hallard brought to the hospitalized Inspector Grant in Josephine Tey's *The Daughter of Time*. The original portrait still hangs in the Gallery, and the bookstore sells postcard reproductions.

In Robert B. Parker's *The Judas Goat*, Spenser spent an afternoon in the National Portrait Gallery staring at portraits of people from another time.

Paintings hung in the Portrait Gallery are chosen for their historical interest and are hung chronologically starting with the oldest paintings on the top floor. That is where you will find the Richard III portrait. You will also find one of Sir

Thomas More, whose *Historie of Richard III* was Shakespeare's source for his play about Richard.

The Gallery houses a number of portraits of mystery writers, among them Charles Dickens, Robert Louis Stevenson, G. K. Chesterton, Graham Greene, E. C. Bentley, and Dorothy L. Sayers. A copy of the Sayers portrait also hangs in the Sayers Room in the tower of St. Anne's Soho, where her ashes are interred.

The National Portrait Gallery, like the National Gallery, the British Museum, and the Victoria and Albert Museum, has an outstanding book and gift store. In it, you can find a wide assortment of books about the mystery surrounding Richard III. According to writer Catherine Aird, Josephine Tey single-handedly kept alive the historical controversy surrounding the ill-fated king.

Outside the Portrait Gallery, turn left and follow Irving Street, which curves its way into Leicester Square. The square, which dates from 1670, is now famous for its movie theaters and restaurants. It was laid out on the site of Leicester House, home of the family of Sir Philip Sidney, the Elizabethan soldier-poet. The painter Sir Joshua Reynolds lived here during the eighteenth century, as did caricaturist and painter William Hogarth. In the nineteenth century, the square became known as the site of music halls such as the Alhambra (now the Odeon).

Today, Leicester Square is a meeting place for tourists, especially the young. It has public lavatories and many fast-food restaurants. It is closed to traffic, making it attractive to the crowds who loiter under the square's tall plane trees or stand in line at the half-price ticket kiosk where same-day tickets are sold for West End shows.

Half-price tickets brought Ann and Lark to Leicester Square. First they tried for *Cats,* but it was too expensive. Finally, they settled for tickets to *Hamlet* the following night at the National Theatre. (*Skylark* by Sheila Simonson)

As Asher hurried along toward Leicester Square, he noted the garish lights from the Empire and the Alhambra. He huddled in the voluminous folds of his ulster and scarf as the day ebbed, having no idea how soon after sunset the vampires began to stir about. (*Those Who Hunt the Night* by Barbara Hambly)

In *The New Arabian Nights* by Robert Louis Stevenson, Prince Florizel of Bohemia and his Master of Horse went about the streets of London in disguise and looking for adventure. They were driven by sleet into an oyster bar in the vicinity of Leicester Square. A young man came into the oyster bar with a tray of cream tarts, which he offered to everyone there. He then invited Prince Florizel to join the Suicide Club. This Stevenson tale was recalled by Lord Peter Wimsey while he and Charles Parker ate snails in a Soho restaurant. (*Unnatural Death* by Dorothy L. Sayers)

Sayers's characters frequented Leicester Square in several books. In *Busman's Honeymoon,* Lord and Lady Peter Wimsey, while waiting to meet with barrister and MP Sir Impey Biggs, killed time by watching an educational film and a Mickey Mouse cartoon in one of the Leicester Square movie houses.

Young Paul Mortimer, of the toy manufacturing family, walked north to Leicester Square from the family factory on the Strand to eat his baker's pie among the grass and flowers and dream of being a great reporter. Later, when his cousin Isabel was being tried for the murder of his father, Paul stumbled by night into the Caravanserai, one of the Victorian brothels in Leicester Square. (*The Blackheath Poisonings* by Julian Symons)

In Anne Perry's *Resurrection Row,* Sir Desmond and Lady Cantlay were heading toward Leicester Square after seeing a production of Gilbert and Sullivan's *The Mikado* when they hailed a hansom cab containing a dead cabbie.

Probably the most fantastic scene in a detective story is set in Leicester Square. In G. K. Chesterton's *The Man Who Was Thursday,* a band of anarchists met in Leicester Square for Sunday breakfast. They sat on a hotel balcony overlooking the Square, "with its sunlit leaves and the Saracenic outline of the Alhambra." Chesterton's hotel was probably the Victorian-looking hotel at the northeast corner of Leicester Square and Leicester Place.

Firzroy Maclean Angel used yuppie Patterson's office phone

to ring Sorrel's number. She wasn't in, so he left a message on her answerphone for her to come to the Vecchio Reccione in Leicester Square at 9:30. (*Angel Touch* by Mike Ripley)

Leave Leicester Square on Leicester Street (at the northwestern corner). Go north on Leicester Street past Manzi's to the next street, which is Lisle Street. This is an area of narrow, rather dirty streets lined with small food shops and cafes.

It was "off Lisle Street" that Sonny Haliwell ran Contemporary Books, an adult bookstore, for a crime syndicate. He became the third victim of the karate-chop killer in Julian Symons's *A Three Pipe Problem.*

Turn left on Lisle Street and follow it to Wardour Street; turn right and take Wardour Street one block to Gerrard Street; turn right again. This street, which is the heart of London's Chinatown, is closed to traffic. Restaurants, as well as shops offering a variety of merchandise, abound here.

Gerrard Street is often mentioned in mystery fiction. This is no doubt the area Martha Grimes wrote of in *The Dirty Duck,* in which she tells of Amelia Blue Farraday, who, becoming bored with the strip joints, blue-movie houses, and cheap restaurants, returned to Berkeley Square and her death.

Look for No. 31 Gerrard Street. It is the site of the first club rooms rented by the Detective Club. The rooms were furnished with secondhand furniture found by Helen Simpson, author of *Enter Sir John.*

In *Clouds of Witness,* Dorothy L. Sayers used No. 31 as the site for her fictitious Soviet Club. The Soviet Club was where Lord Peter was shot at by Lady Mary's former lover, and where the romance between Lady Mary and detective Charles Parker received its first push.

John Dryden's home was on Gerrard Street, as was The Turk's Head pub, now long gone, which was where Dr. Samuel Johnson and Sir Joshua Reynolds founded their famous Literary Club.

In *Great Expectations,* Mr. Jaggers lived in a "stately" house in Gerrard Street, something difficult to imagine as you survey the present street.

Return to Wardour Street turn right; walk past Dansey Place

to Shaftesbury Avenue. Wardour Street is synonymous with the British film industry, which originated here.

Shaftesbury Avenue, named for the nineteenth-century philanthropist Lord Shaftesbury, was cut through Soho in 1886 to connect Holborn and Piccadilly. Today, it is one of London's principal theater streets.

In *From London Far,* Meredith, Michael Innes's amateur detective, set out to walk from the British Museum in Bloomsbury by way of Shaftesbury Avenue to Piccadilly and the Athenaeum for a couple of hours of "light reading" in scholarly journals.

In John Creasey's *The Toff and the Deadly Parson,* Pond Street (fictitious) was described as a dingy thoroughfare off Shaftesbury Avenue. It was where the Toff went to find the disreputable Daisy Club.

Cross Shaftesbury Avenue and continue north on Wardour Street. On the right is the open churchyard of St. Anne's Soho. Bombs in World War II destroyed the church but left its bulbous, Russian-looking tower. George the II worshiped here while Prince of Wales, having "discovered an inclination to come to church." The remains of Theodore, the dethroned king of Corsica, were buried here in 1756, as were those of William Hazlitt in 1830. The tombstones of both can be seen at the foot of the tower. Horace Walpole wrote the epitaph for Theodore.

Detective writer and theologian Dorothy L. Sayers is also buried here. Her ashes lie beneath the floor of the Sayers Room inside the tower. In 1978, a plaque commemorating Sayers was unveiled here, and the portrait which hangs in the tower room was presented by the Dorothy L. Sayers Historical and Literary Society. The tower is kept locked, and you need to be at least six feet tall to see in through the window, but if you are anxious to see inside, you may ask for the tower key at 57 Dean Street, where St. Anne's services are held.

From 1952 until her death in 1957, Sayers was vicar's warden of the parish of Soho, which also included St. Thomas Regent's Street (now demolished) and St. Paul's Covent Garden.

Return to Wardour Street and turn right. Walk north to No. 17. It used to be Pinoli's, the restaurant where the Junior Debating Society (the JDC), the schoolboy literary club to which G. K. Chesterton and E. C. Bentley belonged, held a stag party on the eve of the Boer War.

Continue on Wardour Street to Old Compton Street. This is where Simon Brett's mostly out-of-work actor, Charles Paris, met his cockney-speaking pal, Stan, at the Patisserie Valerie in *Not Dead, Only Resting.*

Turn right on Old Compton Street and go east to Dean Street. Turn right. In Dicken's *A Tale of Two Cities,* Dr. Manett lived at No. 10 Dean Street.

Above a pizza restaurant, somewhere on Dean Street, Oxford don Patrick Grant went to see the agent of his dead actor friend in Margaret Yorke's *Cast for Death.*

Edmund Crispin, in *Swan Song,* had operatic tenor Adam Langley take Elizabeth Harding to dinner in a restaurant in Dean Street. They sat at a table with a red-shaped lamp and were waited on by a garrulous Cypriot.

In one of these streets must be Chang's Club. Inspector Gideon went there to find the hit-and-run killer of the renegade Constable Foster in J. J. Marric's (John Creasey's) *Gideon's Wrath.* Marric's fictional Winter Street, the worst street in Soho, may also be near here.

This is the heart of the Soho restaurant area. Many writers have told us of that character or this one who ate in a restaurant "in Soho."

Soho was the likely location for the fictitious Reeder Street and the Moulin Gris restaurant where Thalia Drummond was taken by one of the members of the Crimson Circle. (*The Crimson Circle* by Edgar Wallace)

In Agatha Christie's *The Big Four,* there was a small foreign restaurant in Soho where Poirot and Hastings often dined.

Somewhere nearby should be the small restaurant that was located on the fictitious Mervyn Street. It was where the Thursday Club met in John Buchan's *The Three Hostages.* Started by some people who wanted to keep in touch after World War I, the club met on the second floor of the restaurant.

You may also be walking by the location of Veglio's, another fictional Soho restaurant, where racist MP Sir Pountney took the TV actress playing Irene Adler in Julian Symons's *A Three Pipe Problem.*

Then of course there is Pesquero's, the Soho restaurant to which Dame Beatrice's secretary, Laura, was taken by her Scotland Yard fiancé in Gladys Mitchell's *Watson's Choice.*

Follow Dean Street south to Romilly Street and turn left. At this point, you are just opposite the parking lot behind St. Anne's. (Dorothy L. Sayers tried to get a multimedia chapel-cum-theater built on the site of St. Anne's Church, but the parking lot was built instead.)

No. 27 Romilly Street was the site of the Moulin d'Or, a restaurant where Sayers liked to eat and on which she based the Au Bon Bourgeois in *Unnatural Death.*

When you walk east along Romilly Street, the first crossing is Frith Street, where Mozart once stayed with his father and sister.

Next, you cross Greek Street where, at No. 5, Au Jardin des Gourmets is. In *Watson's Choice* by Gladys Mitchell, lawyer and murder suspect, Toby Dance, told Scotland Yard that he usually lunched at the Jardin des Gourmets near his office.

Adam Dalgleish, in P. D. James's *Unnatural Causes,* visited the Cortez Club, a pseudo-Spanish disco near Greek Street.

Follow Romilly Street to the end. Here is Cambridge Circus, the crossroads of Shaftesbury Avenue and Charing Cross Road.

It was here, in *The Man in the Queue,* that Josephine Tey's Inspector Grant found the palatial offices of Laurence Murray, "Lucky-FolkBetWithLaury Murray," one of the biggest bookmakers in London.

This rather nondescript traffic center is also the site of the mysterious Circus from which the secret work of Smiley's people was orchestrated in the cold-war thriller *Tinker, Tailor, Soldier, Spy* by John Le Carre.

Cross Cambridge Circus to Earlham Street, directly opposite from where you are. Walk down Earlham Street to the next circle, which is the sinister Seven Dials. It was (and is) the meeting place of seven narrow alleys. In the eighteenth and nineteenth centuries, it was a hangout for thieves. Hogarth used it in his illustrations of "Gin Land," and it was made famous by Charles Dickens in *Sketches by Boz*. Dickens said of the slums around "the Dials," that "the streets and courts dart in all directions [and] unwholesome vapour hangs over the housetops."

A pillar topped by a clock with seven dials stood here until it was torn down in a hunt for hidden treasure.

Inspector Pitt, in Anne Perry's *Bluegate Fields,* went to Seven Dials searching for evidence.

Agatha Christie located the Seven Dials Club at a fictitious address, No. 14 Hunstanton Street. The mysterious secret Seven Dials organization which Lady Eileen (Bundle) spied on was located here in *The Seven Dials Mystery*.

In Julian Symons's *The Blackheath Poisonings,* Paul Mortimer wandered into Seven Dials with a drinking crony who took him to witness a vicious fight between a dog and a rat.

An agent in Seven Dials supplied the phony Father Garnett with heroin in Ngaio Marsh's *Death in Ecstasy*.

Take Mercer Street, which is to the left, and go west out of Seven Dials. When you cross Shaftesbury Avenue again, Mercer Street becomes St. Giles Passage. Follow St. Giles to New Compton Street and turn right on New Compton to St. Giles High Street. Turn left on St. Giles High Street and follow it around the south side of St. Giles-in-the-Fields.

Matilda, the wife of Henry I, founded a leper hospital here in 1101. She dedicated it to St. Giles, the patron saint of outcasts. At her bequest, a "Cup of Charity" was to be given to condemned prisoners as they passed the door of the hospital on their way to Tyburn for execution. By the thirteenth century, a chapel had come to serve parishioners and patients and the "Cup" was passed to the Bow Tavern. There, in one of London's foulest rookeries, the condemned, dressed in their best finery, would be cheered on to their deaths with a cup of ale. John Creasey gives an excellent description of this in *The Masters of Bow Street*.

Turn to the left off St. Giles High Street into the nondescript Denmark Street. Follow it back to Charing Cross Road.

Denmark Street is London's Tin Pan Alley, the mecca of would-be pop singers. Denmark Street will soon bring you to Charing Cross Road, which once was the location of most of London's secondhand bookstores, including the one made famous by Helene Hanff in *Eighty-Four Charing Cross Road.*

Lark's friend Ann wanted to take a stroll along Charing Cross Road and look at the bookshops. (*Skylark* by Sheila Simonson)

In Tey's *The Daughter of Time,* hospitalized Inspector Grant asked his friend Marta Hallard to get someone to go to Charing Cross and buy him a copy of Sir Thomas More's *Historie of Richard III.*

The bookstores on Charing Cross Road are fewer today, but some can still be found. Foyles, a veritable London institution, is there at Manette Street, and next to it is Waterstones. Down the Street at No. 71 is Murder One, a bookstore jammed full of mysteries, romances, and science fiction.

Cross Charing Cross Road and go west on Manette Street past Foyles; this will bring you back to the head of Greek Street. Turn right on Greek Street and go north to Soho Square. At the corner of Greek Street and Soho Square is the fine eighteenth-century rococo House of St. Barnabas. Although it was built as a private home, it was sold to the House of Charity in 1861. Today, it provides temporary accommodations for homeless women.

It was at this corner that "Duds" Morrison and another man were involved in a street fight in Margery Allingham's *Tiger in the Smoke.*

In the green park in the center of Soho Square is a weathered statue of Charles II. It was his illegitimate son, James, the Duke of Monmouth, who gave the square its name.

James, whose mansion was located here, used the hunting call "so-hoe" as his battle cry at Dedgemoor when he fought for the crown against his unpopular uncle, James II.

At the corner of the square, there is a French Huguenot Church, a reminder of the Huguenots who came to Soho as refugees in the seventeenth century.

In Agatha Christie's *The Secret Adversary,* the intrepid

Tommy Beresford followed a gang member from South Audley Street up Shaftesbury Avenue to the maze of mean streets around Soho until he reached a small, dilapidated square.

On the west side of Soho Square, there are still several decayed-looking houses, giving you, despite the encroaching office buildings, an idea of the place about which Christie wrote.

Now take Carlisle Street to the west, out of Soho Square. Go across Dean Street on Carlisle to Great Chapel Street. Turn right on Great Chapel Street and go to Hollen Street. Turn left on Hollen Street, which will shortly become Noel Street. Follow Noel Street, which is in the heart of an old cockney-Jewish neighborhood; it will become Great Marlborough Street.

As you follow Great Marlborough Street you will pass many small shops connected with clothing manufacturing.

While seeking information about the murdered vampire Lotta, Asher found a shop in Great Marlborough Street that was run by a woman named Minette, who described Lotta as a true blonde with green eyes. (*Those Who Hunt the Night* by Barbara Hambly)

You will also pass a very large round sign that marks Carnaby Street. This was the clothing center of the 1960s London youth culture—as well as that of the U.S.

In Mary Stewart's thriller *The Gabriel Hounds,* her heroine asks her cousin Charles, who, disguised as an Arab, has just rescued her from a harem, "Where did you get that Carnaby Street rig anyway?"

Today, Carnaby Street is history. The young and the hip have moved on to new scenes, in particular, Kings Road in Chelsea. Carnaby Street is still worth a stroll, however, if just to put you in the know.

In P. D. James's *The Skull Beneath the Skin,* Cordelia Gray sent her office helper, Bevis, to a Carnaby Street deli to get them lunch.

Continue west on Great Marlborough Street. Across the street is Argyll Street. (Argyll Street is the site of the world-famous Palladium Music Hall.) In Sayers's *The Unpleasantness at the Bellona Club,* Robert Fentiman planned to take Ann Dorland there for an evening's entertainment, proving that she would attract strong, silent men, just as Lord Peter Wimsey had predicted.

In Sax Rohmer's *The Trail of Fu Manchu,* during one of Fu Manchu's efforts to subvert western civilization with eastern magic, a landlady in Limehouse was given tickets to the Palladium by an undercover Scotland Yard man, so that he could gain access to her building in the East End.

At the corner of Great Marlborough and Kingly Streets, you will see the Tudor-timbered back of Liberty's, a department store famous for its beautiful fabrics, cashmere sweaters, lovely scarves, and elegant soaps.

Lord Peter borrowed some of his wife's Liberty ties for his costume the night his son Bredon was born. ("The Haunted Policeman" by Dorothy L. Sayers)

Turn left behind Liberty's and walk down Kingly Street. You are retracing the workaday steps of P. D. James's Cordelia Gray in *An Unsuitable Job for a Woman.* Gray came up from the Oxford Circus Underground and plunged into the "cacophony" of Kingly Street "between the blocked pavement and shining mass of cars and vans which packed the narrow street." She saw the bronze plaque that read "Pryde's Detective Agency, Props. Bernard G. Pryde, Cordelia Gray."

The Detection Club met in rooms in Kingly Street after World War II. Dorothy L. Sayers was able to get the rooms cheaply through her Church of England connections.

Farther along, you will pass the Red Lion Pub at 14 Kingly Street. This is about the right location for The Golden Pheasant, where P. D. James's Bernie and Cordelia lunched, presided over by Mavis.

Kingly Street runs into Beak Street, where the famous Italian painter Canaletto lived at No. 41. He painted scenes of London spires beneath a blue Venetian sky.

Turn left (east) along Beak Street to Upper John Street and then turn left along Upper John Street to reach Golden Square.

Created in 1681, Golden Square was the first square in Soho. Most of the buildings here are now quite modern; they contrast oddly with the statue of George II in a Roman toga, which stands in the park.

On the west side of the square, two eighteenth-century houses remind us of earlier days. At one time they were combined into one building to create the Portuguese Embassy. Margery Allingham may have used this square and that building for her fictional Ivory Art Gallery at Nos. 38 and 39 Sallet Square near Regent Street and the Cafe Royal. (*Black Plumes*)

Cross Golden Square to the east and turn right to take Lower James Street south to Brewer Street. Turn left on Brewer Street and go as far as Bridle Lane.

Somewhere nearby is the fictional Grace Street where Helen MacInnes placed the offices of her superspy Robert Renwick. In *Cloak of Darkness,* he was asked to rendezvous at the Red Lion in Bridle Lane, which was not far from his office.

Turn right and walk back along Brewer Street, then turn left at Sherwood Street and go south toward Piccadilly Circus.

On the left, you will pass Denman Street with the Piccadilly Theatre on the corner across from the Regent Palace Hotel.

Cross Sherwood Street and look into the small, dark gateway that leads into tiny Ham Yard behind the theater. It is very like the description of Goff Place in Margery Allingham's *Tether's End.* Allingham described Goff Place as a cul-de-sac off Deban (Denman) Street, near the Avenue (Shaftesbury). On a dark and rainy night, Goff Place was the scene of a murder by "Major" Gerry Hawker, who made his getaway in a bus with two museum figures in it.

To end this walk, continue to Sherwood Street, which will return you to Shaftesbury Avenue and the Piccadilly Circus Underground Station.

6

MAYFAIR/ OXFORD STREET WALK

BACKGROUND

A Mayfair address speaks of wealth, position, and glamor. It is, in the words of a London friend, ". . .smart, terribly, terribly smart."

Mayfair was not always upscale and sought after. It was originally named for the noisy May Fair that annually took place during the first fifteen days in May. The fair, transferred here in 1686–88, was held in an open area between Berkeley Street and Park Lane, where Curzon Street and Shepherd Market are today. In the mid-eighteenth century, George III's time, the fair was suppressed because the goings-on created a public nuisance.

The whole of modern Mayfair had been covered with houses long before the end of the eighteenth century when the center of gravity for aristocratic London shifted west from Covent Garden and Soho.

First came the townhouses of the landed gentry, some of whom still maintain residences there. Next came the hotels for the aristocrats who couldn't or wouldn't maintain a house in town, but demanded all the amenities of one. Many of the townhouses are gone or have been divided into elegant flats, but the fine hotels are still around to provide, on a London visit, all the comforts one could expect to find in a country manor.

Mayfair is also a noted shopping area. Everything from fine fashions to handmade saddles and luxury motor cars can be found in Mayfair's shops. If you are bent on spending money, this is an ideal area.

The Mayfair walk is a long one, but it can be divided into two or more sessions. If you choose to do it as one walk, it will take a full day. Although what is worn on the walks in this book is the walker's choice, for this one, remember that Mayfair is definitely an upscale area and that hotels such as the Ritz and Brown's, where you may choose to have lunch, tea, or dinner, make ties and jackets de rigeur for men and require comparable attire for women.

LENGTH OF WALK: 6.2 miles

See text for shorter segments. See the map on page 104 for the boundaries of this walk, and page 255–57 for a list of the authors, books, and detectives mentioned.

PLACES OF INTEREST

Sotheby's, 34-35 New Bond Street.

Marlborough Fine Art, Ltd., 39 Bond Street.

U.S. Embassy, Grosvenor Square.

Royal Academy of Arts, Burlington House, Piccadilly. Open daily. Admission charge.

PLACES TO EAT

Cafe Royal, 68 Regent Street. The hotel has the Grill and Le Relais restaurant. Continental food is served in an ornate rococo decor from the days of Oscar Wilde. Reservations required. 071-437-9090; after six o'clock, 071-429-6320.

The Connaught Hotel, Carlos Place. A grill and restaurant are available; English and French food are served in an elegant continental dining room. Reservations are needed. 071-492-0668.

Brown's Hotel Restaurant, 21–24 Dover Street. Afternoon tea in the lounge is noteworthy. Reservations required. 071-493-6020.

Shepherd's Tavern, 50 Hertford Street. This 300-year-old pub with a paneled bar serves real ale. 071-499-3017.

Claridge's Hotel, Brook Street. This elegant 1930s-style restaurant with orchestra has a huge menu. The causerie has a cold buffet. Reservations are required. 071-629-8860.

— MAYFAIR/OXFORD STREET WALK: — PART ONE

Begin this walk by exiting the Piccadilly Circus Underground Station and following the sign for Piccadilly North side, Regent Street South side. As you emerge from the tube station, stop to admire the elegant sweep of Regency buildings on your left. They are part of the graceful crescents that once stretched all the way north to Regent's Park.

You are now on Regent Street. Across the street, the Cafe Royal at 68 Regent Street is on your right. On September 8,1902, Sherlock Holmes was attacked in Regent Street, but escaped his attacker by running through the Cafe Royal. ("The Adventure of the Illustrious Client" by Sir Arthur Conan Doyle) Perhaps that is why the Cafe Royal was for so long the site of the Detection Club's annual initiation rites. (Since 1992, the Detection Club has met at the Savoy.)

Asher took time for dinner at the Cafe Royal and for a nap before he met Ysidro and the other vampire, Grippen. (*Those Who Hunt the Night* by Barbara Hambly)

In *Black Plumes* by Margery Allingham, painter David Field took Frances Ivory to the Cafe Royal for an ice cream sundae and to talk over the strange happening at the Ivory Gallery, 39 Sallet Square, just off Regent Street.

MAYFAIR
OXFORD STREET

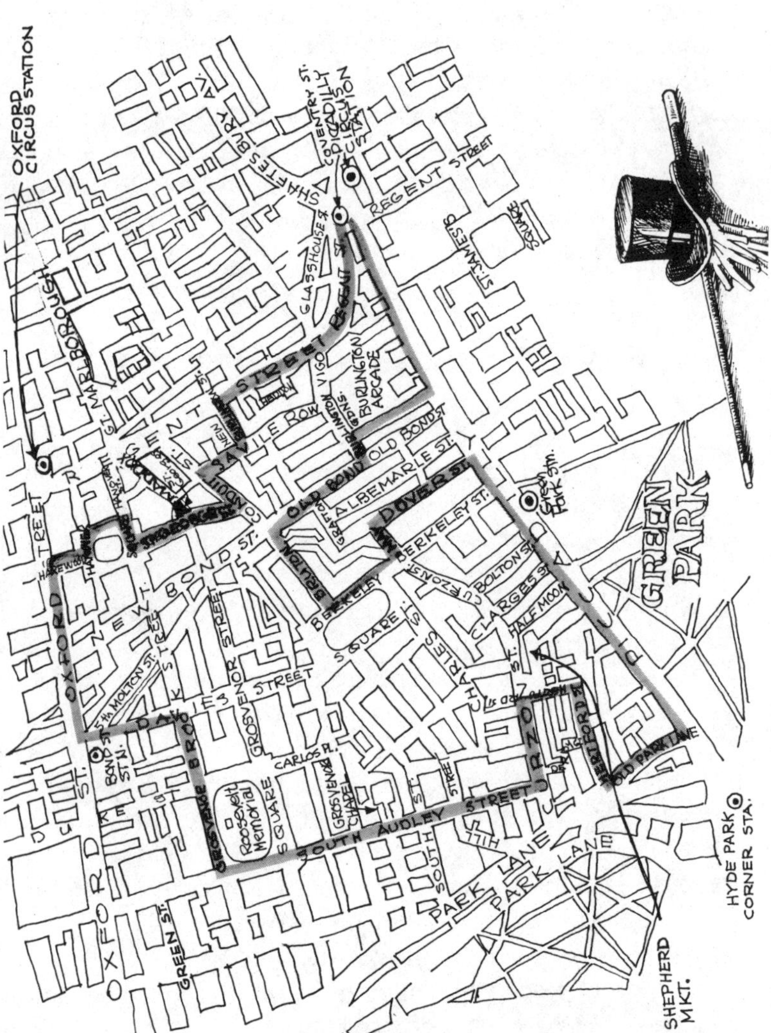

Another restaurant, Oddenino's, was located at 60 Regent Street. It was where Lord Peter Wimsey thought about taking Marjorie Phelps, the sculptress in Dorothy L. Sayers's *The Unpleasantness at the Bellona Club*.

In Ngaio Marsh's *A Wreath for Rivera,* the Metronome Restaurant, a fashionable nightclub that featured Breezy Bellairs's Band, was located somewhere around Regent Street and Piccadilly. Lord Pastern and Baggot played the drums there. One night, Lord Pastern appeared to murder Carlos Rivera in front of the CID's Inspector Alleyn and his wife Troy.

There is no longer a Lyons Teashop along this stretch of Regent Street as there was when Baroness Orczy's Lady Molly and her friend, Mary Granard, stopped for a bit of refreshment after seeing a matinee of du Maurier's *Trilby* (*Lady Molly of Scotland Yard*). Lady Molly always thought that, had they gone to the Mathis Vienna Cafe just across the street, the murder of Mark Culledon would never have occurred.

Regent Street is an excellent place for eating and an equally good place for shopping. In H. R. F. Keating's *Inspector Ghote Hunts the Peacock,* Inspector Ghote, searching for a "real English teapot" for his wife, went into a Regent Street china shop that was much too pricey, then into a seconds shop where he was too humiliated to make a purchase.

Rowena Stanwick apologized for being late to Hannah Greenwood's, explaining that the celebration in honor of Her Majesty's Jubilee created an inordinate amount of traffic and that it "took ages to get down Regent Street." (*Mrs. Jeffries on the Ball* by Emily Brightwell).

Cordelia Gray, on her way to work, sped past early morning shoppers scanning the windows of Dickin and Jones. Arriving at work, she found the body of her partner, Bernie Pryde. After seeing the undertakers about her partner's funeral, Gray took herself back to Dickin and Jones for tea. (*An Unsuitable Job for a Woman* by P. D. James)

In *I Am the Only Running Footman* by Martha Grimes, Jury remembered the time he had come upon Dr. Nancy standing outside Dickin and Jones eyeing the bridal display.

We will not go as far along Regent Street as Dickin and Jones, but do continue on Regent for the time being. Go past the Burberry store, Heddon Street, and the New Burlington Mews. Turn left into New Burlington Street and follow it to Savile Row; turn right. You are across the street from the West Central Police Station.

World-famous for its gentlemen's bespoke tailoring, Savile Row is not a street for window-shopping, as most displays consist of bolts of fabric.

Trevor Worth, Miss Beale's nephew, was a tall, blue-eyed man with a voice like Michael Caine and a suit that "murmured Savile Row." (*Skylark* by Sheila Simonson)

In the *English School Murder* by Ruth Dudley Edwards, Jeremy Buckland, Amiss's old friend from Oxford days, had such sartorial spendor that he made even his most uncouth contemporaries long to head for Savile Row.

At No. 3 Savile Row, the Beatles' company, Apple, had its headquarters. John, Paul, George, and Ringo conducted their business there, and, on January 30, 1969, the final public performance by the Beatles was held on the roof of No. 3.

The eighteenth-century playwright Richard Brinsley Sheridan lived at No. 14 Savile Row, but when he died, in 1816, it was in the front bedroom of No. 17.

The Fortress House is on the right as you continue down the street. Fortress House is a large, official-looking gray building, which contains, among other departments, the Royal Commission on Historical Monuments, as well as a department of British Intelligence.

Tamara Hoyland, Jessica Mann's sleuth, worked there as an archaeologist. She bicycled to work from her flat in Kensington. (*Funeral Sites* by Jessica Mann)

Follow Savile Row to Conduit Street, the site of Weston's, a tailoring establishment that is mentioned often in Regency tales, including Georgette Heyer's *Regency Buck*. Weston's was the tailor of choice for the well-dressed gentleman in the early nineteenth century.

Turn left on Conduit St. and follow it to St. George Street. Turn right and walk north until you come to Maddox Street.

At the corner of St. George and Maddox Streets is St. George's Hanover Square, favored both in literature and life by the upper levels of London society.

St. George's is considered to be the West End's most impressive church. It was built in 1713–24 by John James, a follower of Christohper Wren. The church has a large Corinthian portico and a Baroque tower. The interior resembles St. James's Piccadilly. On either side of the entrance porch sit nineteenth-century cast-iron dogs by Landseer; they seem to be waiting for their master.

St. George's best-known parishioner, the composer George Frederick Handel, had his own pew there. Handel's home for 35 years was nearby at 25 Brook Street. It is where he wrote *The Messiah*, and it is where he died in 1759.

St. George's has long been the scene of fashionable weddings for both the known and unknown, the real and the fictional. The register records the nuptials of Sir William Hamilton and Emma Hart (Lord Nelson's "Dearest Emma") in 1791; Benjamin Disraeli and Mrs. Wyndham Lewis in 1839; J. W. Cross, a New York banker, and Mary Ann Evans (George Eliot) in 1880; and Theodore Roosevelt and Edith Carow in 1886. John Bucan, the first Baron Tweedsmuir, was married here in 1907. In 1814, Percy Shelley and Harried Westbrook were remarried at St. George's to validate their Scottish wedding vows.

St. George's was the choice church for weddings among Georgette Heyer's characters.

The sharp-tongued Helen, Duchess of Denver, thought it was a suitable spot for Harriet and Lord Peter to exchange vows in Dorothy L. Sayers's *Busman's Honeymoon*.

Walk up to St. George Street to Hanover Square. The bronze statue at the south end of the square is of William Pitt the Younger, prime minister in the days of Napoleon. The Hanover Square Rooms, the principal concert hall in London during the late eighteenth century, stood at the corner of Hanover Street on the east side of the square. Turn right and follow the square around to Harewood Street; turn right, then left into Oxford Street.

Oxford Street is London's longest shopping thoroughfare. It runs eastward from Marble Arch to Tottenham Court Road, where it continues as New Oxford Street. The road was laid out in Roman times, possibly even earlier. Until the eighteenth century, it was known as Tyburn Hill, where Marble Arch is today.

In Robert Barnard's *A Scandal in Belgravia,* Andy Frobes said he would never go back to England. "I hear you're knee deep in litter if you walk down Oxford Street these days," he commented.

Oxford Street today is the site of many of London's large department stores. This walk takes you along Oxford Street, across from several well-known stores.

In John Mortimer's *Rumpole of the Bailey,* one of Rumpole's clients, the Reverend Mortimer Skinner, had gone to the Oxford Street summer sales, where he was arrested for shoplifting.

In Margaret Yorke's *Find Me a Villian,* Nina Crowther was in a highly upset state over the breakup of her marriage. After following her husband and "the other woman," she found herself in Oxford Street. She went into John Lewis and then into Woolworth, where she bought herself a cheap china cat that reminded her of her husband's mistress.

In Antonia Fraser's *Quiet as a Nun,* Jemima Shore and her classmate, Sister Miriam of Blessed Eleanor's Tower, lunched at D.H. Evans because it was less expensive than Fortnum & Mason. Tamara Hoyland, in Jessica Mann's *Funeral Sites,* spend an afternoon shopping at Marks and Spencer. She was buying clothing that would serve to disguise the fugitive Rosamund Sholto and allow her to be smuggled out of London.

Follow Oxford Street to Davies Street and again turn left. Follow Davies Street to Brook Street, passing Weighhouse Street and St. Anselm's Place. At the corner of Davies and Brook Street is Claridge's Hotel; it is mentioned in many mystery novels.

Sir Richard Hannay was involved in trying to solve a triple murder when the mysterious Medina summoned him to Claridge's to meet a great master of Eastern lore. Hannay found the hotel bright and commonplace, with people dancing and dining. A turbaned Indian appeared and led him into a small anteroom, furnished with vulgar copies of French furniture, where he met the intriguing Kharama. (*The Three Hostages* by John Buchan)

In Nicholas Blake's *Minute for Murder,* the Director of the Ministry of Morale was directed by letter to ring up his missing brother-in-law at Claridge's.

Dorinda Brown went to Claridge's to apply for a job as secretary to the wife of a wealthy businessman in *Spotlight* by Patricia Wentworth.

John Dickson Carr in *The Skeleton in the Clock,* had the Dowager Countess insist that her granddaughter meet her at Claridge's for lunch, even though the girl had just been reunited with her lost wartime love.

Agatha Christie was very fond of Claridge's. The hotel rivals the Ritz for appearances in her books. Sometimes it is called Claridge's, other times there is a variation of the name. For instance, in *The Golden Ball,* she calls it Harridge's, "Who in England did not know Harridge's where notables and royalty arrived and departed as a matter of course." (As a matter of policy, Claridge's flies the flag of any resident prince, king, or president.)

In *The Secret of Chimneys,* adventurer Anthony Cade met Baron Lolpretzyl of Herzoslovakia at Claridge's to talk about possible kings for Herzoslovakia.

Kramenin, the Russian conspirator in *The Secret Adversary,* had a suite at Claridge's where he dictated to his secretary in sibilant Russian.

One of Mr. Parker Pyne's clients, an unhappy, middle-aged woman, met a gigolo called Claude at Claridge's where they dined and danced in *Mr. Parker Pyne, Detective.*

Agatha Christie was not the only writer to tamper with the name of the famous hotel. Anthony Berkeley, in *The Piccadilly Murder,* refers to Alridge's, where "the air cost several pounds an hour to breathe."

After people-watching for a moment outside Claridge's, turn right and walk west along Brook Street until you reach Grosvenor Square.

The townhouse that belonged to the timid Lord Caterham was located near the west end of Brook Street. In

Christie's *The Secret of Chimneys,* Lady Bundle stayed there with her father.

In *Regency Buck* by Georgette Heyer, Lord Worth rented a Brook Street house for his wards, the Taveners.

Grosvenor Square, which was built between 1725 and 1731, is the site of the American Embassy. The largest of Mayfair's squares, it is second in area only to Lincoln's Inn Fields.

From its earliest days, Grosvenor Square attracted residents of high social rank, and it has never deteriorated socially. This is due, at least in part, to its proximity to Hyde Park, as well as to the careful management by the Grosvenor family.

The square's original large, handsome houses have been rebuilt or have disappeared completely, but there are locations of note to capture your attention. Two that have been much altered are No. 9, at the northeast corner of the square, which was once the residence (1785–86) of John Adams, the first "minister plenipotentiary" and later President of the United States; and No. 38, on the south side of the square, which is now the Indonesian Embassy.

Grosvenor Square has a large and beautiful central park in the center of which stands the British memorial to President Franklin Delano Roosevelt. The American Embassy, built in 1956–60, is on the west side of the square.

In Dorothy L. Sayers's *Clouds of Witness,* Lord Peter Wimsey found it necessary to go to the American Embassy for his papers so that he could hurry to New York after the murdered Denis Cathcart's mysterious mistress.

During the second world war, many of the buildings in the square served as American military headquarters. A plaque at No. 20 indicates the building where General Eisenhower had his headquarters in 1942.

In detective fiction, Grosvenor Square was the home of Julius Ricardo, who served as "Dr. Watson" to A.E. W. Mason's French detective, M. Hannaud.

Just off Grosvenor Square in Carlos Place is the elegant Connaught Hotel. It has a long-standing reputation for impeccable service and outstanding international cuisine. Tea is served in Victorian splendor each afternoon.

According to Jemima Shore in Antonia Fraser's *Cool Repentance,* the Connaught had "arguably the most expensive restaurant in London," and it was where Jemima's boss, Cy Fredericks, lunched each day.

According to Julian Symons in *A Three Pipe Problem,* the Connaught's grill room was where the idea for a Sherlock Holmes TV series sold to the BBC's director of programmes.

The Connaught is also a likely location for the place where Sir Percy Crumble had lunch just a stone's throw away from his office in Berkeley Square. (*Who Is Simon Warwick?* by Patricia Moyes)

Leave Grosvenor Square by its southwest corner. You should now be walking south on South Audley Street. This has always been a very smart neighborhood. Two French kings—Louis XVIII and Charles X—lived here. Queen Caroline, while awaiting her divorce by George VI, also lived here.

In John Creasey's *The Toff and the Deadly Parson,* the wealthy church warden, Mr. Straker, lived in South Audley Street.

The Alpine Club at 74 South Audley Street was one of the clubs to which Sir Julian Freke belonged. His club membership gave Lord Peter a vital clue in Dorothy L. Sayers's *Whose Body?*

Somehow, Colonel M. Worthington made it out of the depths of his leather armchair in South Audley Street, in order to walk to his armchair at Plum's. (*Murder at Plum's* by Amy Meyers)

As you continue along South Audley Street, on your left, you will pass the modest, brown-brick Grosvenor Chapel, which served as chapel for the U.S. armed forces during World War II.

In Sayers's *Unnatural Death,* Miss Climpson trailed Mrs. Forrest up South Audley Street past a chemist's, a florist's, a cafe, and finally to her flat. Then Miss Climpson pretended to conduct a canvass in order to locate the exact apartment. Lord Peter later scaled a drainpipe to Mrs. Forrest's bathroom window so that he could retrieve a glass with fingerprints on it.

The flat of Mrs. Rita Vandermeyer was in Audley Mansions at 20 South Audley Street. She was part of the gang that kidnapped Jane Finn in Agatha Christie's *The Secret Adversary.*

Continue on South Audley Street past Hill Street to Audley Square. No. 2 Audley Square was the Belchester townhouse that Lord Peter Wimsey and his wife Harriet rented for their town home after their wedding in *Busman's Honeymoon.*

The attractive brick-and-stone mansion, now the University Women's Club, was transformed into Bertram's Hotel for the television version of Christie's *At Bertram's Hotel,* starring Joan Hickman.

Follow South Audley to Curzon Street, where you will turn left. In the eighteenth century, Curzon was an elegant street. Today, only one of its great mansions, Crewe House, remains among the offices, shops, and restaurants.

Many of Georgette Heyer's characters had Curzon Street addresses, and in Agatha Christie's *The Mystery of the Blue Train,* 160 Curzon Street was the mansion of the American couple, Ruth and Derek Kettering.

As you continue on Curzon Street, you will come to Chesterfield Street on your left. George (Beau) Brummel, arbiter of taste among the ton, moved into No. 4 Chesterfield Street in 1799. Somerset Maugham's Ashenden lived at No. 36.

Follow Curzon Street to Hertford Street and turn right. This will bring you into Shepherd Market. In 1688, James II decreed that a fair that was then held in the Haymarket be transferred to what was then a wasteland. (A plaque at the corner of Trebeck Street and Shepherd Market commemorates the fair.) Shepherd Market is an area of narrow streets and alleys, with an open marketplace filled with small shops, cafes, and pubs, making it a shopper's delight.

Spenser, Robert Parker's private eye, lunched in the fictional Shepherd Market Pub. It could easily be Shepherd's Tavern at 50 Hertford Street. It is a 300-year-old pub with a bow window, leather seats, and, on the first floor landing, a telephone booth fashioned from an eighteenth century sedan chair.

In Ngaio Marsh's *Death in Ecstasy,* the small but expensive house that was home to Cara Quayne, the murder victim in the House of the Sacred Flame, was in Shepherd Market.

Dmitri, who catered the debutante balls in *Death in a White Tie,* also by Marsh, had his business in Shepherd Market.

In *Death Has Deep Roots* by Michael Gilbert, the Leopard was the pub in Shepherd Market where Nap Rumbold, the junior member of the solicitor's firm of Markby, Wragge and Rumbold, went to enlist the help of Major McCann to create a new defense for Victoria Lamartine. They held a council of war upstairs in the landlord's parlor. The description that Gilbert gives sounds very much like Ye Olde Bunch of Grapes at 16 Shepherd Market.

David Marr, a friend of Ivy Childress, a murdered girl, lived in Shepherd Market not far from the Only Running Footman Pub. (*I Am the Only Running Footman* by Martha Grimes)

The first part of this walk has covered 3.7 miles. If you wish to end the walk at this point, leave Hertford Street and go left on Shepherd Street to White Horse Street, and go right. Follow White Horse Street to Piccadilly. When you reach Piccadilly, turn left and walk up Piccadilly to the Green Park Underground Station at Queen's Walk.

— MAYFAIR/OXFORD STREET WALK: — PART TWO

Begin the second part of the walk by going to the right and following Hertford as it angles to the right. At 10 Hertford Street, there are two blue historical markers. One notes that this was the residence from 1722 to 1792 of General John Burgoyne, whose loss of the Battle of Saratoga to Benedict Arnold helped to pave the way for the Colonials to win the American Revolution; later, from 1795 to 1802, the house was the residence of the playwright and politician Richard Brinsley Sheridan.

American poet Edwin Arlington Robinson stayed at No. 3 on his 1923 visit to London.

Continue on Hertford Street until you reach Old Park Lane. A little to the right is the double roadway called Park Lane. It sweeps along Hyde Park, stretching its way from Hyde Park Corner to Marble Arch. Park Lane is out of the area of this walk but still requires mention. In the fifteenth century, Park

Lane was called Westminster Lane; later, it was called Tyburn Lane because it led directly to Tyburn, the dreaded place of execution. Although once lined with opulent mansions, which gave it the nickname "Millionaires Row," Park Lane is now lined with luxury hotels. Starting from the north end and working south, they are Grosvenor House, the Dorchester, the London Hilton, the Londoner, the Inn on the Park, and the Intercontinental.

According to *Murder Ink* by Agatha Christie, the modern block of flats called Whitehaven Mansions, where Hercule Poirot lived with his secretary, Miss Felicity Lemon, and his manservant, Georges, was on Park Lane.

The townhouses of Lord Charles Lamprey's older brother, the Marquis of Wutherwood, was located on Park Lane. Roberta Grey and Henry Lamprey went to 24 Brummel, Park Lane, to spend the night with Charles's widow after he was murdered. In *A Surfeit of Lampreys,* Ngaio Marsh described "a row of great uniform houses [that] seemed fast asleep. . .[as] a fairy tale was unfolding."

In Dorothy L. Sayers's *Whose Body?,* Sir Reuben Levy lived at 9a Park Lane and in "The Article in Question" (also by Sayers) the Duchess of Medway's townhouse was on Park Lane.

Enough of Park Lane. Turn left into Old Park Lane, which will bring you to Piccadilly. Here you will find the Hard Rock Cafe, a favorite with fans of rock music and American-style hamburgers.

Slightly piqued at her husband Jay, who chose to go to bed at ten, Lark commented that they could "boogie all night at the Hard Rock Cafe." (*Skylark* by Sheila Simonson)

In Alan Scholefield's *Threats and Menaces,* Adrienne Marvell tried to entice Dory out of the apartment with the promise of a double-thick chocolate malted at the air-conditioned Hard Rock Cafe.

Turn left off Old Park Lane onto Piccadilly. Green Park will be across the street from you, on the right.

Continue along Piccadilly, where Ruth Callice, who joined Martin Drake in an adventure seeking prison ghosts, ran a bookshop in *The Skeleton in the Clock* by John Dickson Carr.

The Toff, the West-Ender created by John Creasey who was equally at home in the East End, lived in Gresham Terrace on Piccadilly.

As you walk along Piccadilly you will pass Down Street, Brick Street, White Horse Street, and Half Moon Street, all to the left.

Recently, Half Moon Street gave its name to a Paul Theroux short story on which a Michael Caine film was based.

Bertie Wooster, P. G. Wodehouse's lively creation, lived with his perfect butler, Jeeves, in Half Moon Street.

In Edmund Crispin's *Frequent Hearses,* a member of the theatrical Crane family had a party on Half Moon Street.

The murdered vampire Lotta and a friend had gone to the rooms of another vampire called Edward Hammersmith. He lived in an old mansion in Half Moon Street that his father had owned when he was a man. (*Those Who Hunt the Night* by Barbara Hambly)

The next street is Clarges Street. It is where Edgar Wallace placed the fictional Steyne Square in *The Crimson Circle.* Wallace described a square of large, old-fashioned houses with iron railings.

Julian Kestrel, the aristocratic sleuth in *A Broken Vessel,* Kate Ross's tale of murder in Regency London, lived in rooms let from Mrs. Mabbit in Clarges Street.

Flemings Hotel in Clarges Street, together with Brown's Hotel (Dover Street), served as a model for Agatha Christie's Bertram's Hotel.

Stratton Street, a little farther on, was the location of the car rental place called Hire Car Lucullus in *Forfeit* by Dick Francis. He called it "a small, plushy office off Piccadilly."

The street after Stratton is Berkeley. In Anthony Berkeley's *The Poisoned Chocolate Case,* the Rainbow Club was "in Piccadilly, just around the corner from Sir Eustace Pennefeather's rooms in Berkeley Street."

Continue on Piccadilly to Dover Street and turn left to go to Berkeley Square. Old General Fentiman would leave his rooms and walk along Dover Street to the Bellona Club, which was east on Piccadilly at No. 49. (*The Unpleasantness at the Bellona Club* by Dorothy L. Sayers)

This is a street of shops, small galleries, and pleasant pubs. Brown's Hotel, which often pops up in mystery stories, is at the head of Dover Street. As already noted, Agatha Christie combined Brown's with Flemings to produce Bertram's Hotel in *At Bertram's Hotel.*

Brown's Hotel, which was founded by Lord Byron's valet, is the quintessence of English hotels. When you walk into its lobby, time rolls back and you expect to see Miss Silver, Miss Marple, and their contemporaries gathered for tea. Tea, by way, is served in a lounge decorated, as the magazines would say, in "dignified English country." While we were there gathering local color and enjoying a delightful tea, a group of television actors were ensconced in one corner discussing their trade. When a rather threadbare-looking American clergyman led his wife and five children to a cozy corner, the wife hung back, but her husband soothed her parsimony by murmuring that "yes, it will be costly but it is an experience the children must have."

In *The Dirty Duck* by Martha Grimes, Brown's provided the appropriate, expensive place to house Valentine Honeycut's exclusive Honeysuckle Tours.

Melrose Plant had had tea at Brown's with Lucinda St. Clair. The tea had later escalated into dinner. (*I Am the Only Running Footman* by Martha Grimes)

Oxford University Press is at No. 37 Dover Street, across from Brown's. Just beyond Brown's is Hay Hill where you will turn left.

Hay Hill gets its name from the old Hay Hill Farm which stood on the Aye (or Eye) brook. The brook still runs underground at the foot of the hill. While George IV was still Prince of Wales, he and two friends were accosted here by footpads and robbed of two shillings and sixpence.

Hay Hill will take you to Berkeley Street where you will turn right.

The Thomas Cook office where Katherine Grey, the companion of an old lady from St. Mary Mead, went to get a ticket for Nice was in Berkeley Street. It was there that she met Derek

Kettering, the dissolute husband of Ruth Kettering, the rich American. (*The Mystery of the Blue Train* by Agatha Christie)

Berkeley Street will lead you into Berkeley Square. This is the "Gaunt Square" which figured so prominently in Thackeray's *Vanity Fair* and the "Buckley Square" of the *Yellowplush Papers,* which appeared in *Fraser's Magazine* in 1837–38.

The square was named for Berkeley House, which stood on the south side from 1664 to 1733, when it was replaced by Devonshire House. The square's gigantic plane trees were planted in 1790. The garden in the center of the square is said to be haunted by the ghost of Lord Clive, the conqueror of India, who committed suicide in 1774 in his home at No. 45. Peter Underwood, in his *Haunted London,* calls No. 50 Berkeley Square the most haunted house in London.

The chemist, Joseph Priestley, was librarian in Lansdowne House at No. 54. It was there that he discovered oxygen.

Berkeley Square was the scene of the murder of a member of the Honeysuckle Tours in Martha Grime's *The Dirty Duck.* Only Running Footman pub, which gave Grimes the title for another novel, is located in Charles Street just off Berkeley Square. (*I Am the Only Running Footman* by Martha Grimes)

The opulent office of Sir Percy Crumble, director of the Charlton business, was located in Berkeley Square in Patricia Moyes's *Who Is Simon Warwick?*

The May Fair Inter-Continental Hotel, located off Berkeley Street, was probably the big flossy hotel where Spencer, Robert Parker's private eye, stayed while on his manhunt in London. He ambushed several members of the terrorist gang Liberty there in *The Judas Goat.*

The Hungaria, a Mayfair nightclub once located in Berkeley Square, was where Roberta Grey and the Lampreys went in the 1930s to hear Richard Tauber sing.

The Mirros Club was also in Berkeley Square. It is where Thalia Drummond, the daughter of Scotland Yard's Inspector Parr, dined with cabinet minister MP Raphael Willings in Edgar Wallace's *The Crimson Circle.*

The best-known, most fashionable nightclub in today's

London is Annabel's at No. 44 Berkeley Square. It seems to be the model for the "Over and Under Club" where the MP Sir Pountney took the actress who played Irene Adler. (*A Three Pipe Problem* by Julian Symons)

The author of *The Castle of Otranto,* Horace Walpole, father of the Gothic romance from which the modern detective story is descended, lived the last years of his life in a small house on the east side of Berkeley Square.

In Sax Rohmer's *The Trail of Fu Manchu,* the Secretary for Home Affairs had a gloomy, stone-porched mansion a few paces from Berkeley Square. That was where Scotland Yard's Sir Denis Nayland Smith got permission to open the mausoleum of the Demurases in a London cemetery.

In the Sherlock Holmes story "The Adventure of the Illustrious Client," General DeMerville lived on the east side of Berkeley Square, as did Admiral Sinclair in "The Adventure of the Bruce-Partington Plans." (Dr. Watson spelled Berkeley "Barkeley," the way it is pronounced.)

Leave Berkeley Square at the east side by way of Bruton Street. Queen Elizabeth II was born at No. 17 Bruton Street in 1926.

Follow Bruton Street to Bond Street where you will turn right. Bond Street is really two streets, New Bond to the left and Old Bond to the right. They connect, but, confusingly, they have separate numbering systems. (At best, the numbering system all over London is confusing to North Americans who expect even numbers on one side of the street and odd numbers on the other.)

Both Bond Streets are known for their luxurious shops. Judith Travener drove to Bond Street to purchase a ravishing hat in *Regency Buck* by Georgette Heyer.

Julian Kestrel, who had been seeking an opportunity to approach Lady Gayheart, saw her carriage pull up outside a milliner's in Bond Street. He managed to stroll by in time to hand her out. (*A Broken Vessel* by Kate Ross)

In *The Daughter of Time* by Josephine Tey, hospitalized Alan Grant explained to actress Marta Hallard that you can pick out the normal run of oversexed women any day on a walk down Bond Street between five and six o'clock.

Roger Sheringham, president of the Crimes Circle, went to a Bond Street hat shop after leaving Scotland Yard in Anthony Berkeley's *The Poisoned Chocolates Case.*

The Ambassador Club, a fictional club located at Bond and Grafton Streets, was where Fah Lo Sue, Fu Manchu's daughter, met the governor of the Bank of England, Sir Bertram Morgan, and vamped him into going to meet her father. (*The Trail of Fu Manchu* by Sax Rohmer)

Not knowing what time vampires began to move, Asher bought a silver chain made of the purest metal available at Lambert's, a fashionable Bond Street shop. (*Those Who Hunt the Night* by Barbara Hambly)

George Mortimer, in Julian Symons's *The Blackheath Poisonings,* bought women's underclothing at Baker's in Bond Street.

Follow Bond Street to Grafton Street; at No. 166 you will see the elaborate black, white, and gold facade of Asprey's, one of London's most luxurious shops. In addition to being a goldsmith, silversmith, bookbinder, and manufacturer of leather goods, Asprey's has a particularly important antique clock department that features some items that are of museum quality.

Founded in 1781 and moved to this location in 1847, Asprey's possesses the Royal Warrant. The shop is often mentioned in Georgette Heyer's Regency mysteries, and it is where Mrs. Packington bought a gold cigarette case for her young man, Claude. ("The Case of the Middle-Aged Wife" by Agatha Christie)

In Marian Babson's *Tourists Are for Trapping,* Gerry had been trailed past "so many jewelry shop windows by hinting birds that he must know as much about [jewelry] as anyone." He often joked that had he been born a century sooner he could have hired himself out as an extra hitching post as Asprey's.

In the C. M. Chan short story "Murder at Christmas," Bethancourt was going to Asprey's when he sighted the stocky figure of Detective Sergeant Jack Gibbons.

At Grafton Street, New Bond Street becomes Old Bond Street. Continue on Old Bond Street past Sotheby's, the world-renowned auction house at 34–35 Old Bond Street.

Sotheby's was established in 1744 as a rare-book dealer; it moved to this location in 1917. Above the kiosk to the right of the entrance there is a statue of the Egyptian god Sekmet that dates from circa 1320 BC.

In Gwendoline Butler's *Coffin on Murder Street,* Ellice Eden, reading the paper, saw that there was an auction of theater objects at Sotheby's.

John Dickson Carr probably had Sotheby's in mind when he created the auction house called Willaby's and placed it in Bond Street. Martin Drake was present at Willaby's when a grandfather clock with a skeleton inside was auctioned. (*The Skeleton in the Clock* by John Dickson Carr)

Agnew's, the art gallery at No. 43 which specializes in old masters, was most likely the model for Quinns, the Mayfair art salesroom in John Creasey's *The Baron and the Missing Old Masters.*

Cross Bond Street and turn left on Burlington Gardens. Cork Street, which leads off Burlington Gardens, is the location of many of London's private art galleries. It was on a street very much like Cork Street that Ngaio Marsh located the Wiltshire Gallery in *Death in a White Tie.*

Mr. Fitzjohn, a crony of young Peregrine Tavener had lodgings in Cork Street. (*Regency Buck* by Georgette Heyer)

Turn right from Burlington Gardens and enter the Burlington Arcade, a Regency arcade famous for its small, elegant shops and tall Beadles. The Beadles, who date from the early 1800s, are present to ensure obedience to rules against singing, carrying an open umbrella, large packages (in Regency times, people of quality did not carry packages), or running. At one time, the Beadles were ex-soldiers of the Tenth Hussars, but now any reliable ex-serviceman is considered for the appointment. Walk through the arcade to Piccadilly; if you can resist the urge to shop which will engulf you, well, you are far stronger than most.

Tessa Crichton's friend Lorraine explained that her in-law

Elaine was the type of high-powered shopper that found Boston and New York far too ordinary. She thought it necessary to make a trip to the Burlington Arcade. (*The Men in Her Death* by Anne Morice)

Thalia Drummond, who was accosted on Regent Street by her swain, Jack Beardmore, Jr., escaped through the Burlington Arcade. (*The Crimson Circle* by Edgar Wallace)

Harriet Vane ordered two dozen silk shirts from a Burlington Arcade shop in *Busman's Honeymoon* by Dorothy L. Sayers.

Leaving the Burlington Arcade, turn left on Piccadilly. You will be in front of the Burlington House and the Royal Academy of Arts.

When Nina Crowther was abandoned by her husband, she wandered Mayfair in the rain until she found herself at the bottom of Bond Street, where she paused outside Burlington House. (*Find Me a Villian* by Margaret Yorke)

Burlington House has been the home of the Royal Academy of the Arts since 1868, when it was moved from Somerset House. Burlington House is located on the north side of Piccadilly next to the Burlington Arcade. (The Burlington Arcade was designed originally for Lord Cavendish of Burlington House by Samuel Ware in 1819 to keep passersby from throwing oyster shells and other rubbish into his garden.

Burlington House is the last of the Piccadilly palaces. It is truly a grand sight with banners flying to announce an exhibition. The courtyard features a statue of the Academy's first president, Sir Joshua Reynolds.

In *Grave Goods* by Jessica Mann, Thea, Tamara Hoyland's friend and mentor, decided that she and Tamara should have coffee at the Ritz, although Tamara thought the basement of the Royal Academy would do just as well.

The painter who lodged with John Munting gave the unhappy Harrisons tickets for a private viewing of the annual show at Royal Academy. The portrait of Mrs. Harrison which was painted by Lathom was on exhibit. (*The Documents in the Case* by Dorothy L. Sayers)

Leave the Burlington House courtyard and walk to your

left along Piccadilly. Off to the left is Albany Court Yard. It leads to the most exclusive address in London, which is Albany.

The supercrook Raffles, who made thieving charming, had his chambers in Albany, as did Gregory Chapman, Jessica Green Wood's least-favorite suitor, in Joan Smith's *Behold, a Mystery!* Albany was also the address of Anthony Berkeley's Roger Sheringham.

It was long an ambition of Georgette Heyer to live in Albany. In 1942, she realized her dream by moving into chambers at No. 43 Albany.

Albany has an illustrious history. It was originally the home of the first Lord Melbourne and then of the Duke of York. Its distinguished residents included Lord Byron, Thomas Babington Macaulay, Prime Minister Gladstone, Prime Minister Edward Heath, Lord Beaverbrook, Graham Greene, and J. B. Priestley.

Continue on Piccadilly to Swallow Street; turn left. Walk along Swallow Street to Vine Street where you will see a police station. It is a likely choice for the "Bottle Street Police Station" above which Albert Campion, Margery Allingham's detective, had his flat at 17A.

As they were speeding in a cab toward 17A Bottle Street, Miss Joyce Blount eyed the young man next to her and the Inspector, who sat opposite, and lied. (*Police at the Funeral* by Margery Allingham)

Leave Vine and Swallow and return along Swallow to Piccadilly; turn left.

Before you reach Piccadilly Circus Underground Station, there are just two more observations to be made: Benson, who was posing as Simon Warwick, received a death threat in the middle of Piccadilly, just as he and the crowd were about to surge across the street. (*Who Is Simon Warwick?* by Patricia Moyes)

Dolly Godolphin, in Allingham's *Black Plumes,* dashed into traffic in Piccadilly and was struck by a car; seconds later, he was dead.

But enough. Head for the tube station where you will conclude this walk.

7

ST. JAMES WALK

BACKGROUND

This walk takes place in the area known as St. James, one of the many small villages that make up London. It is a cluster of squares and lanes, narrow streets, cul-de-sacs, and courts in the area between Piccadilly and the Mall, bordered by Green Park and St. James's Park. It is an area long associated with royalty.

When Whitehall Palace burned in 1698, St. James's Palace became the official residence of the monarch, until it was succeeded by Buckingham Palace. Today, although nearly two centuries have passed since it was the monarch's official residence, ambassadors are still accredited to the Court of St. James.

Since his separation from Princess Diana, Prince Charles has maintained his London residence at St. James' Palace.

From the early seventeenth century onward, many fine houses were built in the area of St. James; it later became known for the bachelor apartments of such young men about town as Beau Brummell. The most exclusive gentlemen's clubs are in St. James, as are antique and art dealers, as well as custom shops dealing in everything expensive, from wines, cheese, and tobacco to shirts, shoes, and guns.

The neighborhood is also famous for its hotels, among them Dukes Hotel, which has been called the quintessential small London hotel.

LENGTH OF WALK: 3-plus miles.

See the map on page 125 for the boundaries of this walk and page 258–59 for a list of the authors, books, and detectives mentioned.

PLACES OF INTEREST

St. James's Palace, Cleveland Row. Official seat of royalty built by Henry VIII. Chapel Royal. Open for Sunday services, Oct.–Palm Sunday.

Marlborough House, Pall Mall. Once the residence of Queen Mary, now Commonwealth Conference Centre. Queen's Chapel, adjoining Marlborough House, open for Sunday services, Easter–July.

Buckingham Palace, London residence of HM Queen Elizabeth II. When the Queen is in residence, the Royal Standard is flown. Changing of the Guard: daily, April–Aug. Every other day, Sept.–March. The palace is open to the public for a limited period of time each year. Admission charge.

Queen's Gallery, Buckingham Gate. Open Tues.–Sat. Admission charge.

The Royal Mews, Buckingham Palace Road. Open Wed. and Thur. Admission charge.

Lancaster House, Stable Yard. Open Sat.–Sun.

Christie's International Auction House, 8 King Street.

PLACES TO EAT

Fortnum & Mason, 181 Piccadilly. Two restaurants. 071-734-8040.

The Red Lion, Crown Passage. Pub food. 071-930-4141.

Overton's, 5 St. James's Street. With its gentleman's club atmosphere, Overton's is known for its fish and oyster bar. Book ahead. 071-493-8181.

St. James

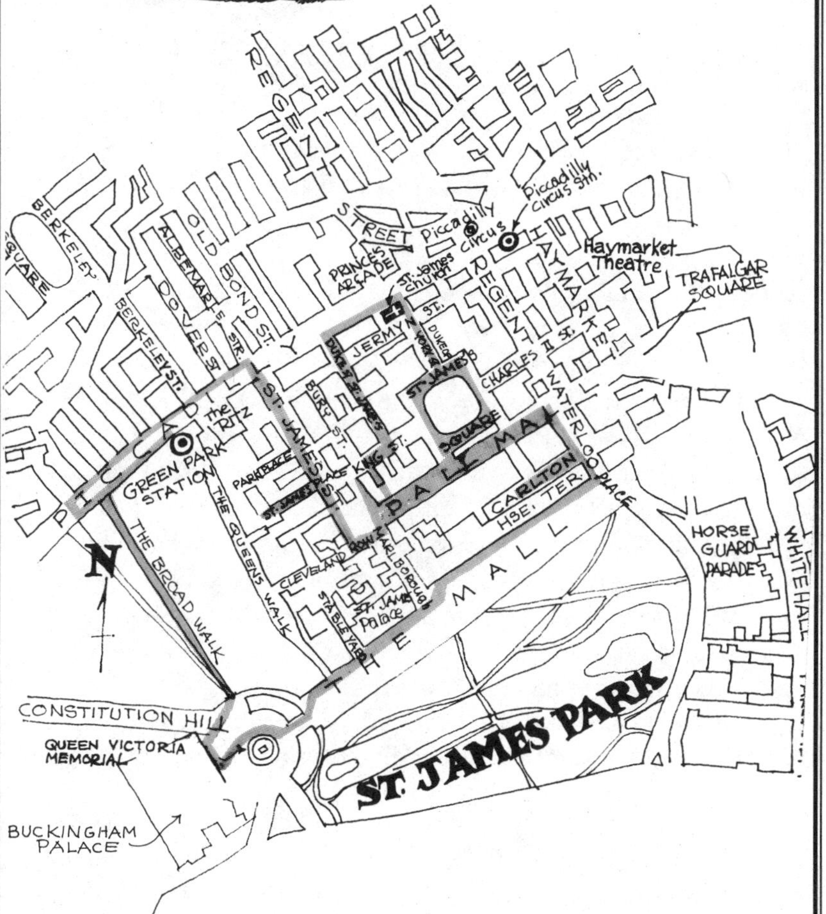
N
W
E
S
REGENT
STREET
BERKELEY SQUARE
BERKELEY ST.
ALBEMARLE STR.
OLD BOND ST.
DOVER ST.
PICCADILLY
Piccadilly Circus
Piccadilly Circus Stn.
HAYMARKET
Haymarket Theatre
TRAFALGAR SQUARE
PRINCE'S ARCADE
St. James Church
JERMYN ST.
DUKE ST. ST. JAMES'S
DUKE OF YORK ST.
ST. JAMES'S SQUARE
REGENT
CHARLES II ST.
WATERLOO PLACE
the RITZ
GREEN PARK STATION
PARK PLACE
ST. JAMES'S PLACE
ST. JAMES'S ST.
BURY ST.
KING ST.
PALL MALL
CARLTON HSE. TER.
THE QUEEN'S WALK
CLEVELAND ROW
MARLBOROUGH
ST. JAMES Palace
STABLE YARD
THE MALL
HORSE GUARD PARADE
WHITEHALL
THE BROAD WALK
N
CONSTITUTION HILL
QUEEN VICTORIA MEMORIAL
BUCKINGHAM PALACE
ST. JAMES PARK

ST. JAMES WALK

Begin this walk at the Green Park Underground Station. When you leave the tube, turn left and walk west along the south side of Piccadilly. This street, laid out in the seventeenth century, runs for almost a mile from Hyde Park Corner to Piccadilly Circus. The name comes from a sixteenth-century mansion known as Pickadill Hall because its owner, Robert Baker, manufactured pickadills—lace frills such as those favored by Elizabeth I and her courtiers.

In *A Wreath for Rivera* by Ngaio Marsh, Inspector Roderick Alleyn was caught in one of Piccadilly's many traffic jams opposite Green Park.

Any of the numerous building that stretch along Piccadilly opposite the park could have been used as sites for the various flats and rooms located "across from the Park" by Agatha Christie, Dorothy L. Sayers, Edgar Wallace, and the like.

Lord Peter Wimsey lived in a luxury flat with the address of 110A Piccadilly; it was directly across from Green Park and technically in Mayfair. (Note that Sayers deliberately played with Sherlock Holmes's address, 221B Baker Street when assigning a residence to her own master sleuth.)

In *Whose Body?,* Sayers gives a detailed description of Wimsey's flat. It had "black and primrose walls lined with rare editions (occasionally attracting burglars), deep chairs and a Chesterfield sofa suggesting the embraces of the houris, a black baby grand, a wood fire in an old-fashioned hearth and Serves vases filled with flowers of the season. . .a place not only rare and unattainable, but friendly and familiar, like a colourful and gilded paradise in a medieval painting."

When you have walked the length of the park on Piccadilly, cross the street and return in the direction of the underground station.

Notice the Naval and Military club at No. 49 Piccadilly; it is known as "The In and Out" because of its driveway signs. It was the site Sayers picked for the Bellona Club, where in *The Unpleasantness at the Bellona Club,* old General Fentiman was found dead in his chair on November 11.

Adjacent to the Naval and Military Club, note the blue historical marker that identifies a onetime residence of Lord Palmerston. It was his statue in Parliament Square on which a drunken Lord Peter climbed, after his brother, the Duke of Denver, was acquitted of murder by the House of Lords. (*Clouds of Witness* by Dorothy L. Sayers)

Cross the street (you may use the Green Park pedestrian subway walk that also leads to the station). You will be back at the Green Park Tube Station. Ahead on your right is the Ritz Hotel.

Willow King stopped outside the Green Park Tube Station to buy a copy of Gripper's *Daily Mercury*. Dazed by the headline, she retraced her steps to a small cafe where she ordered coffee. (*A Common Death* by Natasha Cooper)

Walk toward the Ritz. It is one of London's old-line luxury hotels, despite the misleading exterior which resembles nothing more elegant than a train station.

The lobby, which has been restored to all its Louis XVI–style grandeur, is resplendent in gold, marble, and crystal. The rooms and suites are everything any guest could desire. Absolutely nothing has been overlooked to assure comfort.

The restaurant is good, expensive, and French. Tea, which is served in the Palm Court, is both hearty and elegant. It is also absolutely English. Tea at the Ritz has become such an institution that it is necessary to book a table several days in advance.

Almost without exception, if Agatha Christie characters were in London, they popped in and out of, stayed in, or ate at the Ritz. In *The Secret Adversary,* for instance, Julius Hersheimer, a rich American, was staying at the Ritz while looking for his missing cousin, Jane Finn. Tommy and Tuppence also stayed there as soon as they had the means.

The Ritz became the Blitz in Christie's *The Golden Ball.* Jane Cleveland was sent to the hotel to impersonate an American journalist. She was also ready to take the place of the "Grand Duchess of Pauline of Ostrova."

It is impossible to recount the number of times the Ritz is mentioned in crime fiction. Dorothy L. Sayers, for one, was fond of it. In Sayers's *Whose Body?,* Sir Reuben Levy dined at the Ritz with friends before keeping an appointment with Sir Julian Freke in Battersea.

In *Fog of Doubt* by Christianna Brand, Raoul Vernet, who was later murdered during a thick "London Particular" (fog) in a house in Maida Vale, came to London from France and stayed at the "Ritzhotel."

Edgar Wallace renamed it the Ritz-Carlton, then sent Thalia Drummond there to dine with a member of the Crimson Circle. (*The Crimson Circle*)

Take a look around the Ritz's lobby if you are so inclined; then return to Piccadilly and walk east to St. James's Street, where you will turn right and walk along the west side of the street. Although St. James was laid out early in the seventeenth century, it was not built up until St. James's Square was completed in 1675.

St. James Street is known as the home of a number of elegant gentlemen's clubs. These clubs evolved from the coffee and chocolate houses that became fashionable for gossip and gambling in mid-seventeenth-century London. By Regency times, the street was the hangout of dandies and beaus, who would mercilessly ogle any female who came into view. For that reason, no respectable female would set foot on St. James. Her reputation would be gone if she did.

In Georgette Heyer's *Regency Buck,* a Regency mystery/romance, Sir Geoffrey Fairford stayed in the Reddish Hotel in St. James's Street.

From where you are on the west side of the street, note the elaborate iron railings and entrance lamps of No. 37 across the way. This is White's, the oldest and most famous club of them all. It was founded in 1693 as a chocolate house.

White's was the model for every other club of this sort in London. The bow window, which was added in 1811, was a cause of wonder in many Regency novels. White's reputation was and is for Conservative arrogance and hard drinking. Appropriately, Sir Julian Freke belong to White's. (*Whose Body?* by Dorothy L. Sayers)

Boodles, at No. 28, is just down the street from White's. It too has a bay window, which was added in 1824. Founded in 1762 by William Almack as a social club, it quickly lost all political involvement. Named for its first manager, the club originally met at Almack's in Pall Mall, but it moved to its present elegant clubhouse in 1783. Beau Brummell was a member and liked to gamble here. Ian Fleming was also a member. The M Club in his James Bond stories is based on Boodles.

According to Janet Morgan in *Agatha Christie,* Dame Agatha and her husband liked to entertain friends at Boodles. She was especially fond of the veal dishes and the Orange Fool.

In his quest to find friends of the late Lord Arvid Pendenning, Duke of Denning, Bow Street Runner Jeremiah Dimm had trekked up and down St. James's Street gong from "White's to Brooks's to Boodle's, chatting up the various doormen and majordomos." (*A Suspicious Affair* by Barbara Metzger)

To your right you will see Park Place, an almost unspoiled, eighteenth-century cul-de-sac. At one time, streets such as this abounded with bachelor lodgings and gambling hells.

Continue your walk past John Walker and Sons, Ltd. Since mystery reading and writing and whiskey drinking often go together, you may find Walker's of interest.

Lord Peter's Egotists' Club was located in this vicinity. In *Murder Must Advertise,* Lord Peter arrived there disguised as a policeman from Scotland Yard. He took Harriet Vane to dinner there in *Gaudy Night,* and she mislaid a postcard from the Shrewsbury College poison pen. Sayers gave no address for the Egotists' club, but the Eccentric Club is at No. 9 Ryder Street, off to your left.

As you continue south along St. James's Street, pause outside No. 69 (on the west side of the street). This is the site of the Carlton Club, originally known as Arthur's because it was founded in 1832 by Arthur Wellesley, Duke of Wellington.

On June 25, 1990, the Carlton Club was badly damaged by an IRA bomb. One man was killed and six others were injured. The Carlton's membership is heavy with Tories, including the prime minister.

In *Murder Must Advertise,* Major Milligan, a drug runner, belonged to the Carlton Club, but at its pre–World War II Pall Mall address.

Continue past Blue Ball Yard; turn right at St. James's Place for a look at Spencer House. Built in the Palladian style, it is the London residence of the Earls of Spencer. Princess Diana was Lady Diana Spencer before marrying the Prince of Wales in 1981.

The Polish composer, Chopin, once had rooms at St. James's Place.

At the end of the gaslit cul-de-sac is Dukes Hotel, the most perfect small hotel in London. There is an aura here reminiscent of the Sherlock Holmes era. The roadway is just wide enough for a horse-drawn hansom cab. This cul-de-sac was once the home of George II's mistress.

Return to St. James's Street, where you will see Berry Brothers and Rudd Ltd., Wine Merchants, on the east side of the street. Although the firm as established in 1680, these premises date only from 1730. An excellent selection of port and single-malt whiskies, plus superb wines, are stocked in this relatively unaltered shop.

Next to Berry Brothers is a narrow, totally unspoiled alleyway that leads to Pickering Place. To get a closer look, walk to the bottom of St. James's Street, cross, and walk back. Go through the archway into the courtyard. If the gate is closed, you will know that you are at Pickering Place by the number 3. The alleyway retains its eighteenth-century timber wainscotting, on which a plaque is posted that notes that the diplomatic office of "The Republic of Texas Legation 1842" was located here.

Here in Pickering Place it is easy to imagine oneself in a long-gone era. As you walk along the alleyway, note the panelling and the flagstones underfoot, and when you reach the tiny courtyard, note the hanging lamps.

Lady Hamilton—Lord Nelson's mistress—lived at No. 5. In *Regency Buck* by Georgette Heyer, No. 5 was designated a gambling hell.

The last duel in England was fought in this small square.

Graham Greene lived in a flat here and placed Colonel Daintry, who was investigating security in *The Human Factor,* in the same location. Daintry had a two-room flat looking out over the tiny, ancient courtyard. A back entrance to Overton's at No. 5 St. James's Street leads from the courtyard. Colonel Daintry usually ate in the famous oyster bar.

Leave Pickering Place and return to St. James's Street. To the right, across the street from Overton's, at the corner of St. James's Street and Little St. James's Street, was Rumplemeyer's the fancy ice cream parlor where the Dowager Duchess took Harriet Vane after a session with Murbles over the will in Sayers's *Busman's Honeymoon*.

Now turn left and walk to the end of St. James's Street and cross Cleveland Row to St. James's Palace. This red and blue brick minipalace was commissioned as a manor house for Anne Boleyn by Henry VIII. St. James's Leper Hospital for Women had previously occupied the site. Only the clock tower, the Chapel Royal, and the sentry station remain from Tudor times.

Each new monarch is proclaimed from the balcony of St. James's Palace. It is also the official headquarters of the Yeomen of the Guard. Tourists gather at the gateway to photograph the sentry. Because of the increase in terrorism, you can no longer go inside the Palace except to attend Sunday services at the Chapel Royal.

The offices of the Royal Household, including that of the Lord Chamberlain, who used to censor all plays in England, is located off the stable yard. In 1941, the Lord Chamberlain removed several witty lines from the play *Love All* by Dorothy L. Sayers.

When you are ready to move on, recross Cleveland Row and turn to your right across the bottom of St. James's Street at Pall Mall. You can walk back up St. James's Street to Pickering Place or head down Pall Mall for a few yards and turn left into Crown Passage, which will take you through to King Street. The Red Lion Pub, located in Crown Passage, is a good place to stop for refreshments. Superb homemade pies and sandwiches, along with assorted brews, are served in its two tiny rooms. Graham Greene undoubtedly ate here.

Continue along Crown Passage, with its minute shops, wine bars, and its strong sense of the seventeenth century, until you reach King Street. Turn right and enjoy its varied art and antique shops until you sight Christie's International Auction House at 8 King Street (on the corner of King and Bury Streets). Christie's, which was founded in 1766, traditionally flies a blue and white standard. Visitors are welcome, but Christie's is closed in August.

When Lord Peter Wimsey made his first fictional appearance in *Whose Body?,* he was in a taxi on his way to Christie's.

Christie's is probably the site of the auction at which Martin Drake met Sir Henry Merrivale and his long-lost sweetheart, Jenny, in John Dickson Carr's *The Skeleton in the Clock.*

After dinner with Lieutenant Tom Worth, Willow King, in the guise of Cressida Woodwruffe, took a taxi to Christie's. After perusing various items, she left Christie's and turned left along King Street. (*Poison Flowers* by Natasha Cooper)

The Savage Club, to which John Dickson Carr's Martin Drake belonged, was on King Street.

General Sir Arthur Fredericks, on his way to Plum's, turned his attention to the "Cheap-Jack trader" on the corner by King Street. For sixpence, he was offering a pocketknife with blades, scissor, corkscrew, and a glazier's diamond for glass cutting. (*Murder at Plum's* by Amy Meyers)

The St. James Theatre, which has been torn down, stood in King Street. It was where the Mortimer family went to see a performance of Oscar Wilde's *Lady Windermere's Fan.* (*The Blackheath Poisonings* by Julian Symons)

Walk east along King Street to Duke Street St. James's. Almack House is at 26–28 King Street. It is on the site of the famous Almack's Assembly Rooms, which figure prominently in eighteenth- and early nineteenth-century novels, such as the Regency mysteries and romances of Georgette Heyer.

Turn left and walk north on Duke Street St. James's, a street of elegant shops, small restaurants, and flats, to Jermyn Street.

Stop a moment to explore Jermyn Street before returning to follow Duke Street St. James's to Piccadilly.

Jermyn Street, which was laid out in the late seventeenth century, is a quietly charming street that recalls a London of more elegant days. There are many fashionable shops along

Jermyn Street, but gentlemen's shirtmakers, like Endicott's in Sayer's *Have His Carcase,* have predominance. Harvie & Hudson, London's largest and best-known shirtmaker, is located at No. 97 Jermyn Street. The shop has one of London's finest examples of mid-Victorian shop fronts.

In Margaret Truman's *Murder on Embassy Row,* the British ambassador to Iran, Geoffrey James, had his club certification on file at Harvie & Hudson so that he could purchase his club ties there.

Paxton and Whitfield, Cheesemonger to the Queen, is at No. 93 Jermyn Street. Castle, Graham Greene's Secret Service officer, bought cheese there while on his lunch hour. (*The Human Factor* by Graham Greene)

When she finished her research, Willow decided to go home via Jermyn Street and window-shop on the way. (*Poison Flowers* by Natasha Cooper)

In Agatha Christie's *The Seven Dials Mystery,* Bundle went to Jimmy Thesiger's flat at No. 103. The door was opened by an expressionless gentleman's gentleman, who let her into a "comfortable sitting room containing leather armchairs of immense dimensions."

The ne'er-do-well playboy husband of Ruth Van Aldin had a flat in Jermyn Street. (*The Mystery of the Blue Train* by Agatha Christie)

In *Duplicate Death* by Georgette Heyer, the flat of Mr. Seaton-Carew was located in Jermyn Street. Seaton-Carew was selling drugs and had blackmailed Beulah Birtley into working for slave wages for Mrs. Haddington.

In *The Thirty-Nine Steps* by John Buchan, Richard Hannay, fresh from South Africa and bored by civilized London, had dinner at a Jermyn Street restaurant, where he ate little but drank the best part of a bottle of burgundy. He then walked down to the corner of Duke Street St. James's, where he passed a group of young men in evening dress who attacked him. He finally broke free and dashed through Pall Mall, into St. James's Park, and south into Birdcage Walk.

Leave Jermyn Street and go to your left up Duke Street St. James's to the south side of Piccadilly. Fortum & Mason will be to your right. This elegant store with its green-trimmed, small-paned display window is the grocery store of the Royal Family. It is world-famous for its unusual wares, morning-coated assistants, restaurants, and the great clock above the front door, where on the hour, the figures of Mr. Fortnum and Mr. Mason come out to the tune of the Eton Boating Song. The store was established in 1707 by Mason, an experienced grocer, and Fortnum, one of Queen Anne's footmen. Fortnum & Mason is an excellent spot for afternoon tea.

Arnold Vereker, who was later murdered, had been in the habit of arriving at his weekend cottage with a hamper from Fortnum & Mason, so that he and his lady friend would not be obliged to shop. (*Death in the Stocks* by Georgette Heyer)

In Sayers's *Unnatural Death,* Lord Peter Wimsey was able to detect that the ham in a sandwich left beside a dead girl in Epping Forest had come from a Fortnum & Mason pig.

Spenser, in Robert Parker's *The Judas Goat,* eyed the gorgeously packaged foods in Fortnum & Mason's windows and thought what fun it would be to stroll there with Susan and buy some quail's eggs, a jellied game hen, or something imported from the Khyber Pass.

In Margaret Yorke's *Find Me a Villian,* as the wretched Nina Crowther went into the muted, fragrant bustle of the grocery department, the Fortnum & Mason clock began to strike. She went upstairs to the mezzanine restaurant, where she met Priscilla Blunt and got a job house-sitting.

Archie Roylance, a comrade in arms of Richard Hannay, went to Fortnum & Mason to stock up on delicatessen food and liqueurs before leaving on a secret mission to Norway in John Buchan's *The Three Hostages.*

In *English School Murder* by Ruth Dudley Edwards, when Rich went out to buy supplies for a Sunday afternoon picnic, he went to Fortnum & Mason for a hamper.

Just east of Fortnum & Mason, at No. 187 Piccadilly, is the black and white facade of Hatchard's, its three bow windows brimming with tempting books. Hatchard's and Fortnum & Mason, which were established in 1707, are the sole remaining representatives of a thriving eighteenth-century shopping are that once lined Piccadilly.

In Georgette Heyer's *Regency Buck,* Judith Tavener marveled at the bookshop, its bow windows filled with all the latest publications, and almost fancied that she saw the great Sir Walter Scott, poet and author of the *Waverley* novel, there.

After indulging herself on Jermyn Street, Willow King salved her conscience by dropping into Hatchard's on Piccadilly for a book about English wildflowers. (*Poison Flowers* by Natasha Cooper)

Today Hatchard's is the best bookstore in London. Here you will find a wide selection of your favorite mysteries and every other book under the sun, just as you would expect from the bookseller to the Queen, the Duke of Edinburgh, the Queen Mother, and the Prince of Wales.

Continue along Piccadilly to the right, until you come to St. James's Church, one of the loveliest and, to Christopher Wren, the most practical of the churches he designed. It was bombed heavily during World War II, but the carvings by Grinling Gibbons were saved. St. James's is a popular spot for weddings and memorial services, but it is more than this. It is a living, thriving church serving the changing London community with services to the homeless and other needy people.

Leave St. James's Church and take Church Place to your right, around the church. Turn right again on Jermyn Street and walk the short distance to Duke of York Street. Turn left into Duke of York Street and make your way to St. James's Square. In Duke of York Street, you will pass another pub called the Red Lion (remember the one in Crown Passage?). This Red Lion is a small Victorian "gin palace" with some exceptional cut glass as well as glossy mahogany.

St. James's Square was the first of the West End's squares. It was built in 1673 by Henry Jermyn on land presented to him by Charles II. During its early years, the square was perhaps the most fashionable address in London; at one time, six dukes and seven earls had housed in St. James's Square. Most of the present buildings date from the eighteenth century or later.

The equestrian statue in the center of the square is of William III. A rather macabre touch is the inclusion in the monument of the molehill over which William's horse stumbled at Hampton Court in 1702. The king died from complications resulting from that fall.

As you turn right into the square, you pass Chatham House at Nos. 9–10; three prime ministers have lived there; William Pitt the Elder, Lord Derby, and William Ewart Gladstone, G. K. Chesterton's boyhood hero.

Plum's Club for Gentlemen was on the north side of St. James's Square in Amy Meyer's *Murder at Plum's.*

The London Library is at No. 14 in the northwest corner of the square. It is a venerable subscription library, open to members only.

In Jessica Mann's *Funeral Sites,* fugitive Rosamund Sholto hid in the newspaper room of the library only to bump into her cousin, Harriet. Sholto had been given a life membership in the London Library when she was 21. Georgette Heyer was a member of the London Library and used its facilities extensively in her research.

After leaving Christie's, Willow King, in her guise of Cressida Woodruffe, hurried to St. James's Square where she took time to do research in the London Library. (*Poison Flowers* by Natasha Cooper)

In Georgette Heyer's *Regency Buck,* the home of Peregrine Tavener's crony, Fitzjohn, was in St. James's Square.

The fictional 38 St. James's Square was the address of the mansion of Caroline Ross, who married Dick Derwent in Newgate Prison. Both Caroline and her "wedding" guests saw Napoleon's captured eagles brought to Lord Castlereagh's home at No. 8 after the Battle of Waterloo. (*The Bride of Newgate* by John Dickson Carr)

Bill Eversleigh, Lady Bundle's intended, parked his car in St. James's Square in Agatha Christie's *The Secret of Chimneys.*

Sallet Square, in Margery Allingham's *Black Plumes,* was most likely modeled on St. James's Square.

In 1984, a violent episode in the history of St. James's

Square occurred when a policewoman was shot to death from the Libyan Peoples Bureau, which occupied No. 5.

As you walk about the square noting the various houses, take special notice of No. 31. It stands on the site of Norfolk House, which was demolished in 1938. This is where, according to the plaque, General Eisenhower established the First Allied Forces Headquarters for World War II.

Come back to the southwest corner of the square and turn left to walk to Pall Mall. Pall Mall is named for the seventeenth-century French version of croquet, "paille maille," which was first played along a tree-lined avenue on the north side of Pall Mall.

Cross Pall Mall and turn left; walk toward Waterloo Place. Pall Mall, like St. James's Street, hosts a number of exclusive clubs. At No. 71 is the Oxford and Cambridge Club, where Sir Julian Freke, in *Whose Body?* by Dorothy L. Sayers, was a member.

The Reform Club, home of liberalism, and the Travellers, originally established for those who had taken the Grand Tour, stand side by side in identical Italian palaces. Next door, at No. 107 at the corner of Waterloo Place, is the prestigious Athenaeum Club.

The Athenaeum is built on the site of the Prince Regent's Carlton House. It was at Carlton House that Judith Tavener was propositioned by the Regent himself and fainted dead away. (*Regency Buck* by Georgette Heyer)

A pale stucco building with a neoclassical look, the Athenaeum is distinguished by its portico and the gilded statue of Palla Athena above it. Inside, the first-floor drawing room is considered one of the grandest of London.

The Athenaeum is known for its distinguished members. It is favored by the hierarchy of the Anglican Church, as well as prominent men from the arts, literature and science. Among its members were Sir Humphrey Davy, about whom E. C. Bentley wrote his first schoolboy clerihew, and Bentley's boyhood chum, G. K. Chesterton, who became a member in 1936.

In *From London Far* by Michael Innes, the absent-minded quotation-loving scholar, Meredith, left the British Museum bound for the Athenaeum with a valuable manuscript under his arm. His intention was to spend a couple of hours doing some light reading in recent issues of the *Journal of Classical Archaeology,* but he never reached his destination.

Another absent-minded fellow, Canon Pennyfather, had an early dinner at the Athenaeum before he, too, disappeared. (*At Bertram's Hotel* by Agatha Christie)

Turn right into Waterloo Place and walk over to take a look at the statue of the Duke of York high up on a pink granite column. This is Frederick, the second son of George III. He was the subject of the nursery song "The Grand Old Duke of York," in which the duke, who was commander of the army, marched his men up to the top of the hill and then marched them down again.

It has been suggested that the memorial, which measures 124 feet from its base to its head, is sufficiently high to keep the duke away from his creditors. The Duke owed £2 million by the time he died. The memorial was financed by stopping one day's pay from every soldier in the army.

Near the Duke of York memorial is the Crimean War Memorial and a statue of Florence Nightingale with her lamp. To the south and east is lovely Carlton House Terrace, built on the site of Carlton House, the mansion of the Prince Regent, which was demolished in 1829. (Its columns are now part of the facade of the National Gallery in Trafalgar Square.)

In Agatha Christie's *The Secret Adversary,* Carlton House Terrace was the home of Sir James Peel Edgerton, whom Tuppence Cowley bravely confronted about the disappearance of Jane Finn and Tommy.

At the corner of Carlton House Terrace is a curiously poignant little monument. In the enclosed garden area, if you look closely beneath the foliage, you will see the tombstone of a little dog called Giro, who died in 1934. Giro belonged to Leopold von Hoesch, Hitler's ambassador to England before World War II.

Leave Carlton House Terrace, return to Waterloo Place and turn right into the wide, pink-surfaced Mall. This is the royal processional road. It leads straight to Buckingham Palace. The Mall was remodeled in 1910 as part of the monument to Queen Victoria.

As you walk along the Mall, St. James's Park is on your left. It is the oldest of London's royal parks. Like all the city's royal parks, it was created by Henry VIII from land he seized from Westminster Abbey.

St. James's is famous for both its wonderful views and for its bird sanctuary. You will find the views quite romantic as you look toward both Whitehall and Buckingham Palace from the center of the lake's modern bridge.

In *Funeral Sites* by Jessica Mann, Rosamund Sholto was driven along the Mall by her eccentric cousin Harriet, only to jump out of the car and make tracks for Cambridge.

As you continue your walk along the Mall, just before you reach the Queen Victoria Memorial, you will pass, on the right, three royal residences that are really part of the Palace of St. James.

The first is the Wren-designed Marlborough House, once the residence of the termagant Duchess of Marlborough and later of Queen Mary, widow of George V. It was for Queen Mary's birthday that Agatha Christie wrote a radio play for the BBC. She called it *The Mousetrap.* Later the play was rewritten by Christie into a drama suitable for the stage. It opened in the West End in 1953 and has been playing there ever since.

Marlborough House is now a Commonwealth Center. You can, however, attend Sunday services there in the Queen's Chapel, which was designed by Inigo Jones.

Beyond Marlborough House is Clarence House, where Queen Elizabeth lived when she was first married; the Queen Mother lives there today. If you are nearby on August 4, you may hear the bagpipes being played to celebrate the Queen "Mum's" birthday. They are a reminder that she was born in Scotland in Macbeth's Glamis Castle.

Lancaster House, the third royal residence, is beyond Clarence House and adjoins the Queen's Walk through Green Park. Built for the Grand Old Duke of York, it now is the scene of official banquets and meetings.

Buckingham Palace, at the end of the Mall, is the principal residence of the British sovereign. Most of the building is early nineteenth century; it was built soon after King George IV came to the throne. He announced that Carlton House was not sufficiently grand enough for the King of England and should be demolished, and a new palace built to replace Buckingham House, his parents' London house where he and all his brothers and sisters had been born. After much wrangling with Parliament, he managed to get his way.

The royal family's private apartments are in the north wing overlooking Green Park, while the State Apartments are on the first floor in the west wing.

After the opening of Parliament, the Trooping of the Colour, a royal wedding, or some other suitable occasion, the royal family make their appearance on the balcony over the main entrance. From there they wave to the crowds. The palace itself is open to the public only for a brief period of time each October. The Queen authorized the opening of the palace to raise money after a fire at Windsor Castle in 1992 did extensive damage. The Queen's Gallery and the Royal Mews, which are both within the palace grounds, may be visited throughout the year.

In *The Judas Goat* by Robert Parker, Spenser went to Buckingham Palace to see the Changing of the Guard: "He stood outside and stared at the wide, bare, hard-paved courtyard. 'How you doing, Queen,' he murmured."

The Changing of the Guard is held in the forecourt of the palace. During the summer, the ceremony takes place every day at 11:30 AM—weather permitting. From September through March, the ceremony is held on alternate days.

There are five Guards regiments who take turns guarding the Queen: The Grenadier, the Scots, the Welsh, the Irish, and the Coldstream Guards, all with distinctive uniform details. Recent downscaling of the military in Britain as in the United States may have some effect on the configuration of the Queen's Guards.

A. A. Milne described the Changing of the Guards ceremony in his poem "Buckingham Palace," which is about Christopher Robin's nursery maid who was marrying one of the guards. Many people who can recite this poem and others by A. A. Milne are unaware that he also wrote a classic detective story, *The Red House Mystery,* which Julian Symons (in *Mortal Consequences*) called the most entertaining book of its kind written in the 1920s.

Patrick Grant drove his friend, visiting Greek police officer Manolakis, past Buckingham Palace in Margaret Yorke's *Cast for Death.*

In *A Splash of Red* by Antonia Fraser, Jemima Shore and her friend, Detective Chief Inspector "Pompey" Portsmouth, agreed that "Buck House is the best alibi in the world."

The Boomer, current ruler of Ng'ombwana and prep school friend of Roderick Alleyn, dined royally at Buckingham Palace, while Alleyn and the CID sweated out an assassination attempt in *Black As He's Painted* by Ngaio Marsh.

Take the Broad Walk from the Queen Victoria Monument north across Green Park toward Piccadilly as Spenser did. This will return you to the Green Park Underground Station and the end of this walk.

8

MARYLEBONE/ REGENT'S PARK WALK

BACKGROUND

This walk takes you through Marylebone, where Sherlock Holmes once lived (at 221B Baker Street). It is also the location of the 275-acre Regent's Park. The first part of the walk explores Regency town planning at its best and the remnants of the medieval village of Marylebone. The village was on the Tye Bourne, or Tyburn, River, which ran into the Thames.

When Holmes lived in Baker Street, the Adam brothers had already developed Marylebone as a suburban garden. Then John Nash made it part of his Royal Mile, which began at the Prince Regent's Palace at St. James's. The area, much of it laid out in handsome squares, has remained fashionable. It contains the best-known art collection in London, as well as the "medical" streets, Harley and Wimpole, where brass nameplates announcing doctors and their specialties decorate nearly every door. (Harley and Wimpole Streets are often mentioned in crime fiction for any number of reasons.)

There are many detective story locales in the area that surrounds Marylebone/Regent's Park. Unfortunately, most are too far removed and too scattered to be covered in this walk, but, before getting underway, we will mention several to you. Using the Oxford Street exit from the Marble Arch Tube Station as your point of orientation, note that to the right and northwest is Edgware Road, the old Roman Watling Street. In *The Man Who Was Thursday* by G. K. Chesterton, Sunday, the gigantic anarchist, abandoned his taxi on Edgware Road when traffic was stopped by a fire engine. He sprang at the fire engine, threw himself onto it, and rode off talking to the astonished firemen.

Farther north, Edgware Road becomes Maida Vale (not shown on the map). Baroness Orczy's *Lady Molly of Scotland Yard* and her friend Mary Granard lived in a little flat in Maida Vale while Lady Molly tried to clear the name of her husband, who was in prison.

Christiana Brand originally set the scene of *Fog of Doubt* in Kensington Gore, south of Hyde Park. Then, because another author had used the same title, she moved her locale to Maida Vale and called her mystery *London Particular* (the Dickensian name for a real pea-souper fog). When the book crossed the Atlantic, the title was changed to *Fog of Doubt*.

West of Edgware Road is Paddington Station, source of numerous detective story references. For instance, Loretta Lawson, London University lecturer and sometime-investigator, hurriedly left the curriculum meeting at the university and hurried to Paddington Station when her friend Bridget Bennet's frantic phone call summoned her back to Oxford. (*What Men Say* by John Smith)

Asher, in his attempt to keep Ysidro from knowing that Lydia was in London, took the underground the long way round, through Victoria and the City, before going back to Euston. He wanted to be nowhere near Paddington when Lydia arrived. (*Those Who Hunt the Night* by Barbara Hambly)

The TV studios where Charles Paris worked may have been near the Regent Studios "somewhere in Marylebone," where Keating's Inspector Ghote reluctantly interviewed the pop singer Johnny Bull. The fictional Tagore House on Hyde Park Terrace, where Inspector Ghote stayed, must have been just past Edgware Road, near Hyde Park Square and Hyde Park Crescent. This was also the neighborhood of the fictional 12 Delaney Street, a cul-de-sac off Lisson Grove, where P. D. Jame's Philippa Palfrey and her mother rented a cheap flat over the greengrocer's shop.

The second part of the walk introduces you to Regent's Park, originally known as Marylebone Park, the northernmost part of Henry VIII's great belt of hunting forest. The part Nash developed can be seen today in the magnificent circles and terraces, which share the park with the Gardens of the Zoological Society of London, better known simply as the Zoo.

LENGTH OF WALK: 4.5 miles (not including walking in or through Regent's Park or wandering about the Zoo)

See the maps on pages 146 and 158 for the boundaries of this walk and pages 259–61 for a list of the authors, books, and detectives mentioned.

PLACES OF INTEREST

221B Baker Street, on the opposite side of the street from the Sherlock Holmes Museum and gift shop. Museum open daily. Admission charge.

Broadcasting House (BBC), Portland Place.

London Planetarium, Marylebone Road. Open daily. Admission charge.

London Telecom Tower, (Post Office Tower), Maple Street. Free.

Madame Tussaud's, Marylebone Road. Open daily. Admission charge.

Regent's Park

London Zoo. Open daily. Admission charge.

Queen Mary's Gardens. Free.

Open Air Theatre. Open July–Aug. Shakespeare and other plays. Charge for tickets.

Wallace Collection, Manchester Square. Open daily. Free.

PLACES TO EAT

Madame Tussaud's, Marylebone Road. Cafeteria. 071-935-6861.

Regent's Park:

The Rose Garden Buffet, Queen Mary's Gardens. Self-service English food can be eaten outdoors when the weather is good.

The Zoo: Regent Restaurant on first floor; *Regent Cafeteria* on ground level. Both restaurants are licensed and serve lunch and tea. In addition, in the Zoo grounds there are the *Pavilion Bar, Mappin Cafe,* and *Garden Cafe,* all serving light refreshments (no alcohol).

— MARYLEBONE/REGENT'S PARK WALK —

MARYLEBONE

Begin this walk by taking the Oxford Street exit from the Marble Arch Underground Station. This is the tube station where H. R. F. Keating's Inspector Ghote of Bombay, in London for the first time, happily observed typical British behavior. Ghote was in London to attend a conference on drugs and took the underground to his meeting in the City. The tube was crowded, but the people were very orderly, ignoring each other with magnificent calm. (*Inspector Ghote Hunts the Peacock* by H. R. F. Keating)

Footer, who was daft on football, knew Lovejoy immediately. After protesting that he felt like a "friggin rabbit," he agreed to make the delivery at marble Arch, where Dutch would be waiting. (*The Very Last Gambado* by Johathan Gash)

James Cox, the inquiry agent Tessa Crichton hired to follow Jocelyn Hunt, trailed him by bus to Marble Arch where Hunt changed to another bus that took him to Notting Hill. (*The Men in Her Death* by Anne Morice)

In the Leslie Charteris short story "The Beauty Specialist,"

MARYLEBONE

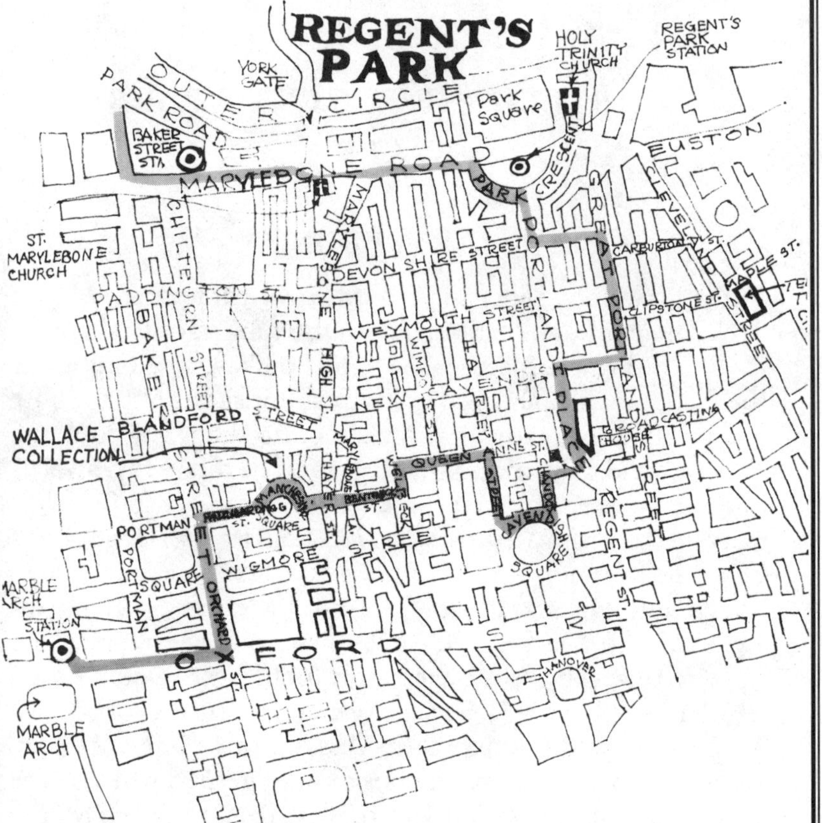
REGENT'S PARK
HOLY TRINITY CHURCH
REGENT'S PARK STATION
YORK GATE
OUTER CIRCLE
PARK ROAD
Park Square
BAKER STREET STA.
MARYLEBONE ROAD
EUSTON
PARK CRESCENT
ST. MARYLEBONE CHURCH
CHILTERN
DEVON SHIRE STREET
CARBURTON ST.
MAPLE ST.
CLEVELAND STREET
PADDINGTON ST.
CLIPSTONE ST.
WEYMOUTH STREET
BAKER STREET
HIGH ST.
NEW CAVENDISH
BLANDFORD STREET
WALLACE COLLECTION
BROADCASTING HOUSE
QUEEN ANNE ST.
PORTLAND PLACE
GREAT PORTLAND STREET
MANCHESTER SQUARE
PORTMAN SQUARE
PORTMAN
WIGMORE STREET
CAVENDISH SQUARE
REGENT ST.
MARBLE ARCH STATION
ORCHARD ST.
OXFORD STREET
HANOVER
MARBLE ARCH

Simon Templar made a note of Beatrice Avery's address, which was 21 Parkside, Marble Arch.

Turn left and walk along the north side of Oxford Street. This is a major London shopping street, always crowded with people, especially during the Christmas season, when it reminds you of the unpleasant individual who hated being shoved, in Marian Babson's *The Twelve Deaths of Christmas.*

In Julian Symons's short story "'Twixt the Cup and the Lip," Oxford Street was wearing its holiday decorations, as Mr. Payne walked along on perfect December day.

Oxford Street is also a favorite shopping location in H. R. F. Keating's mysteries. Writing as Evelyn Hervey in *The Man of Gold,* Keating's redoubtable governess, Miss Unwin, took a cab to the largest bookstore on Oxford Street to purchase *Potherton on Poisons.*

Cross Old Quebec Street, staying on Oxford Street. You will come to Portman Street; continue one more block to Orchard Street. Selfridges, the largest London department store, occupies the block on Oxford Street between Orchard and Duke Streets. Selfridges was founded by Chicagoan Godon Selfridge in 1908. It is famous for its lavish decorations at Christmas, as well as other national holidays.

In *The Unpleasantness at the Bellona Club* by Dorothy L. Sayers, artist Marjorie Phelps gave Lord Peter Wimsey a small statue of himself dressed in a Sherlockian dressing gown with a book on his knee. Thanking her, Lord Peter asked if he would find copies of it on sale at Selfridges.

In Ann Granger's *Say It with Poison,* Sara's friend, the model Fiona, was late for a photographic session. She asked Meredith for a lift "up West." Meredith offered to drop her in Orchard Street "down the side of Selfridges."

Turn left on Orchard Street and walk north three short blocks to Portman Square. Laid out in the late 1800s, it has a number of elegant hotels, a green garden forbidden to all but tiny dogs, and a few original, elegant town residences. Portman Square is a likely location for the townhouse of the Dowager Duchess of Denver, where Lord Peter Wimsey and Harriet Vane's wedding reception was held in *Busman's Honeymoon.*

In Sayers's *Whose Body?,* Sir Reuben Levy's uncle lived in

Portman Square, as did old Lady Dormer, with her companion, Ann Dorland, in *The Unpleasantness at the Bellona Club.*

Lady Dormer's elderly brother, General Fentiman, came there to call on her for the first time in years.

Septimus Crottle, who was kidnapped in A. E. W. Mason's *The House in Lordship Lane,* lived at 41A Portman Square.

No. 20, on the northwest corner of Portman Square, was built by Robert Adam for an ancestor of former Prime Minister Sir Alec Douglas-Home (Lord Home) and restored by Samuel Courtauld, the notable art collector. Courtauld left the house and his superb collection of Impressionist and Post-Impressionist paintings, including the collection of Bloomsbury's Roger Fry, to the University of London. The collection has been housed since 1990 in Somerset House on the Strand.

North of Portman Square is narrow Montagu Square. Developer Sir Richard Lionnel offered Jemima Shore a flat in Montagu when the police moved her out of his Adelaide Square flat in Antonia Fraser's *A Splash of Red.*

In Wilkie Collin's *The Moonstone,* Lady Verinder's townhouse was in Montagu Square.

Walk along Portman Square's east side to the northeast corner and turn right on Firtzharding Street. Continue heading east to Manchester Square. On the north side of Manchester Square you will see Hertford House, a large, reddish mansion which houses the world-famous Wallace Collection.

The Wallace Collection is one of the world's finest private art collections. Among its highlights are Frans Hal's *The Laughing Cavalier* and Nicolas Poussin's *A Dance to the Music of Time.* It is a frozen collection, which means that it is never added to. There are several paintings by Sherlock Holmes's great-uncle, Emile Vernet, and the Greuze painting called *Innocence* may be the original of a Professor Moriarty forgery from the case of "The Valley of Fear."

Anthony Cade, the gentleman adventurer in Agatha Christie's *The Secret of Chimneys,* was talking with a friend who had rescued the old Prime Minister of Herzoslovakia from muggers in Paris. Cade asked his friend if the Prime Minister had told him any state secrets. The friend replied that the Prime Minister said he knew where the Koh-i-noor [one of the Crown Jewels] was kept. Cade replied, "We all know that, they keep it in the tower. . . . Did Stylptitch say. . .he knew which city the Wallace Collection was in?"

Hertford House has other associations with literature. Nineteenth-century writer William Makepeace Thackeray used a Marquis of Hertford as a model for his libertine Marquis of Steyne in *Vanity Fair*.

Go left past Hertford House to the northeast corner of Manchester Square; then turn right to reach Hinde Street. You will be passing a number of eighteenth-century houses, most of which are now used as offices. Novelist Rose Macaulay lived in No. 20 Hinde Street until her death in 1941.

Turn left and go along Hinde Street to Thayer Street. At this point, Hinde Street becomes Bentinck Street. Between 1833 and 1834, Charles Dickens's family lived here at No. 18.

Continue walking along Bentinck Street. At No. 7, Edward Gibbon completed the first part of his monumental *Decline and Fall of the Roman Empire*.

Next cross the southern end of Marylebone High Street, here called Marylebone Lane. Once a winding village lane, it is now a shopping area with good restaurants, pubs, and smart shops; however, the area around the high street is still full of tiny streets and alleys. A pleasure garden similar to Vauxhall and Ranelagh was once located here. Later, it became a haunt of vice, and finally was engulfed by the city's northern development.

This was probably the location of the "Fields of Eden" mentioned in the mysterious kidnap note in John Buchan's *The Three Hostages*. With this faint clue, Richard Hannay and Archie Roylance investigated a Marylebone mews behind an old furniture storage building.

Continue east along Bentinck Street until you come to Welbeck Street. This is the intersection where Sherlock Holmes was nearly killed by a runaway van in "The Final Problem."

Somewhere on Welbeck Street was the doctor's office to which a heavily drugged James Tyrone managed to drive his polio-stricken wife in *Forfeit* by Dick Francis.

Novelist Wilkie Collins was born in No. 11 in 1824, T. S. Eliot called Collin's *The Moonstone* "the first and the greatest of English detective novels." Collins was the creator of Sergeant Cuff, the first detective in English literature.

Turn left and walk north up Welbeck Street to No. 34, where Anthony Trollope died in a nursing home in 1882. Other who lived in Welbeck Street in the days before the use of house numbers became mandatory, includes James Maclean, the highwayman who held up and robbed Horace Walpole.

In 1817, John Keats's first volume of poems was published at No. 3 Welbeck Street. Lord George Gordon addressed the mob from the balcony of No. 64 in Charles Dickens's *Barnaby Rudge*.

Continue along Welbeck for a few steps to Queen Anne Street; this was a fashionable residential street in the eighteenth century. In the "The Adventure of the Illustrious Client," Dr. Watson had his surgery offices at 9 Queen Anne Street.

Turn right and follow Queen Anne Street to Wimpole Street. You are now in the heart of the British medical establishment. Wimpole Street, together with Harley Street, is associated with medical practitioners of all specialties. It is also, in the literary minded, associated with poet Elizabeth Barrett, whose life and love story, as well as her elopement with poet Robert Browning, was dramatized in the play *The Barretts of Wimpole Street.* (The Barrett house was No. 50.)

Wilke Collins, who died in 1889, spent the last months of his life at No. 82 Wimpole Street.

It was in Wimpole Street that Richard Hannay found Dr. Newhover's office in "one of those solid, dreary erections which have the names of half a dozen doctors on their front doors . . .with a drab waiting room furnished with Royal Academy engravings, fumed oak, and an assortment of belated picture-papers." (*The Three Hostages* by John Buchan)

Continue along Queen Anne Street to Harley Street—this street is world-renowned for medical specialists. In *At Bertram's Hotel* by Agatha Christie, Lady Selina Hazy, one of the old ladies who gave the hotel lobby that "olde English atmosphere," had gone "to Harley Street to see that man about my arthritis." He had "wrung" her neck for her, and it was much improved.

Before the doctors moved in around 1845, Harley Street was a fashionable residential street. J. M. W. Turner lived at No. 64 from 1804 until 1808.

The young governess in Henry James's *The Turn of the Screw* came up from the country to answer an ad at a Harley Street address. There, in his big house filled with the "spoils of travel and the trophies of the chase," she met her employer, a handsome bachelor in the prime of life, who bewitched her into taking charge of his uncanny wards, Miles and Flora.

In Dorothy L. Sayers's *The Unpleasantness at the Bellona Club,* young Dr. Penberthy had his office in Harley Street. This made it easy for old General Fentiman to come and see him when Fentiman was taken ill at his sister's house in Portman Square.

Society doctor, Sir Daniel Davidson, had his offices at 50 St. Luke's Chambers, Harley Street, where Inspector Alleyn found a very luxurious office with an Adam fireplace and handsome gifts from grateful patients. (*Death in a White Tie* by Ngaio Marsh)

In Sayer's *Whose Body?,* neurologist Sir Julian Freke, who had treated Lord Peter Wimsey for his nerves, had an office at 282 Harley Street.

P. D. James described an old-fashioned but very shrewd Harley Street practitioner called Dr. Crantley-Mathers in *The Skull Beneath the Skin.*

After her much publicized ten-day disappearance in December 1926, Agatha Christie consulted a Harley Street psychiatrist.

In *Those Who Hunt the Night* by Barbara Hambly, Asher and Ysidro stood in the shadows at the corner of Harley Street at 3:00 AM. The vampire, Ysidro, listened intently to discern any sound in Horace Blaydon's "tall brown-brick house" in Queen Anne Street.

Turn right on Harley Street and go south into Cavendish Square. Dating from the early eighteenth century, this square began the suburban development of the old village of Marylebone.

From 1859 to 1864, Wilkie Collins and his mistress lived in No. 12. Lord Byron lived at No. 21.

In *The Unpleasantness at the Bellona Club,* Lady Dormer's elderly brother, General Fentiman, hailed his grandson George in Cavendish Square, then took him for a taxi ride through Regent's Park while lecturing him on his treatment of his wife.

In Georgette Heyer's *Regency Buck,* Lord Worth had his townhouse in Cavendish Square. It was a great stucco-fronted house with an imposing portico. This was where the young Taveners arrived uninvited.

Also in *Regency Buck,* the Four-Horse Club, a select gathering of all the best whips in London (in the ton, of course) met on the first and third Thursdays in May and June in Cavendish Square and drove in yellow-bodied barouches to Salt Hill.

In Josephine Tey's *The Man in the Queue,* Miss Dinmont, the nice Scottish girl who had befriended a fugitive and come down to London to help him, stayed at a club in Cavendish Square.

From the northeast corner of Cavendish Square take Chandos Street north, passing by Chandos House, a beautiful example of Robert Adam's best work.

Go to Portland Place and turn right, then walk east to Langham Place. The Langham Hotel is at the corner of Portland Place and Queen Anne Mews.

The Langham Hotel was once a very exclusive Victorian hotel, where the King of Bohemia stayed in the Sherlock Holmes case, "A Scandal in Bohemia."

Today it houses some of the BBC offices as well as the BBC Club Bar. It was in the Club Bar that Charles Paris found actor Martin Sabin in Simon Brett's *Not Dead, Only Resting.*

Continue on Portland Place. John Buchan lived at No. 76 Portland Place in 1914 when he wrote *The Thirty-Nine Steps.* In the novel, the protagonist, Richard Hannay, also lived in Portland Place.

Portland Place, the widest roadway in London, was designed by the Adam brothers as a parkway surrounded by the mansions of the wealthy. These plans were changed by Nash's sweeping drive north with Regent Street, which he ended at Langham Place with All Souls Church.

The church has a circular, columned porch and a conical church spire; inside, it is done in gold and cream. Today, both the church and Langham Place are dominated by their taller, heavier neighbors, especially by Broadcasting House, a 1930s skyscraper, where BBC radio programs are still produced. (The TV studios are in Shepherd's Bush.)

The BBC's massive front has a sculpture of Prospero and Ariel by Eric Gill, a friend of G. K. Chesterton, who also designed the monument for Chesterton's grave in Beaconfield.

BBC radio is a British institution. Chesterton was one of its early successes, first in debates with George Bernard Shaw, then in his weekly book review program.

During the 1930s, Detection Club members Agatha Christie, Dorothy L. Sayers, Hugh Walpole, E. C. Bentley, Anthony Berkeley, Clemence Dane, Ronald Knox, and Freeman Wills Crofts collaborated on two radio serials for the BBC, "Behind the Screen" and "The Scoop." Sayers, who was in charge of "The Scoop," wrote to Agatha Christie that the BBC producer didn't seem to want a detective story but rather a "simple love-tale or something."

The radio dramas, as well as the Detection Club's collaborative mysteries, *The Floating Admiral* and *Crime on the Coast,* have been reissued by long-time mystery publisher Victor Gollancz.

Follow Portland Place north to Cavendish Street, now cross Portland Place and go east on Cavendish Street to Great Portland Street. This area has a number of automobile dealerships. George Fentiman, in Sayers's *The Unpleasantness at the Bellona Club,* was hired as a car salesman in Great Portland Street. (Sayers herself was very much enamored with cars and motorcycles. She had a love affair with a mechanic—which may or may not be related to her love of vehicles. When she did marry, her husband, Atherton Fleming, wrote advertising copy for Daimler.)

Turn left and walk up Great Portland Street, stopping at Clipstone Street and looking to the right where you will see the London Telecom Tower, usually referred to as the Post Office Tower. The 620-foot tower is the tallest structure in London. It was built to make telecommunications possible without interference of tall buildings. The entrance is east on

Maple Street. The tower was originally built with a revolving restaurant at its top, but threats by terrorists forced the restaurant to close.

At the time Spenser was in London chasing down the terrorist group, Liberty, the restaurant was in full swing and he was much taken by it. (*The Judas Goat* by Robert Parker)

Continue along Great Portland Street, which skirts the western edge of Bloomsbury in the area around Tottenham Court Road, where a variety of pubs, small cafes, and restaurants abound.

At Devonshire Street, turn left and go to Portland Place; turn right onto Portland Place and walk north into Park Crescent. Park Crescent is a perfect semicircle of gleaming buildings with Ionic colonnades. It was designed by the Regent's architect, John Nash, to provide a formal approach to Regent's Park. The crescent was restored after being badly damaged by bombs during World War II.

Directly to the north is Park Square, with Holy Trinity Church, which was built by Sir John Soane.

In 1935, Penquin Books began publication in Holy Trinity's crypt. Soon the green and white paperbacks, with many crime and mystery novels among them, became a familiar sight.

You have now arrived at the Regent's Park Underground Station. At this point you may end the walk or continue to Baker Street and the Regent's Park segment of the walk.

MARYLEBONE ROAD/BAKER STREET

From Regent's Park Underground Station, go halfway around Park Crescent to the left until you reach Marylebone Road. This street was built in the mid-1800s to connect Paddington and Islington with the north of London.

Go west along Marylebone Road. You will see a 1965 bust of President John F. Kennedy in front of the International Students' House. Continue past Park Crescent Mews, Harley Street, and Devonshire Place, until you reach Marylebone High Street, the beginning of the old medieval village.

Young Dr. Arthur Conan Doyle would walk from Montague Place in Bloomsbury to his consulting room in Devonshire Place, where he waited for patients from ten until four. When none came, he used the time to write of Sherlock Holmes.

From 1839 to 1851, Charles Dickens lived in a house at the corner of Marylebone Road and Marylebone High Street. Ferguson House, the building which marks the site, has a bas-relief showing Dickens and some of the characters from the novels written there: *Barnaby Rudge, The Old Curiosity Shop, Martin Chuzzlewit, A Christmas Carol, David Copperfield,* and *Dombey and Son.*

The Marylebone Police Court, where Thalia Drummond was sentenced for stealing in Edgar Wallace's *The Crimson Circle,* was located in this general area. Thalia and her lady's maid "appeared" to live on Marylebone Road in a luxurious flat.

In *Jemima Shore Investigates,* the Prideaux brothers had a flat in a large Edwardian mansion block near Marylebone Road. When Jemima Shore visited them to find out why they had tried to murder the Duchess of Montford, she decided that these mansions were on their way up in the world again but that the Prideaux brothers were probably going down. (Like her creator, Antonia Fraser, Jemima Shore is very sensitive to London's architecture.)

On Marylebone Road, just opposite the formal entrance into Regent's Park at York Gate, is St. Marylebone Parish Church, where Elizabeth Barrett and Robert Browning were secretly married in 1846. In the north aisle, there is a stained-glass window dedicated to the Brownings.

This is also the church where Paul Dombey was christened in *Dombey and Son* by Charles Dickens.

The fictional Bear and Staff pub, where Sheridan Haynes, an actor who portrayed Sherlock Holmes on television, met with his group of Baker Street Irregulars (a groups of traffic wardens), was in this area. (*A Three Pipe Problem* by Julian Symons)

Continue on Marylebone Road past Oldbury Place, Nottingham Place, and Bingham Place to Luxborough Street. These are all short blocks, filled with modern buildings and occasional

Georgian ones. Cross Luxborough Street and then Marylebone Street to reach the London Planetarium.

The planetarium is next door to the world-famous Madame Tussaud's Exhibition of Waxworks. This is one museum that as a reader of crime and mystery fiction you most definitely must see. A number of the exhibits here relate to murder and to mystery.

Madame Tussaud herself was a real person. She was employed by the Court of Louis XVI to make wax figures. She was imprisoned during the French Revolution when she made wax models of the heads of guillotine victims. Madame Tussaud, in her bonnet and steel-rimmed spectacles, escaped to London in 1802, bringing her wax heads with her. First, she opened a shop in the Strand, but then moved to Baker Street in 1835. After a fire in 1884, the waxworks was moved to its present site on Marylebone Road, just east of Baker Street.

Madame Tussaud's features wax figures of notable and notorious persons both living and dead. The figures are life-size and wear authentic clothing. Other props, such as a guillotine, are also authentic.

The guillotine is in the Chamber of Horrors, as is the replica of a Victorian street in the East End where Jack the Ripper can be stalked.

As you would expect, there is a wax figure of Sherlock Holmes, although most Holmes buffs find it somewhat inferior to the one in the case of "The Mazarin Stone." At one time, the wax figure of Sherlock Holmes's creator, Sir Arthur Conan Doyle, was also on display, but now the only mystery writer so honored is the late Dame Agatha Christie, who knew Madam Tussaud's well. In *At Bertram's Hotel,* Miss Marple, while on her nostalgic visit to London, rather shamefacedly chose to revisit Madam Tussaud's.

Madame Tussaud's may bring to mind the smaller, private museum at *Tether's End* whose wax figurines were used to commit a crime in Margery Allingham's tale by that name (*Tether's End*).

Leave Madame Tussaud's on Marylebone and turn to the right. Cross Chilton Street to reach the real hub of this neighborhood: Baker Street. This is where Sherlock Holmes lived at No.

221B. You will pass the Baker Street Underground Station, the original terminus of the Bakerloo Railway, which opened in 1906. The station itself has been grandly redecorated with large ceramic tile pictures from seven of Sherlock Holmes's best-known cases.

In the area of Baker Street is Montague Mansions, the fictional residence of Miss Silver, Patricia Wentworth's intrepid old tabby.

Nearby was the boardinghouse run by Maude Daneson in Marion Babson's *The Twelve Deaths of Christmas*.

Today Baker Street is a major traffic route from the north. Only a few of the shops and buildings of Holmes's day remain. Nostalgia for the good old days is one reason modern traffic and its wardens are a vital clue in Julian Symons's *A Three Pipe Problem*. Television actor Sheridan Haynes lived in a flat on Baker Street that was furnished like the museum room created for the 1951 Festival of Britain (now in the Sherlock Holmes Pub, No. 10 Northumberland Street).

Haynes, an ardent Holmes buff, who liked to play at detecting, preferred the foggy London of Holmes's time without the noisy motor traffic. When a rare fog hit London (the Clean Air Acts have cut down on the pea-soupers), Haynes found it a pleasure to have Baker Street transformed with soft yellow gaslight and people crowding the pavements, even though the fog made the traffic jam worse than ever.

Turn right at Baker Street and walk north. The Sherlock Holmes Museum gift shop occupies one of the many places where Holmes might have lived. Across the street is the Sherlock Holmes Museum. (Because the area has been renumbered, it is difficult to determine exactly where 221B Baker Street would have been).

The Marylebone part of this walk is now complete. Return to the Baker Street Underground Station.

REGENT'S PARK

This walk is related to and adjoins the Marylebone walk and begins at the Baker Street Underground Station. Leave the sta-

REGENT'S PARK

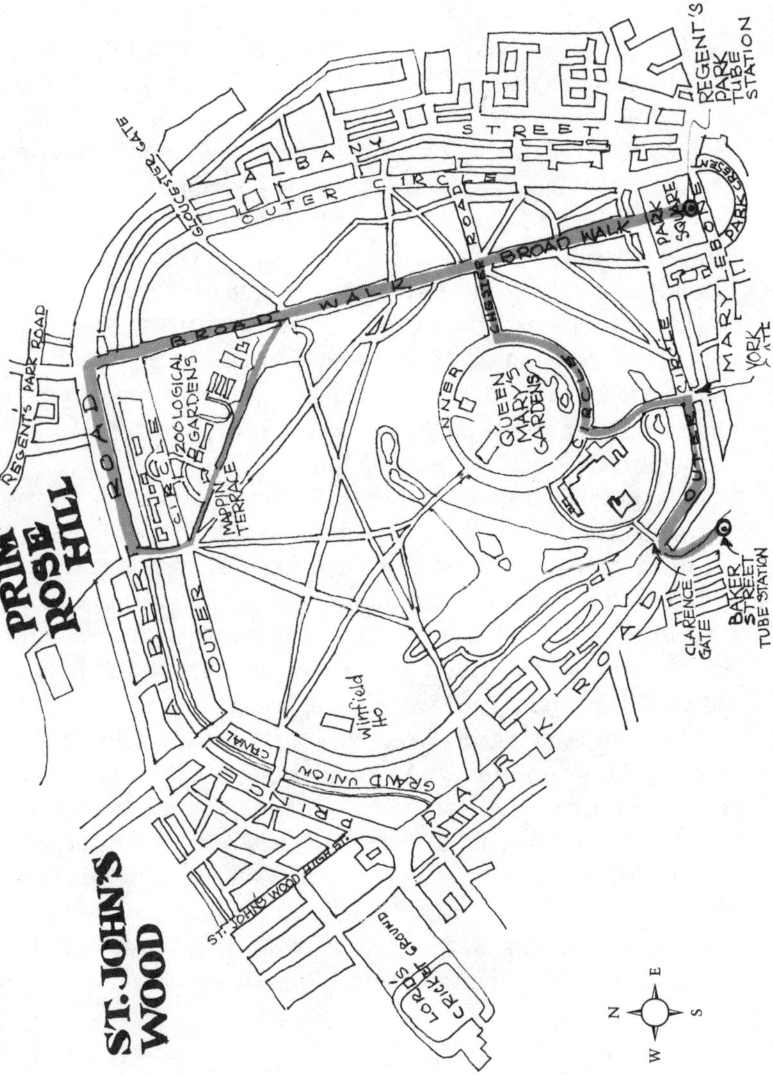

tion at Baker Street and turn right. Take Baker Street north to Park Road. To the left, northwest of Regent's Park, lies St. John's Wood, a hilly, wooded section of suburban London. Artists and writers from E. C. Bentley to Dorothy L. Sayers, Agatha Christie, Michael Gilbert, E. X. Ferrars, and Patricia Moyes have lived in or written about St. John's Woods.

Cross Park Road to your right to reach Clarence Gate and go into the park. Turn right on the Outer Circle, built as a carriage drive and lined with a spectacular row of Georgian houses, many of which are now government offices. The Outer Circle goes around Regent's Park to the other Nash terraces to the east.

Nigel Strangeways came to 35 Outer Circle to interview Alice Lake, the wife of Ministry of Morale Director Jimmy Lake. (*Minute for Murder* by Nicholas Blake)

The houses here have been beautifully restored, but in Blake's book, which is set just after World War II, Strangeways found the house on the curve of the "noble crescent. . .Stucco discoloured and peeling, the magnificent row of houses was gapped in two places, where bombs had fallen, but its grandeur had not departed from the place."

When George Fentiman and his uncle, old General Fentiman, were driven around Regent's Park, the Outer Circle is no doubt the route that was followed. George got out at Gloucester Gate to go home to Finsbury.

When you reach York Gate, turn left and walk north to the Inner Circle, just to the east of the lake filled by the Tyburn, which surrounds Queen Mary's Gardens, with its outdoor restaurant and Open Air Theatre.

In Marian Babson's *Bejewelled Death,* the kidnapper asked Alstair if he knew Chester Road, which cut through Regent's Park from the Outer Circle to the Inner Circle around Queen Mary's Gardens.

In P. D. James's *Innocent Blood,* Philippa Palfrey and her mother came to spend a quiet Sunday afternoon among the roses, only to meet, face to face, the man who was stalking them.

The killer in Marian Babson's *The Twelve Deaths of Christmas* found a young punk lying drunk in the Rose Garden and cut his throat because "blood makes an excellent fertilizer for roses."

Circle to the right to reach Chester Road and then go left to take the Broad Walk north to the "Zoo."

The Gardens of the Zoological Society were begun in 1828 by the Zoological Society of London. One of the founders was Sir Humphrey Davy, about whom E. C. Bentley wrote his first schoolboy clerihew. Today, although the zoo is in deep financial difficulties, it still has the finest and most representative collection of animals in the world.

In *English School Murder* by Ruth Dudley Edwards, according to Mrs. Clarke, the trouble with Wally was that he thought he could run anything in the country, including the London Zoo.

In Joan Smith's *A Masculine Ending,* the woman who had invited Loretta to dinner asked her to arrive a bit later than originally planned because the woman had promised to "take Elinor and one of her school friends to the zoo."

James Tyrone, the sportswriter in *Forfeit* by Dick Francis, was picked up by some racecourse crooks and driven to Regent's Park Zoo to meet the boss at the lions' cages. Tyrone was later driven back into Regent's Park by the same crooks, but managed to cause them to crash their limousine in the Regent's Canal.

The Zoo's Mappin Terraces are a reinforced concrete amphitheater where bears and other animals wander freely without bars. In *A Splash of Red* by Antonia Fraser, Jemima Shore commented unfavorably on the Lionnel building in Adelaide Square, Bloomsbury, saying it resembled the Mappin Terraces at the London Zoo.

Spenser followed his potential "judas goat" to Regent's Park. He then checked the entire zoo to be certain he could not be jumped unexpectedly. He went past the cranes, geese, and owls at the north gate entrance and, using the tunnel by the insect house, came out by the restaurant and a cafeteria with flamingos in a grass park. The next day Spenser returned by the south gate near Wolf Wood and sat in the zoo's cafeteria watching a gang member. Finally, he followed a girl gang member around the northern edge of the park on Prince Albert

Road, along Albany Street, and across Marylebone Road to her flat on Carburton Street.

It was this route that was taken in reverse by Sunday in G. K. Chesterton's *The Man Who Was Thursday.* Sunday jumped off the fire engine and climbed a high railing to vanish into the zoo. He then reappeared riding an elephant down Albany Street on his way to Hyde Park and the Albert Memorial.

To the north of Regent's Park lies Primrose Hill, which is over 200 feet high. On a clear day, Primrose Hill gives you a view south across London into Kent and Surrey. In "The Woman in the Big Hat," by Baroness Orczy, Lady Molly was told that Elizabeth Lowenthal was out taking a brisk walk on Primrose Hill when Mark Culledon was murdered. This gave her an alibi of sorts.

To end this walk, walk back south through Regent's Park on the Broad Walk to the Regent's Park Underground Station in Park Square.

9

WESTMINSTER WALK

BACKGROUND

This walk takes place in the city of Westminster, originally a village west of London on the Thames River. Since 1965, the official area of the city of Westminster has included almost everything from Temple Bar to Chelsea and from Paddington and Marylebone to the Thames.

The everyday Londoner uses the term to designate a much smaller area—that in the vicinity of Westminster Abbey, the Houses of Parliament, and Buckingham Palace. For the purpose of this walk, our definition is closer to that of the everyday Londoner.

Since the eleventh century, kings have been both crowned and buried in Westminster Abbey and have governed from Westminster's royal palaces. Although Henry VIII was the last king to live in the palace between the river and the abbey, Westminster continues as the center of England's government.

Such writers as James Boswell, Sir Edmund Spenser, John Milton, and John Cleland are associated with Westminster, and of course, the greats of British Literature are buried or memorialized in Westminster Abbey.

For the mystery lover, however, Westminster's chief interest is that it is the home of Scotland Yard, the nerve center of law enforcement, where my London detective stories either begin or end. On this walk, we pass both Old Scotland Yard and the "newest" Scotland Yard, located since 1967 at 10 Broadway.

The walk covers three distinct localities: Whitehall, the seat of the Crown, or executive government; Westminster, the home of parliamentary, or legislative, power; and Victoria, the neighborhood behind Victoria Station, which includes St. James's Park.

LENGTH OF WALK: 3.3 miles

See the map on pages 165 and 179 for the boundaries of this walk and pages 261–63 for a list of the authors, books, and detectives mentioned.

PLACES OF INTEREST

Trafalgar Square.

Whitehall Banqueting House, Whitehall. Admission charge.

Mounting of the Guard, Horse Guards.

New Scotland Yard, 10 Broadway.

Westminster Abbey. Admission charge for Royal chapels and Poets' Corner.

Westminster Cathedral (Roman Catholic), Ashley Place. Admission charge for lift in campanile.

Houses of Parliament, Queue at St. Stephen's Porch or contact an MP.

PLACES TO EAT

Sherlock Holmes Pub, 10 Northumberland St. Pub food is offered on the ground floor. Reservations are needed for the upstairs restaurant. 071-930-2644.

The Albert Tavern, 52 Victoria St. This Victorian pub has a carvery restaurant upstairs. 071-222-5577.

Shepherds Restaurant, Marsham Ct., Marsham St., This restaurant offers a traditional British menu and sounds the Division Bell to summon members of Parliament to vote. 071-834-9552.

WESTMINSTER WALK

Take the Trafalgar Square exit from the Charing Cross Underground Station. This will bring you into Trafalgar Square, London's most dramatic open place, whose north side is the columned National Gallery. To the west lies Canada House; to the east, South Africa House; and to the south, Whitehall, with the equestrian statue of Charles I at its head. It is from Charles's statue that all distances in London are measured.

Created by Charles Barry and designed by Nash to celebrate the great naval victory by Lord Nelson in 1805, Trafalgar Square replaced a jumble of buildings and stables with a handsome open space dominated by the 170-foot Nelson Monument. It is guarded by four huge lions by Landseer.

Nearby is a fountain designed by Luytens. It is all very impressive. No wonder that, in *The Judas Goat* by Robert Parker, American private eye Spenser, in London to track down a terrorist group, walked to Trafalgar Square like any tourist to see "Nelson and the lions and the National Gallery and the goddamned pigeons."

John Dickson Carr's publicity-seeking Mad Hatter placed the homburg of a well-known war profiteer on a lion in Trafalgar Square, and Lord Peter Wimsey, in the guise of Death Bredon, led Scotland Yard a merry chase up Whitehall, doubling back around the Cenotaph, before his sensational capture in the middle of Trafalgar Square. (*Murder Must Advertise* by Dorothy L. Sayers)

In *The Hound of the Baskervilles* by Sir Arthur Conan Doyle, Stapleton caught a cab in Trafalgar Square in order to tail Henry Baskerville.

Trafalgar Square is the scene of many of London's open-air meetings, revivals, rock concerts, and demonstrations.

WESTMINSTER

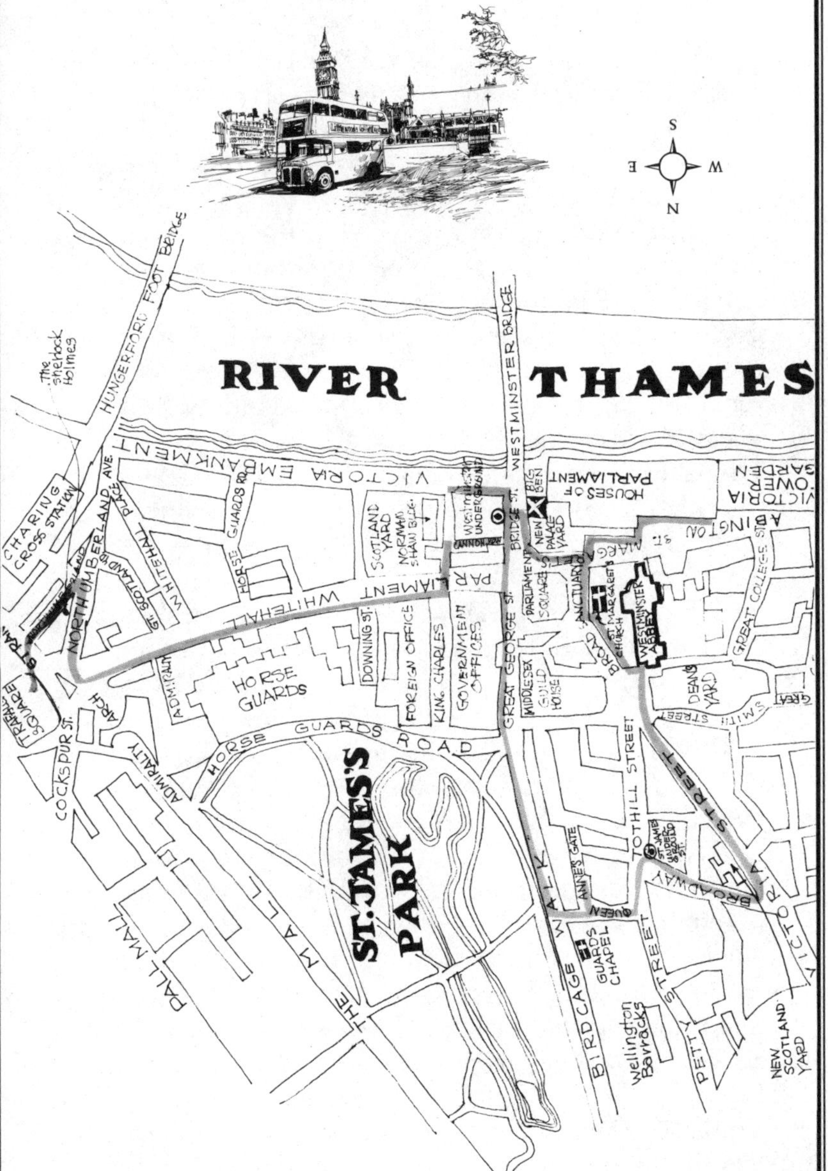

It was not surprising that Jemima Shore saw a photograph in the *Times* of her lover, MP Tom Amyas, taking part in a Trafalgar Square rally for Welfare Now. (*A Splash of Red* by Antonia Fraser)

In Agatha Christie's *The Secret Adversary,* the Labor Day meeting that was meant to begin a general strike was thwarted by the sudden death of Sir James Peel Edgerton. Instead, speeches in Trafalgar Square and a straggling procession singing the "Red Flag" were substituted.

Cross the street to South Africa House and turn right and cross the Strand. Turn right again to Northumberland Street (not Avenue). Walk down Northumberland Street to Craven Passage, where you will find the Sherlock Holmes Pub. At one time, the pub was called the Northumberland Arms. Sir Henry Baskerville stayed there when he came to London. (*The Hound of the Baskervilles* by Sir Arthur Conan Doyle)

Now the pub features mementos of Sherlock Holmes's cases and a replica of the sitting room at 221B Baker Street. The sitting room can be viewed through a window at the head of the stairs.

In Julian Symons's *A Three Pipe Problem,* this replica, built for the Festival of Britain, was placed in the flat of amateur detectives Sheridan Haynes, who played Sherlock Holmes in a TV series.

Across Craven Passage from the Sherlock Holmes is the Midland Bank Building. It once housed Nevill's Turkish Bath, which was patronized by Holmes and Watson.

Leave the Sherlock Holmes and turn left to walk toward the river. At the point where Northumberland Avenue runs into Whitehall Place is the building which houses the Ministry of Defense. It was once the exclusive Hotel Metropole, which figured in Sherlock Holmes's case of "The Noble Bachelor."

Turn right and walk back along the south side of Northumberland Avenue to Trafalgar Square and the statue of King Charles I, which faces down Whitehall toward the site of the royal palace of Whitehall. Charles I was executed on January 30, 1649, outside the Banqueting House, all of the palace that remains today. Royal processions pass down Whitehall, a wide avenue that leads to Westminster Abbey and the Houses of Parliament. It follows an earlier roadway called King Street. Since a "white hall" at one time meant a grand hall built for public occasions, the entire area came to be known as Whitehall.

After the palace fire of 1698, royalty moved from Whitehall, but the name remained synonymous with government.

In detective stories, characters often report to mysterious officials "at Whitehall."

In Margaret Yorke's *Cast for Death,* intent on showing him the famous sights, Patrick Grant drove Manolakis, the visiting Greek policeman, down Whitehall.

In *All Hallows' Eve* by Charles Williams, Lester Furnival, unaware that she had died in a plane crash, walked up Whitehall from Westminster Bridge, finding the offices and shops full and furnished with everything—except people.

As you go south on Whitehall, walk on the west side of the street until you cross Whitehall at Derby Gate. Along the way, take note of Admiralty Arch, near Trafalgar Square, which leads to the Mall and Buckingham Palace. Beyond it is the Old Admiralty, where Lord Nelson received his orders. Next door is the red-brick Admiralty House, entered from an internal courtyard where, in John Buchan's thriller *The Thirty-Nine Steps,* Foreign Office Permanent Under-Secretary Sir Walter Bullivant took Richard Hannay to determine where to look for those mysterious "39 steps."

In "The Priory School," Sherlock Holmes knew the Duke of Holdernesse, who was First Lord of the Admiralty, and it was in Admiralty House that the British naval codes were changed in "His Last Bow."

Across Whitehall to your left is the entrance to Great Scotland Yard, originally the palace of the kings of Scotland and later, until 1890, the first home of the Metropolitan Police.

Between Whitehall Place and Horse Guards Road, on the river side of Whitehall, is the ponderous Victorian War Office where, in Nicholas Blake's *Minute for Murder,* war hero Charles Kensington reported for duty after a secret mission in which he captured a top Nazi.

Next on the west side of Whitehall is the Horse Guards,

a low, Portland-stone building with a courtyard and an archway with a clock tower. Two mounted sentries are stationed there daily in twin sentry boxes. If there aren't too many tourists about, walk close and see for yourself what Spenser meant when he said that the two mounted sentries had "young and ordinary faces." (*The Judas Goat* by Robert Parker)

The Mounting of the Guard is carried out weekdays at eleven and at noon on Sunday by one of the two regiments of the Household calvary: the Life Guards in red tunics and white plumes, or the Royal Horse Guards in blue tunics and red plumes. On the second Saturday of June, the Queen's official birthday, there is a Trooping of the Colour on Horse Guards Parade westward through the arch.

Directly across Whitehall, you can see the Portland-stone Banqueting House, all that remains of the Palace of Whitehall.

The Banqueting House was designed by Inigo Jones in 1619; it has a glorious ceiling painted by Peter Paul Rubens. A plus is that it is one of the lesser-visited tourist stops along Whitehall. Usually you can drop in and be quite alone.

Historically, the Banqueting House is also important because of its association with the execution of Charles I on January 30, 1649. On that date, the doomed king walked through the vast room and stepped through one of its windows. Outside, a scaffold had been erected. Dressed in an extra shirt against the January chill, Charles became the only English king ever to be executed, or, as is often suggested, murdered, by judicial decree.

Beyond the Banqueting House is Welsh Gwydyr House, then the Ministry of Defense in front of which is a statue of Sir Walter Raleigh.

On the west side of Whitehall, you will find the Scottish Office, the Treasury, and, finally, tiny Downing Street, the official residence of the Prime Minister. For security reasons, Downing Street is now closed to all visitors.

Topaz's lawyer winced when Nell Bray introduced herself to him. She observed that lawyers often are cautious when faced with people who've served prison sentences for throwing bricks through the window of 10 Downing Street. (*Sister Beneath the Sheet* by Gillian Linscott)

In Edgar Wallace's *The Crimson Circle,* Inspector Parr, whose daughter Thalia Drummond had infiltrated the Crimson Circle, went to No. 10 to talk with the Prime Minister about the murder of Cabinet Minister Raphael Willings.

The mysterious Foreign Office Official, "Mr. Carter," talked with the Prime Minister about Sir James Peel Edgerton's sinister plot. (*The Secret Adversary* by Agatha Christie)

In *A Splash of Red* by Antonia Fraser, Sir Richard Lionnel's watertight alibi for the time his mistress was murdered was that he was attending a meeting at No. 10 Downing Street.

The Mad Hatter planned to use a crossbow bolt to pin the top hat of the old-fashioned patriot Sir William Bitten to the door of No. 10 in *The Mad Hatter Mystery* by John Dickson Carr.

Directly across Whitehall from Downing Street is Richmond Terrace. In the Sherlock Holmes case "The Second Stain," Whitehall Terrace, the building where the Secretary for European Affairs lived, was located there. Also, Sax Rohmer's Sir Denis Nayland Smith had his residence in "Westminster Court or Mansions, next door to Scotland Yard," probably in Richmond Terrace.

The Foreign Office, with its elaborate Italianate front, occupies the entire block, stretching south from Downing Street along the west side of Whitehall to King Charles Street.

In Charles Williams's *All Hallows' Eve,* Richard Furnival served at the Foreign Office during the war.

In *Gaudy Night,* Harriet Vane learned from Freddy Arbuthnot that Lord Peter Wimsey was abroad doing what he called "plumbing" for the Foreign Office, and, in *Black As He's Painted,* Ngaio Marsh's delightful Mr. Whipplestone, having retired from the Foreign Office with two solid Georgian gravy-boats, impulsively adopted the stray cat Lucy Lockett.

In "His Last Bow," the Foreign Minister himself persuaded Sherlock Holmes to take on the mission against Von Bork.

Nicholas Blake placed the wartime Ministry of Morale somewhere in this area. From a window there, Nigel Strangeways, in *Minute for Murder,* looked out on discolored plane trees and the rubble of bombed houses near the park just before the director's secretary was poisoned.

Helen, Duchess of Denver, Lord Peter Wimsey's estimable sister-in-law, was probably also employed by the Ministry of Morale during World War II. In real life, the Ministry of Information turned Dorothy L. Sayers herself down for a position because she was "too difficult and loquacious."

Carter Dickson (aka John Dickson Carr) had Sir Henry Merrivale, known as the "Old Man," nap "in a rabbit warren behind Whitehall."

The Cenotaph stands in front of the Foreign Office, in what is now called Parliament Street; it is Britain's chief monument to her war dead. An annual remembrance service is held at the Cenotaph on the second Sunday in November.

Cross Parliament Street at King Charles Street to Derby Gate. You are at the rear of (old) New Scotland Yard. This was the home of the Metropolitan Police for almost a century. Then, in 1967, the CID moved to No. 10 Broadway, which also is called New Scotland Yard; (old) New Scotland Yard is now called the Norman Shaw Building after its architect. It is a massive, red and white striped brick hulk, crouching between the Italianate Whitehall buildings to its north and the Gothic towers of Westminster: It is a tiger among the bureaucratic lions here in C. P. Snow's "corridors of power."

Despite the move, it is the Shaw building most pursuers of crime fiction imagine when they think of Scotland Yard.

To reach the front of the Shaw building, walk toward the river on Derby Gate. Turn right when you come to Cannon Row. Follow Cannon Row past the Cannon Row Police Station (to create confusion, there is also a Cannon Row Police Station in the City). Go left on Bridge Street past the Westminster Underground Station and a clutch of souvenir shops and snack bars.

Stop here for a minute to take in the aspect of the Gothic-style Houses of Parliament and the impressive St. Stephen's

Clock Tower, which houses the famous bell Big Ben. This is the sight that spells London to people around the world.

The distinctive sound of Big Ben, made famous around the world by the BBC, is probably the result of a crack made in the bell when it fell from the cart taking it to the Clock Tower.

In *The Trail of Fu Manchu,* Sax Rohmer wrote that Big Ben was clearly visible in the night as Sir Denis chased off to Limehouse after Fu Manchu.

In Ngaio Marsh's *A Surfeit of Lampreys,* New Zealander Roberta Grey heard a clock strike a single great note and asked Henry Lamprey what it was. "I suspect it was Big Ben, you hear him all over the place at nighttime." "I've only heard him on the air before," was her reply. "You are in London now," he told her.

In Sayers's *Clouds of Witness,* Big Ben solemnly stuck "11 deep ones" as the trial of the Duke of Denver opened in the House of Lords.

Leave Ben and Parliament behind and turn left, walk north along the Embankment to the impressively ornate iron gates at the entrance to the Norman Shaw building or (old) New Scotland Yard, if you prefer.

Although this is no longer the headquarters of the Metropolitan Police, there is still security, and the ordinary tourist is not a welcome visitor. A police sentry will ask your business and then politely decline your admittance.

In support of the authenticity of crime fiction, recall that in *Mortal Consequences,* Julian Symons stated that before the founding of Scotland Yard by Sir Robert Peel in 1829, there were likely more than 10,000 murders in Britain every year. Today, despite cries concerning the degenerating state of modern society, that number has shrunk considerably.

Symons credits Charles Dickens with creating the popular idea of Scotland Yard as the protector of society and G. K. Chesterton with calling the policeman on the beat the modern "knight-errant."

John Creasey wrote a history of the formation of the London police in *The Masters of Bow Street.* The highly readable *The*

Story of Scotland Yard by Sir Basil Thomson covers the Yard from its founding until the early 1930s. John Dickson Carr in *Fire Burn!,* which is set in 1829, also describes the founding of Scotland Yard.

You may wish to take a break from walking and settle down with a drink in a nearby cafe and reflect on the number of times your favorite sleuths found their way to this building.

Although Sherlock Holmes (a Nietzschean Superman, according to Julian Symons) on occasion made his way to Scotland Yard, he usually would receive Inspector Lestrade in the evening in Baker Street.

In *Tether's End* by Margery Allingham, Albert Campion closed the door of Chief Superintendent Yeo's room and walked up two flights of stairs to tap on the door of the room that belonged to the newest superintendent, Charles Luke. Campion and Oates had been "hunting companions" since the days when Oates was an inspector.

By the time of his "last" case, Philip Trent was so well acquainted with Inspector Murch that Trent visited him at home, met his wife, and played with his children. (*Trent's Last Case* by E. C. Bentley)

Dr. Gideon Fell lived on the Embankment at No. 1 Adelphi Terrace, making it possible to be "called over" by Chief Inspector Hadley. Sir Henry Merrivale, Carr's (aka Carter Dickson) "Old Man," worked across the way in Whitehall but was handy for consultations.

In *The Poisoned Chocolates Case,* his mystery about the Detection Club, Anthony Berkeley (aka Francis Iles) had President Roger Sheringham invite Inspector Moresby of Scotland Yard to the club's monthly dinner, then persuaded Moresby to let the club try to solve a murder.

The French detective Valentin, a creation of G. K. Chesterton, headed for Scotland Yard upon his arrival in London.

Several of Agatha Christie's characters worked out of the Yard. Wooden-faced Superintendent Battle was a man of the utmost discretion, according to the nervous Foreign Office dignitary, George Lomax. Julius Hersheimer, the rich, young

American seeking his kidnapped cousin, Jane Finn, called upon the services of Scotland Yard. (*The Secret Adversary*)

Inspector Japp, a friend and colleague of Hercule Poirot, worked with him on such cases as *The Big Four*.

Ngaio Marsh often placed Roderick Alleyn at the Yard, usually late at night, sometimes with reporter Nigel Bathgate in tow, but always with his team of Fox, Curtis, Bailey, and Thomson.

In Dorothy L. Sayers's *Whose Body?*, Sir Andrew Mackenzie, the head of Scotland Yard, is a Wimsey family friend, and Detective-Inspector Charles Parker was first a close friend to Lord Peter and later became his brother-in-law. In Parker's last appearance in Sayers's unpublished work, *Thrones, Dominations,* when Lord Peter came calling, Parker was sitting in his Scotland Yard office sorting through reports of possible assassins likely to attend the funeral of King George V.

Josephine Tey's detective Alan Grant was in love with London, as was Marsh's Roderick Alleyn. One night, after putting away the gilt dagger that had been used to stab a man in a theater queue, Grant came out of his office onto the Embankment to find a fine night "with a light frosty mist in the air." He decided to walk home through the city that he found even more beautiful by night than by day.

Enough of Scotland Yard for now. Cross the street to the Victoria Embankment that runs along the Thames. Here, just before Westminster Bridge, is a great bronze statue of the Icenian Queen Boadicea. In AD 60, she sacked Londinium in her drive against the Romans.

Westminster Pier is where you can pick up the river tour boats that go east to the Tower and past the Port of London to Greenwich, or west to Kew, Richmond, and Hampton Court.

In Josephine Tey's *The Daughter of Time,* Inspector Grant promised a trip by river to Greenwich to his young American researcher who had asked him what was "at Greenwich?"

If you look north, you will see the skyline of the City with the great dome of St. Paul's Cathedral and the spires of many of Wren's churches.

Westminster Bridge stretches over the Thames beside you. Since it was build as London's second bridge in 1748, it has been immortalized by such poets as Wordsworth and such painters of the London scene as Turner, Constable, and Monet.

Westminster Bridge has not escaped the attention of the crime writer. Spenser, Robert Parker's private eye, stood musing on Westminster Bridge. Below, he saw the platform where excursion boats loaded, and he was struck with the realization that Shakespeare himself must have crossed the river here (there would have been ferry boats in Shakespeare's day) to reach the Globe Theatre on the other side. (*The Judas Goat* by Robert Parker)

At the end of Margery Allingham's *Black Plumes,* when David Field and Frances Ivory went for a walk down Whitehall, they reached the bridge and paused to look over the parapet: "Big Ben blinked down on them and the coloured advertisement signs from upriver stained the water below."

In Ngaio Marsh's *A Surfeit of Lampreys,* Chief Inspector Alleyn crossed the Embankment and, leaning on the parapet, looked down into "the black shadows of Westminster Pier where the river slapped against the wet stones."

In *All Hallows' Eve* by Charles Williams, Lester Furnival, who had died in a plane crash, stood on Westminster Bridge and saw the huge body of the plane that killed her, lying half in the river and half on the Embankment.

In *Cast for Death* by Margaret Yorke, as soon as he heard about a corpse found in the river, Patrick Grant rang up Detective Inspector Colin Smithers at Scotland Yard, only to learn that the body was that of his friend Sam.

The promising film ingenue Gloria Scott's suicide from Westminster Bridge began a chain of murders in Edmund Crispin's *Frequent Hearses.*

The poet Gabriel Syme came down river in a tug from an underground meeting in an old Chiswick pub. He landed at Cleopatra's Needle, where we was met by another anarchist, who walked with him to Sunday's breakfast. (*The Man Who Was Thursday* by G. K. Chesterton)

From Westminster Bridge you can look north along the

Embankment and see Cleopatra's Needle, the oldest monument in London. One of a pair (the other is in New York's Central Park), it records the deeds, not of Cleopatra, but of Thothmes and Ramses II. It was given to London in 1819 by the Viceroy of India but was not set up until 1878.

Turn back and walk west along Bridge Street, across the top of Parliament Square. Bridge Street soon becomes Great George Street. This is where the spy, Adolph Meyer, lived in the Sherlock Holmes case "The Adventure of the Bruce-Partington Plans."

Continue on Great George Street, which becomes Birdcage Walk. On his first day in London, Spenser walked along Birdcage Walk to Buckingham Palace.

To the right at St. James's Park, you will see a sign pointing to the Cabinet War Rooms in Horse Guards Road. It was in this underground bunker that Winston Churchill and his Cabinet met and masterminded Britain's defense during World War II.

St. James's Park was once a marsh. It was drained by Henry VIII and turned into a royal deer park. Charles II allowed the people of London in to see him feeding the birds. Later it became a public park and bird sanctuary, famous for its pelicans. Today, St. James's is a favorite lunchtime spot for Whitehall's civil servants. If you wish to join them, purchase a sandwich from one of the vendors and find yourself a vacant deck chair. An attendant will collect a small fee for the chair. On most days during the summer, a military band performs between 1:00 and 2:00 PM.

G. K. Chesterton proposed to Frances Blogg during a St. James's Park lunch hour.

In Agatha Christie's *The Secret Adversary,* Tuppence, having left Tommy Beresford after they had had tea in a Lyons Corner House, walked home across St. James's Park. She was followed by "Mr. Whittington."

At the first stoplight on Birdcage Walk, turn left and cross to Queen Anne's Gate. The street is difficult to identify because there are no street signs, only a faded gatepost set into the black railings. A row of attractive red-brick houses that rank among the best examples of early eighteenth-century domestic architecture in London line the way. The headquarters of the National Trust is at No. 42. A stone statue of tragic Queen Anne, the last Stuart to sit on the throne of Britain, stands before No. 15.

In *The Piccadilly Murder* by Anthony Berkeley, Major Lynn Sinclair of the Guards, whose barracks were just beyond the Guards Military Chapel, had a flat in Queen Anne's Gate.

In John Buchan's *The Thirty-Nine Steps,* Richard Hannay came to Queen Anne's Gate to the home of Sir Walter Bullivant. The house was in the narrow part of Queen Anne's Gate. It had a wide hall with rooms on both sides.

In Buchan's day, Lord Haldane, who was head of the Foreign Office before he became Lord Chancellor, lived in No. 28. No. 16 was the home of Admiral Lord Fisher, who was the actual First Sea Lord from 1905 until 1910 and again from 1914 through 1915. No. 50 Queen Anne's Gate now houses the Home Office.

After giving in to the Home Secretary's urgings, Willow King left the Home Office. She paused on the steps comparing London with Berkshire; There was nothing moving in Queen Anne's Gate, not even a taxi. (*Bitter Herbs* by Natasha Cooper)

When the likes of Hercule Poirot and Lord Peter Wimsey found it necessary to consult or report to the Home Office, they reported to the former offices in a building on Whitehall.

Hercule Poirot and Captain Hastings visited the Secretary of State for Home Affairs, the Right Honorable Sydney Crowther, in his offices at the Home Office. (*The Big Four* by Agatha Christie)

In *The Documents in the Case* by Dorothy L. Sayers, after the Reverend Mr. Parry's dinner party, writer John Munting and a professor friend of his hunted up Sir James Lubbock at his Bedford Square home. They went with him to his Home Office laboratory late that night.

Queen Anne's Gate intersects with Petty France to the right and Broadway to the left. Broadway will shortly turn to the south and lead to Victoria Street. Turn left onto Broadway and follow it as it turns to the right at St. James's Park Underground Station. Turn right and follow Broadway to Victoria Street.

To the right, as you walk south on Broadway, is Caxton Hall, which is named for the printer William Caxton. He set up his business here during the reign of Richard III. Today it is often the scene of fashionable out-of-church weddings. No doubt it is the site of Carr's Westminster Registry Office where artist Martin Drake and his long-lost love, Lady Jennifer, were going to be married by special license in John Dickson Carr's *The Skeleton in the Clock.*

As you continue along Broadway, you will pass the towering twenty stories of granite and glass that is the current home of the Metropolitan CID, New Scotland Yard. P. D. James described it as "a bastion of concrete and glass."

In James's *An Unsuitable Job for a Woman,* Adam Dalgleish called Cordelia Gray into Scotland Yard for questioning in connection with the suicide of her business partner, Bernie Pryde, and the murder of Cambridge student Mark Callender.

American policeman Jay Dodge found Scotland Yard disappointing. His wife, Lark, in London on "bookseller's business" thought that "he wanted something hung with gargoyles and flying buttresses." (*Skylark* by Sheila Simonson)

The flat of the Honorable Edward Manx, theater critic and nephew of eccentric Lord Pastern, was located beyond New Scotland Yard, somewhere in a cul-de-sac "off Victoria Street." Manx took his cousin Carlisle there after she was grilled by Inspector Alleyn in Ngaio Marsh's *A Wreath for Rivera.*

In *Trent's Last Case* by E. C. Bentley, Trent and Mrs. Manderson's uncle Burton Cupples walked together along Victoria Street after leaving the St. James's Park flat of Manderson's former secretary, Marlowe.

Father Brown and the private detective Flambeau walked along Victoria Street on their way to see Flambeau's new office in a modern "skyscraper." ("The Eye of Apollo" by G. K. Chesterton)

Continue on Broadway to Victoria Street; turn left. Take note that to the right you will find the Army and Navy Stores where Agatha Christie shopped with her grandmother and where Miss Marple shopped when she stayed at Bertram's Hotel in the novel of the same name.

As you walk east on Victoria Street, you will see the twin towers of Westminster Abbey. When Victoria Street becomes Broad Sanctuary, cross Storey's Gate to the open driveway called the Sanctuary, and enter Westminster Abbey at the west porch.

The abbey is a minster, or mission church. Originally, it was built to the west of London. According to legend, the first church was built in the seventh century by King Sebert of the East Saxons on the instructions of St. Peter, who materialized at its construction. King Edward the Confessor rebuilt the church about 1050. Nothing of Edward's church remains, but it is depicted in the Bayeux Tapestry as having a central tower and transepts covered with a lead roof.

The present church—with the exception of the twin towers, which were added in the early eighteenth century—is the work of King Henry III, who rebuilt it in 1245 as a shrine to Edward the Confessor, his patron saint.

Officially known as the Collegiate Church of St. Peter's at Westminster, its dean is answerable only to God and the Queen.

Kings and queens are crowned, married, and buried in Westminster Abbey. It survived the Cromwellian Reformation, despite having its monastery dissolved. Today the abbey is both a large, handsome thirteenth-century church and a vast and cluttered memorial to British monarchs and heroes from all walks of life. Patrick Grant took the Greek policeman who was visiting London to see the memorials in Westminster Abbey in Margaret Yorke's *Cast for Death*.

From the perspective of the crime story enthusiast, there are certain parts of the abbey that must be seen.

Upon entering the abbey, go down the north aisle through the nave and the choir to the sanctuary where the kings and queens are crowned. (Please do a little looking along the way.) Pay your admission fee at this point, and continue on.

The abbey has close associations with the boy-king Edward V, whose purported murder by his uncle Richard III

Westminster Abbey

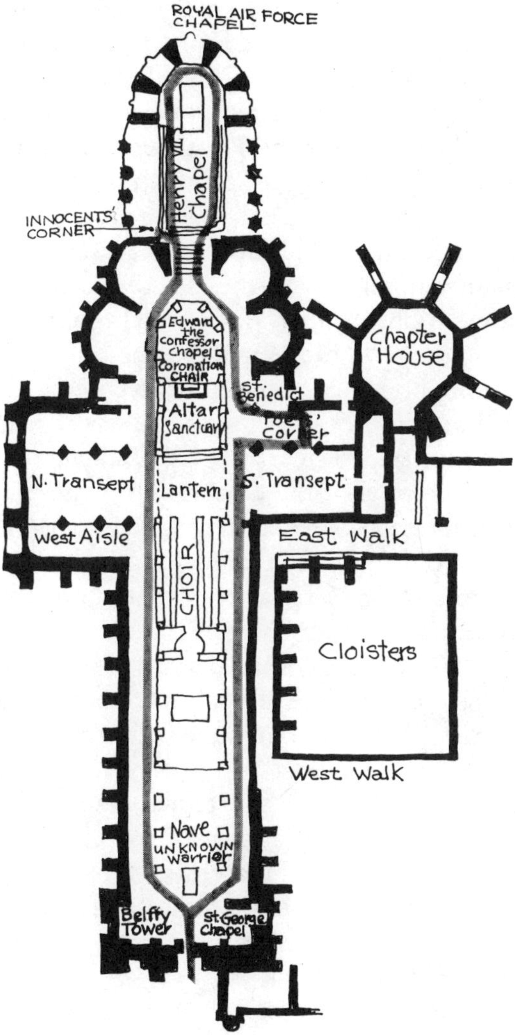

ROYAL AIR FORCE CHAPEL
Henry VII Chapel
INNOCENTS' CORNER
Chapter House
Edward the confessor chapel
Coronation CHAIR
St. Benedict
Altar
Sanctuary
Poets' Corner
N. Transept
Lantern
S. Transept
West Aisle
East Walk
CHOIR
Cloisters
West Walk
Nave
UNKNOWN Warrior
Belfry Tower
St. George Chapel

exercised the mind of Inspector Grant in Josephine Tey's *The Daughter of Time.*

Not only was Edward V born in the abbey while his father, Edward IV, was in exile, but his mother, Elizabeth Woodville, bolted her sanctuary and, taking young Richard, Duke of York, with her, fled at the time of Edward IV's death. Go by the High Altar and the Chapel of Edward the Confessor, where you can see the old and scarred, wooden Coronation Chair with the shelf beneath for the Royal Scottish Stone of Scone. Continue past the Plantagenet tombs into the northern aisle of Henry VII's beautiful chapel. There, just beyond the tomb of Elizabeth I, you will find Innocents' Corner, with the tombs of two infant daughters of James I. Above them is a casket designed by Sir Christopher Wren which contains the bones of two boys found at the White Tower during the reign of Charles II. The bones are commonly accepted as those of Edward V and his brother. Writing in *Murderess Ink,* Catherine Aird points out that just by writing *The Daughter of Time,* Josephine Tey has kept alive the doubts about the murder of the boys and continued to provoke questions about the authenticity of the Shakespearean portrait of Richard III.

Walk across Henry VII's chapel. The starkly modern blue window is dedicated to the flyers of the battle of Britain. Now go into the south transept, known as Poets' Corner. This area, surrounding the burial place of English literature's father, Geoffrey Chaucer, is filled with tombs and memorials to British writers, artists, and musicians.

Be certain to hunt out the tablet memorializing Henry James, the American-born author of the chilling *Turn of the Screw.* Also locate the burial place of one of mystery writing's grand masters, Charles Dickens. (Although Dickens's body was buried in Westminster Abbey at the request of Queen Victoria, his heart was buried in Rochester.)

William J. Palmer's *The Highwayman and Mr. Dickens* opens with a reminiscence of Charles Dickens's "ceremonious funeral in the Abbey."

The newest memorial in Poets' Corner is to the Irish-born playwright, Oscar Wilde. The witty Wilde is commemorated in a window unveiled in 1995.

Leave Westminster Abbey and turn to your right to cross the parkway to the small church at the abbey's northeast corner. This is St. Margaret's Westminster, the parish church of the House of Commons. It was built in 1500 and since then has been the scene of many fashionable weddings, including John Milton's in 1655 and Sir Winston Churchill's in 1908. The church has a 1501 window that celebrates the betrothal of Catherine of Aragon to Prince Arthur. The headless body of Sir Walter Raleigh is buried beneath the altar. He was executed across the street in Old Palace Yard.

Crime fiction characters take note of weddings and funerals just as everyone else does. In Jessica Mann's *Funeral Sites,* Phoebe Sholto was married to Aidan Britton in a society wedding in St. Margaret's.

Cub reporter Hector Puncheon of the *Morning Star* had to get down to St. Margaret's by 10:30 A.M. to cover the wedding of a fashionable beauty who was being married in the strictest secrecy. (*Murder Must Advertise* by Dorothy L. Sayers)

According to Baroness Orczy, Captain Huber de Mazaren and Lady Molly of Scotland Yard (heroine of the popular short story series) were married in St. Margaret's by special license on April 22, 1904.

It is highly likely that it was at this St. Margaret's that the disinterred corpse of Lord Augustus Fitzroy-Hammond was found keeling in the family pew. (*Resurrection Row* by Anne Perry)

A memorial service for Dorothy L. Sayers was held in St. Margaret's on January 15, 1958. It was attended by a representative of the Archbishop of Canterbury, the Red Dean, and five other bishops of the Church of England. The panegyric written by C. S. Lewis was read by Bishop Bell of Chichester, who had persuaded Sayers to write a play for Canterbury (leading her, a schoolboy wrote, "from a life of crime to the Church of England"). The first lesson was read by her former BBC producer, Val Gielgud, and the second by His Honour Judge Gordon Clark (detective writer Cyril Hare).

Leave St. Margaret's and cross Broad Sanctuary to Parliament Square, where the first traffic roundabout system was introduced in 1926. Note the statues of Prime Ministers

Churchill, Canning, Derby, Disraeli, Peel, and Palmerston, as well as one of Abraham Lincoln, which is reminiscent of the Saint-Gaudens statue in Chicago's Grant Park.

Rose Mills, Tansy's sister, explained that she owed her life to Bobbie Fieldfare, "She pulled me out from under the hooves of a police horse in Parliament Square." (*Sister Beneath the Sheet* by Gillian Linscott)

Cross Parliament Street east to New Palace Yard and Westminster Hall, the oldest remaining part of the Palace of Westminster. This is where the Royal Courts sat until the nineteenth century. It was built by William Rufus, the Conqueror's son; Richard II added the glorious hammerbeam roof. A massive statue of Oliver Cromwell, booted and spurred, stands outside, seemingly guarding Parliament.

A number of historical trials were held in Westminster Hall, including those of Edward II, Richard II, Guy Fawkes, and Sir Thomas More. In recent years, terrorist threats have closed the hall to tours. Perhaps the present easement in tensions will see a change in that policy.

Beyond Westminster Hall, continue south along St. Margaret's Street to St. Stephen's Porch. This is the public entrance to the Houses of Parliament. You can join the queue for a seat in the Public Gallery of the House of Commons or the Strangers' Gallery of the House of Lords.

The House of Commons is to the north. It was rebuilt after being destroyed by bombs during World War II. The House of Lords is to the south. Beyond it are the Royal Gallery, the Sovereign's Robing Room, and the Royal Entrance under Victoria Tower. (Victoria Tower, at 336 feet, is the world's highest square stone tower.) The entire group of buildings making up the Houses of Parliament were rebuilt after a fire in the Victorian era. They represent the neo-Gothic imaginations of Sir Charles Barry and Augustus Pugin.

As an MP (Member of Parliament), Antonia Fraser's Tom Amyas spent his evenings at the House of Commons, where Jemima Shore sent him unsigned notes congratulating him on a telling speech or arranged to later meet him at their favorite little trattoria "behind Victoria."

The Wimseys came to the House of Commons to meet with Sir Impey Biggs, who had defended the then Harriet Vane. They wished to engage him for Crutchley's defense in Dorothy L. Sayers's *Busman's Honeymoon.*

In Agatha Christie's *The Secret of Chimneys,* the Honorable George Lomax declared that "St. Stephen's is ruined, absolutely ruined. . .by women in politics."

There is a Members' Terrace on the river; it is mentioned in Sayers's *Murder Must Advertise.* The office boy, Ginger Joe, while checking alibis for Lord Peter, discovered that Mr. Vibart's alibi was that he was "at Westminster making a sketch of the Terrace of the House of Commons for Farley's Footwear."

The House of Lords also has its moments in crime fiction. In Sarah Caudwell's *Thus Was Adonis Murdered,* Timothy Shepherd had a case on the Companies Act coming up in the House of Lords and was weeks behind in his paperwork.

One of the House of Lords' more impressive appearances occurs in Dorothy L. Sayers's *Clouds of Witness.* The Duke of Denver, a peer of the realm, was tried for the murder of Denis Cathcart. The Royal Gallery was packed, while the witnesses were held in the Royal (Sovereign's) Robing Room, and the Garter-King-of-Arms tried to make 300 or so sheepish peers stay in line in order of rank.

Outside the Houses of Parliament, cross to the Jewel Tower, a small stone tower set in a tiny moat. Part of the old Palace of Westminster, it was built by Edward III to hold his royal plate and jewelry.

Now turn right and retrace your steps toward Parliament Square, where, after the Duke of Denver was acquitted, the crowd began to stir. When he appeared, a bullet crashed through the window of the Denver limousine. A bearded man was chased by the crowd to Westminster Bridge where he was struck by a taxi and killed.

Much later, after all the excitement had died down, Inspector Sugg came upon a cabbie seeming to argue with the statue of Lord Palmerston. A closer look revealed that Palmerston was sharing his pedestal with a gentleman in evening dress. It was Lord Peter Wimsey, who, together with Charles Parker and

Freddy Arbuthnot, had been celebrating the acquittal of the Duke. Sugg saw them all safely stowed in cabs just as the members of the House of Commons came out after a late-night sitting.

This completes the Westminster walk. Cross Bridge Street to Westminster Underground Station.

10

BROMPTON/ HYDE PARK WALK

BACKGROUND

Brompton, early called "Broom Farm," was first recorded in 1294. It was an outlying village of Kensington on its southern boundary. Also called Knightsbridge, it lies directly south of Hyde Park.

Early in its history, Brompton (Knightsbridge) served as the Knights Bridge over the Westbourne, another London stream that runs into the Thames. Before going off to war, the knights who owed service to the Bishop of London, rode across the bridge to his palace at Fulham for a blessing. In later years, Queen Caroline used the waters of the Westbourne to create the Serpentine, or the Long Water, in Kensington Gardens.

Today Brompton is known for its shops, especially Harrods, and its museums.

Harrods is one of the world's largest stores. It was founded in 1849 by Henry Charles Harrod, a wholesale tea merchant from Eastcheap. Today it is renowned for its selection of merchandise and for its unique food halls.

The area museums were built on land purchased with the proceeds from the Great Exhibition of 1851. The Exhibition was organized by Prince Albert, Queen Victoria's husband. The main building was the Crystal Palace, a glass and iron exhibition hall designed by Sir Joseph Paxton. The Crystal Palace was later moved to Sydenham and, in 1936, was destroyed by fire.

The second part of the walk takes us to Hyde Park, the largest park in London. Together with the adjoining Kensington Gardens, it covers over 630 acres. Queen Victoria was born in the Royal Palace of Kensington located here. Like St. James's Park and Green Park to the east and Regent's Park to the north, Hyde Park was originally part of the monastery land seized by Henry VIII for his own use.

The name Hyde came from the Saxon word "hide," a unit of land measurement.

Henry's daughter, Elizabeth I, reviewed her troops in Hyde Park. In 1637, under Charles I, it was opened to the public. During the Civil Wars, Parliament fortified Hyde Park. Under the later Stuarts, after the failure of the Commonwealth and the return of Charles II, Hyde Park became society's favorite riding place, as well as a haunt of highwaymen and a site for duels.

Hyde Park is London's beach in summer and its skating rink in winter; but, above all else, Hyde Park is the place Londoners go to walk.

LENGTH OF WALK: 3 miles

See the maps on pages 188 and 196 for the boundaries of this walk and page 263–65 for a list of the authors, books, and detectives mentioned.

PLACES OF INTEREST

Albert Memorial, Kensington Gardens (near the site of the Crystal Palace).

Geological Museum, Exhibition Road. Extensive rock collection, including moon rock.

Harrods, Knightsbridge and Brompton Roads. Best-known London department store, where you can buy anything from fresh meat to a riding horse.

Hyde Park/Kensington Gardens.

Marble Arch (Tyburn Hill).

Hyde Park Corner.

Wellington Monument.

Royal Artillery Memorial Wellington Museum (Apsley House). Admission charge.

Kensington Palace, State Apartments.

Formal Gardens, Open year-round; gates close at dusk.

The Round Pond, The Broad Walk, Kensington Gardens.

Statues, Peter Pan and Physical Energy.

Natural History Museum, Cromwell Road. One of the world's finest natural history collections. Admission charge.

The Oratory, Brompton Road. Italian Baroque, known for musical services. Where Cardinal Newman served after he became a Roman Catholic.

Royal Albert Hall, Kensington Gore. Largest concert hall in London.

Science Museum, Exhibition Road. Collection of scientific, engineering, and industrial exhibits. Admission charge.

Victoria and Albert Museum, Cromwell Road. One of the world's greatest museum of the fine and applied arts. Admission charge.

PLACES TO EAT

Harrods, Brompton Road. The store offers a variety of restaurants ranging from inexpensive to luxurious, all licensed. 071-230-1234.

Paxton's Head, 153 Knightsbridge Road. This pub, opposite the Knightsbridge Gate to Hyde Park, commemorates Sir Joseph Paxton. 071-589-6627.

Victoria and Albert Museum, Cromwell Road. Both a licensed restaurant and a self-service cafe are available.

BROMPTON

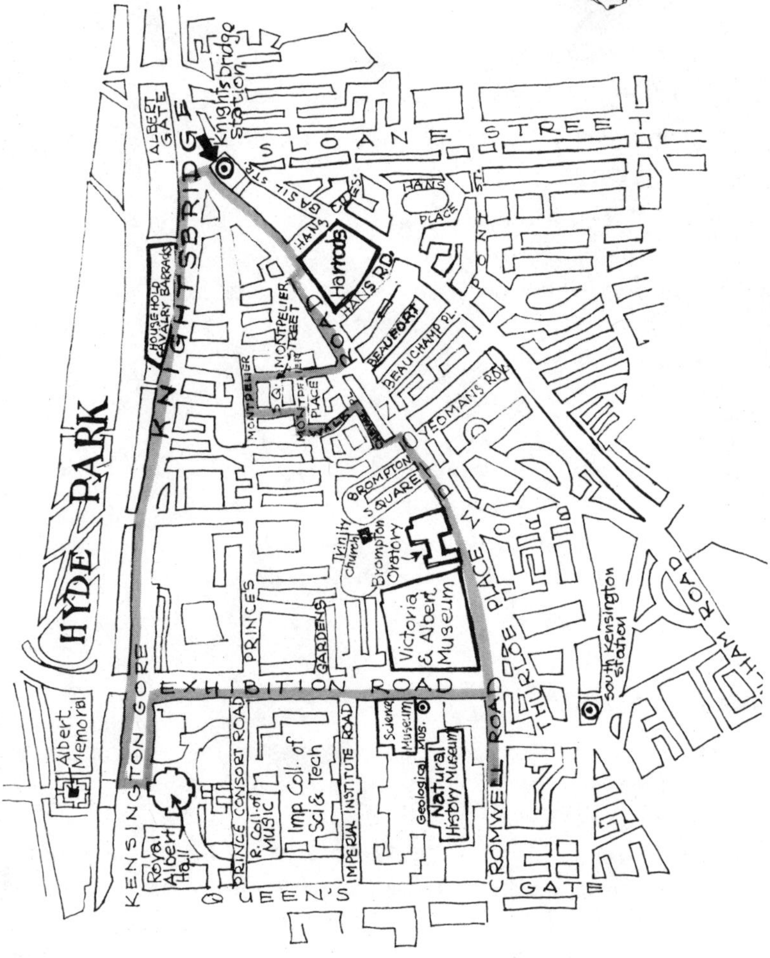
N
E
S
W
HYDE PARK
Albert Memorial
ALBERT GATE
HOUSEHOLD CAVALRY BARRACKS
KNIGHTSBRIDGE
Knightsbridge Station
SLOANE STREET
BASIL ST.
HANS CRES.
HANS
HANS PLACE
PONT ST.
Harrods
HANS RD.
BEAUFORT
BEAUCHAMP PL.
YEOMANS ROW
MONTPELIER
MONTPELIER SQ.
MONTPELIER STREET
MONTPELIER PLACE
WALK
BROMPTON ROAD
BROMPTON SQUARE
Trinity church
Brompton Oratory
PRINCES GARDENS
Victoria & Albert Museum
THURLOE PLACE
South Kensington station
EXHIBITION ROAD
KENSINGTON GORE
Royal Albert Hall
PRINCE CONSORT ROAD
R. Coll. of Music
Imp. Coll. of Sci & Tech
IMPERIAL INSTITUTE ROAD
Science Museum
Geological Mus.
Natural History Museum
CROMWELL ROAD
QUEEN'S GATE

— BROMPTON/HYDE PARK WALK —

Begin your walk by coming out of the Brompton Road exit of the Knightsbridge Underground Station and walking southwest (left) along Brompton Road. There is an exit marked Harrods which also may be used.

Harrods is housed in a block-long Edwardian building made of terra-cotta. The elaborate green awnings over its display windows are outlined with a myriad of tiny lights that give it an almost magical appearance.

The Queen does her Christmas shopping at Harrods. Virtually anything can be purchased there—from school uniforms to a country estate. Of course, there is also a supply of tea towels decorated with the red Harrods bus for the souvenir hunter on a budget.

Harrods is well worth a visit, if not a shopping trip, but be warned that, like London itself, the store is an international mecca for tourists and is jammed year-round, but particularly when it runs its annual sale.

In Antonia Fraser's *A Splash of Red,* artist Kevin John Altlone did a funny, but biting, imitation of a Harrods lady shopper for Jemima Shore.

In order to evade the pursuit of reporters, Anne and Lark planned an escape to Harrods, ". . .the most confusing store I've ever been in." They felt encouraged when "the arrogant gray bulk of Harrods" was within sight from their taxi. (*Skylark* by Sheila Simonson)

In Jessica Mann's *Funeral Sites,* fugitive Rosamund Sholto tried to escape pursuit by using her Harrods credit cards to buy a disguise. She dashed about in a variety of departments until she realized that her trail had already been picked up by her pursuers, who had used her credit cards to trace her. During the chase, Rosamund kept remembering with nostalgia the days when Harrods had been her family store, where she and her sister bought their school uniforms and had their hair cut.

In *The Blackheath Poisonings* by Julian Symons, the box of chocolates that Paul Mortimer used to poison his Uncle George came from Harrods.

In Anne Morice's *The Men in Her Death,* Tessa's friend

Lorraine, who was in London to track down her missing relative, announced that she would not terminate her visit without "setting foot in Harrods."

At the beginning of Brompton Road, just outside Harrods, there used to be a famous horse market called Tattersall's. This was where all the young Regency bucks bought their horseflesh.

In Jane Austen's *Persuasion*, Sir Walter Eliot tried to give consequence to his ungrateful heir by taking him to Tattersall's; and, in the Regency mystery *Regency Buck* by Georgette Heyer, Lord Worth took his spirited ward, Judith Tavener, to Tattersall's to buy a matched pair. She later incurred his anger when she drove the team in a race to Brighton against her brother.

Leave Harrods by the Brompton Road exit on the north side of the store. Cross Brompton Road, turn left, and walk along the north side of Brompton Road. Despite its heavy traffic, Brompton Road is wide and tree-lined, with a fascinating number of specialty shops.

No. 70 Brompton Road is the headquarters of the Independent Television Commission.

Ngaio Marsh favored this general area. She lived at several different area addresses herself and placed many of her characters here as well.

After crossing Knightsbridge Gate and Lancelot Place, you will come to Montpelier Street. Turn right and follow Montpelier Street past Montpelier Place into Montpelier Square. To the west is Montpelier Terrace, which runs into Montpelier Walk.

Walk around Montpelier Square, a pretty private garden. Ngaio Marsh lived in Montpelier Walk during one of her periodic stays in England. She said that her house "[was] on the sunny side of the street, looking towards the dome of the [Brompton] Oratory." She furnished her home with secondhand goods from Fulham Road and enjoyed Montpelier Square's "decorous pub," the Prince of Wales.

The Montpeliers, as we might call them, all contain nicely kept, small terrace houses with tiny balconies and delicate ironwork railings. They were built in the 1830s.

There are also antique shops filled with Victoriana and, in

Montpelier Street there are the Bonham auction rooms with very good buys in pictures and furniture. These are interesting places to investigate if you are a reader of Jonathan Gash's Lovejoy series.

This little enclave must have been the model for the delightful group of streets, mews, and squares that Marsh called "the Capricorns" in *Black As He's Painted.* In that mystery, a tiny terrace house at 1 Capricorn Walk was impulsively purchased by Mr. Whipplestone, a retired Foreign Office official. One bright morning he left his dark and boring flat, and after a ten-minute walk across Hyde Park, he came through "Baronsgate" into Brompton.

Once in Brompton, Whipplestone followed a small cat called Lucy Lockett into a pleasing street that Marsh described as "narrow, orderly, sunny, with a view, to the left, of tree-tops and the dome of the Baronsgate basilica [Brompton Oratory]." The houses were small, well-kept Georgian and Victorian residences with iron railings and at one corner there was a pub, the Sun in Splendour.

Marsh's fictional Capricorn Place led into Capricorn Square, where there was a tiny grocery store, the Napoli, and the sinister Piggy Potterie, where two fat African emigres manufactured pottery pigs and ceramic fish. Lucy Lockett liked to steal the fish and bring them home.

The Capricorns were just "around the corner" from the Ng'ombwana Embassy in Palace Park Gardens, probably the Princes' Gardens on Exhibition Road, north of the Victoria and Albert Museum. (It can be reached from Montpelier Square through a series of mews and lanes.) "The Boomer," Superintendent Alleyn's prep school pal, who was the Ng'ombwana head of state, was staying at the embassy when the murder was committed.

After walking around Montpelier Square, take Montpelier Walk south to Cheval Place. Turn right on Cheval Place and follow it as it turns south again to Brompton Road. Yeoman's Row is just west of Beauchamp Place, on the south side of Brompton Road. It has some nice red-brick, late-Georgian houses.

In Marsh's *Death in Ecstasy,* Jenny Jenkins had a flat on Yeoman's Row at No. 99. Jenny was the girlfriend of drug user Maurice Pringle, and both were initiates of the House of the Sacred Flame and later suspected of murder.

In the 1930s, Ngaio Marsh and her friend "Charlot Lamprey" opened a very successful gift shop on Brompton Road. Unfortunately, when they moved to larger quarters in Beauchamp Place, the shop failed.

In Marsh's *A Surfeit of Lampreys,* the fictional Lampreys also moved to a duplex flat on Beauchamp Place to "economize."

Continue walking on the north side of Brompton Road to Brompton Square. It is a long, narrow, half-circle with elegantly kept houses and the Brompton Oratory looming up next door. Officially, the Oratory is the London Oratory of St. Philip Neri; the Order was brought to England and moved to Brompton by Cardinal Newman in 1854. The landmark dome is 200 feet high. The Oratory itself is built in an ornately Italian Baroque style. It is well known for the choral music performed there.

In *Behold, Here's Poison* by Georgette Heyer, the widow, Mrs. Matthews, reported to her bereaved family that, finding herself in Knightsbridge (shopping), she slipped into the oratory for a few moments. "There was something in the whole atmosphere of the place which I can hardly describe," she gushed. Her matter-of-fact sister-in-law doubtfully suggested that it must have been the incense.

Across the Brompton Road from the Oratory stands the Hotel Rembrandt. Ngaio Marsh lived there one winter while getting ready to help run the gift shop with Charlot Lamprey. Weat of the oratory, Brompton Road becomes Cromwell Road. Here the impressive Victorian-Gothic Victoria and Albert Museum stretches its impressive length along Cromwell to Exhibition Road. An extraordinary collection of English furniture, costumes, and much more is housed in this enormous museum. At any given time, only a portion of the collection is on view.

Take time to go inside. The domed lobby is done in cream and black marble. It is not uncommon to feel time rushing backward and find the Victorian age seeming to encompass you.

In Josephine Tey's *The Daughter of Time,* Marta Hallard, Inspector Grant's actress friend, compelled a V&A curator called James to accompany her to a print shop to find portraits of famous criminals from history. She thought that they would amuse the hospitalized Grant.

In *Death and the Oxford Box* by Veronica Stallwood, Rose was determined to get the box back from Theo before Granny came to Oxford. She had read about the nineteenth-century mourning objects at the V&A exhibit, *The Art of Death.*

Leaving the Victoria and Albert turn right into Exhibition Road. This area is really "museum row," considering the Victoria and Albert which you have just left; beyond, fronting on Cromwell Road is the Natural History Museum; and beyond it, the Royal College of Art.

In *Murder Must Advertise* by Dorothy L. Sayers, the police found reporter Hector Puncheon unconscious on the second floor of the Natural History Museum. The police had been following Puncheon, who, in turn, had been following the man in evening dress who had given him drugs in a Covent Garden pub. Unfortunately for Puncheon, the police had spent too long looking at birds on the first floor. (These birds are found in a gallery to the left of the main entrance.)

In *Skylark* by Sheila Simonson, Lark jogged across Cromwell Road to the Natural History Museum.

The Geological Museum and, behind it, the Science Museum are on Exhibition Road the route this walk will follow.

In Dick Francis's *Odds Against,* Sid Halley's father-in-law borrowed a special rock collection from the Geological Museum in order to entrap a racecourse criminal.

Continue along Exhibition Road past the Imperial College of Science and Technology and the Royal College of Music.

Elspeth rang Peter Proctor to tell him that No. 35 Exhibition Road had been listed for nearly twenty-five years as the number for Forbes, F. in *A Scandal in Belgravia* by Robert Barnard.

Cross Prince Consort Road and continue on Exhibition Road to Kensington Gore where you will turn left. Walk the short distance along Kensington Gore to Royal Albert Hall, a great oval auditorium built facing Hyde Park and the Albert Memorial.

In G. K. Chesterton's *The Man Who Was Thursday,* Sunday, on his wild ride from Leicester Square, flew past the Royal Albert Hall riding the elephant he had stolen from the zoo.

In Evelyn Anthony's *Avenue of the Dead,* an internationally known pacifist was assassinated at a mass meeting in Albert Hall.

In *Death in the Stocks,* Georgette Heyer sent the young artist, Kenneth Vereker, to a charity ball at Albert Hall on the night his brother Roger was murdered in his flat in Kensington Gore.

Albert Hall is best known for the concerts and recitals held there. In Baroness Orczy's *Lady Molly of Scotland Yard,* Elizabeth Lowenthal took pride in her performances there.

The Albert Memorial is across the street from the Royal Albert Hall. The Memorial stands at the border between Hyde Park and Kensington Gardens on the spot where the Crystal Palace once stood. (As a tiny child, when his family lived on Campden Hill just west of Kensington Gardens, G. K. Chesterton could see the fairy glitter of the Crystal Palace in the distance.)

The Albert Memorial, which at present is undergoing restoration, is a large Victorian Gothic edifice designed by Sir Gilbert Scott. It presents a seated statue of Prince Albert beneath an arched cathedral roof. The Prince Consort, holding a catalogue of the Exhibition, sits facing south, as if blessing the vast array of museums that the Exhibition spawned.

Although Kensington Gardens, located behind and to the left of the memorial, is associated in most peoples' minds with children and their nannies, it does appear in a number of crime novels.

In P. D. James's *Innocent Blood,* the malicious young aristocrat, Gabriel Lomas, told Philippa Palfrey that he became addicted to gossip during childhood afternoons spent in Kensington Gardens about the Round Pond, listening to nannies chat.

In an attempt to work out her frustration, Willow King found herself in Kensington Gardens at the end of a long walk across Hyde Park. (*Poison Flowers* by Natasha Cooper)

After bearding the arch traitor himself in his Carlton Terrace

House, Tuppence Cowley walked all the way across Hyde Park and into Kensington Gardens.

In *Black As He's Painted* by Ngaio Marsh, Superintendent Alleyn's friend Boomer wanted to go look at Peter Pan in Kensington Gardens.

The statue of Peter Pan by Sir George Frampton is located near the Long Water. To the south is *Physical Energy,* a rampaging bronze horse by G. F. Watts. (Watts also did the murals for the rebuilt Houses of Parliament.)

The statue was used as secret rendezvous by the members of the terrorist organization Magma in Geoffrey Household's *Hostage: London.*

Comtemplation of the Albert Memorial and Kensington Gardens concluded, turn back the way you came and at Exhibition Road, go to the right on Kensington Gore, which becomes Kensington Road, which becomes Knightsbridge. This is the southern boundary of Hyde Park.

Lark left Kensington Gardens by the main gate and jogged in place while waiting for the lights on Kensington to turn green. (*Skylark* by Sheila Simonson)

Hyde Park was opened to the public in the seventeenth century and soon became quite fashionable, particularly on May Day.

When William III came to live at Kensington Palace he had 300 lamps hung from the branches of the trees along the *route du roi* (from which Rotten Row takes its name) between the palace and St. James's. It was the first road in England to be lit at night. The hope was that the lighting would deter highwaymen who were active in the park. One bizarre incident involved a woman who was killed by a highwayman after she swallowed her wedding ring rather than surrender it to the villain. He was later hanged for his crime. The hanging did not put an end to the robberies. In 1749, Horace Walpole was stopped by two highwaymen who threatened him with a blunderbuss and took his watch and eight guineas.

The park was also known as a dueling ground. It was here, in 1722, that the playwright Richard Brinsley Sheridan fought Captain Matthews over Miss Linley.

Hyde Park

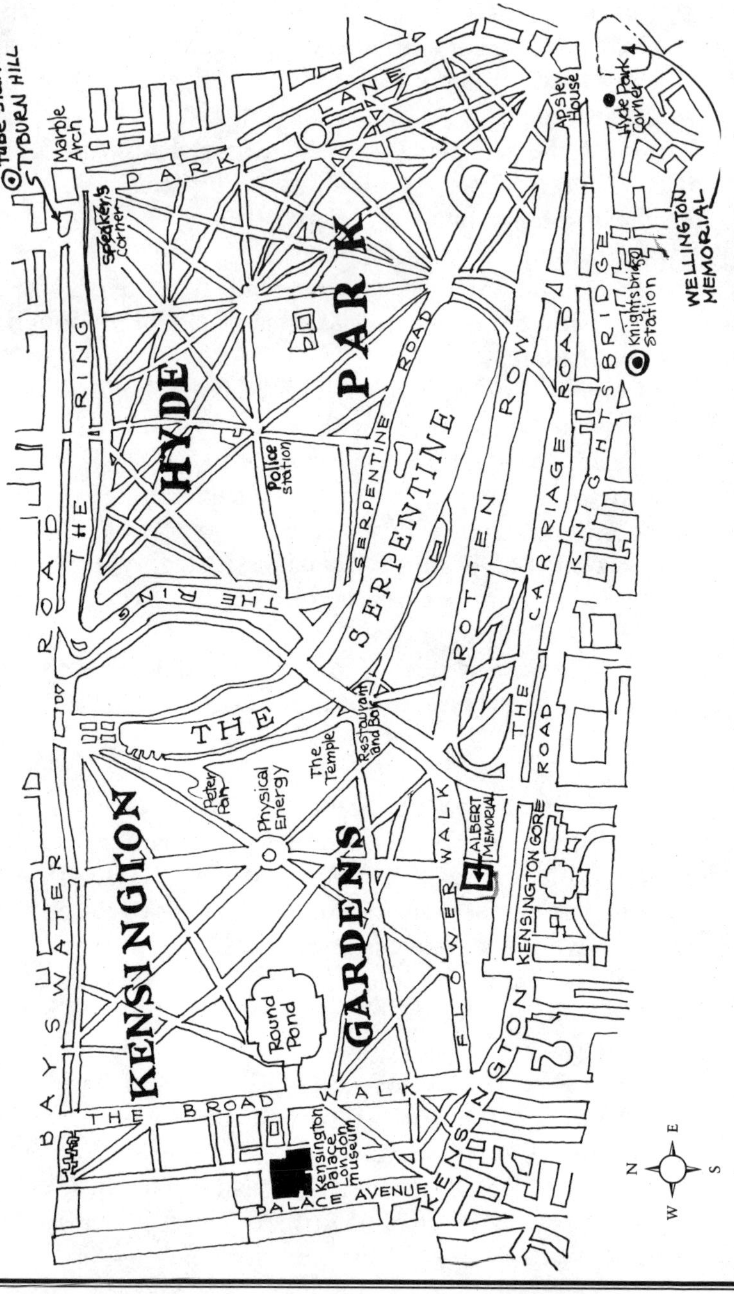
Marble Arch Tube Station
TYBURN HILL
Marble Arch
Speaker's Corner
PARK LANE
HYDE PARK
Police station
Apsley House
Hyde Park Corner
WELLINGTON MEMORIAL
Knightsbridge station
KNIGHTSBRIDGE
THE CARRIAGE ROAD
ROTTEN ROW
THE SERPENTINE
SERPENTINE ROAD
THE RING
BAYSWATER ROAD
Restaurant and Boat
The Temple
Physical Energy
Peter Pan
KENSINGTON GARDENS
ALBERT MEMORIAL
KENSINGTON GORE
FLOWER WALK
Round Pond
THE BROAD WALK
Kensington Palace London museum
PALACE AVENUE
KENSINGTON ROAD
N
E
S
W

As you walk along Kensington Road, you will very likely see riders on Rotten Row. Horses may still be hired there today, and you can experience a bit of history by joining the other riders in a canter along the famous way.

Ray Marcable, star of the musical comedy *Didn't You Know?*, was photographed riding in Rotten Row in Josephine Tey's *The Man in the Queue*.

In Julian Symons's *A Three Pipe Problem,* Sherlock Holmes enthusiast Sheridan Haynes wondered if Holmes and Watson ever walked in [Hyde] Park. He decided that they must have, and that idea made Haynes feel as if he too were back in the nineteenth century. He strolled toward the Serpentine, where he saw two borzois galloping and a boxer trotting beside a girl. He saw children on horses and felt that England was again the way it had been, gentler and more attractive. Later in the story, however, Haynes was lured into Hyde Park at night by reporters; there he tripped over the body of the actress who played Irene Adler.

In Alan Scholefield's *Threats and Menaces,* Mr. Pargeter told seven-year-old Dory that if he didn't have arthritis, he would take her to Hyde Park. When she saw a heron fly overhead, she remembered that Mr. Pargeter had said that it would be going to the Serpentine in Hyde Park. Later, Dory found Alice asleep on a bench in the park—just beyond the Marlborough Gate.

While he was in London, Spenser, the American private eye in Robert Parker's *The Judas Goat,* jogged daily along the Serpentine.

Willow King, attempting to walk off her sense of frustration, left Chesham Place and walked through Lowndes Square and across Knightsbridge into Hyde Park. Soon she was picking her way across the grass to the Serpentine. As she circled the lake, she was surprised to see that there were still uniformed nannies pushing prams and looking very much as they did in those pictures from before the war. (*Poison Flowers* by Natasha Cooper)

In Agatha Christie's *The Big Four,* Hastings was crossing Hyde Park when he was stopped by Countess Vera Rossakoff in a limousine. The countess leaned out to tell him not to mourn for Poirot (who was playing dead) but to go back to his wife in South America.

In Robert Barnard's *A Scandal in Belgravia,* Laurence Cornwallis took pictures of Andy Frobes and Timothy Wycliffe when they went to Hyde Park to swim in the Serpentine on a Sunday afternoon.

The headless body of Captain, the Honorable Oakley Winthrop RN was found slumped in a gently rocking boat on the Serpentine in Anne Perry's *The Hyde Park Headsman.*

In Regency days, Judith Tavener was taught that ladies who wished to be seen in polite society could promenade—properly chaperoned of course—in Hyde Park between the hours of 5: 00 and 6:00 PM.

Monolakis, the Greek policeman who was visiting don Patrick Grant in Margaret Yorke's *Cast for Death,* informed Grant that he greatly admired Hyde Park.

Kensington Road has become Knightsbridge. In Susan Moody's *Death Takes a Hand,* Cassandra Swann was scheduled to appear in a charity bridge tournament at the Hyde Park Hotel on Knightsbridge.

Continue east past the Hyde Park Barracks, the Knightsbridge Gate, and the Edinburgh Gate. Beyond the Knightsbridge Underground Station is Hyde Park Corner, the official entrance to the park.

Mrs. Jefferies, the sleuth in Emily Brightwell's Victorian mystery series, belonged to the prestigious Hyde Park Literary Circle. (*Mrs. Jeffries on the Ball* by Emily Brightwell)

Hyde Park Corner is the busiest traffic corner in Europe. The corner's official title is Duke of Wellington Place, in honor of the great duke who defeated Napoleon. The monument to Wellington is the Wellington Arch, placed opposite Constitution Hill, which leads to Buckingham Palace. The Wellington Arch is topped by a quadriga, or four-horse chariot, driven by the figure of Peace.

As Roberta Grey and Henry Lamprey were on their way by taxi to the Wutherwood mansion in Mayfair, she looked up and saw "four heroic horses snorting soundlessly against a night sky. (*A Surfeit of Lampreys* by Ngaio Marsh)

The headless body of a bus conductor was discovered in an

abandoned jig that was holding up Hyde Park Corner traffic in Anne Perry's *The Hyde Park Headsman.*

On the north side of Hyde Park Corner is Apsley House, No. 1, London, which was Wellington's home. It is now a museum. On an island across the roadway, you can see a bronze statue of Wellington riding his favorite horse, Copenhagen, who at his death was buried with full military honors.

In Georgette Heyer's *An Infamous Army,* Judith Tavener (now Lady Worth) flirted with the Duke of Wellington at the great Brussells ball before Waterloo.

Take the underpass (subway) to reach Park Lane. Walk north on Park Lane along Hyde Park to Speaker's Corner. There you can climb up on a soap box and speak on any subject that strikes your fancy.

At the intersection of Park Lane and Oxford Street is the Marble Arch. It was designed by John Nash based upon the Arch of Constantine in Rome. It was erected in 1827 in front of Buckingham Palace. According to some, it was too narrow for the State Coach, but that is disputed. Anyway, it was, for whatever reason, moved to the northeast corner of Hyde Park in 1851 and islanded in 1908.

In *The Case of William Smith* by Patricia Wentworth, Katherine Eversley had her taxi drop her at the Marble Arch tube station so that no one could figure out where she lived.

The infamous Tyburn, London's principal place of execution from 1388 until 1783, was located west of Marble Arch. The gallows were built in the shape of a triangle and as many as fifteen men, women, and children could be hanged at a time. Executions took place every six weeks and were a public event. An estimated 20,000 spectators witnessed the hanging of highwayman Jack Shepherd in 1724.

Today a triangular memorial stone in the traffic island at the junction of Edgware and Bayswater Roads marks the approximate site of the gallows.

The executions were quite grisly. The prisoners were brought from Newgate Prison and the Tower and were hanged and sometimes drawn and quartered. Their bodies were then displayed at the gates of London as a warning to others.

John Creasey's *The Masters of Bow Street,* opens with a hanging at Tyburn which is being watched by a small boy.

Dr. Samuel Johnson deplored the end of these public executions, because they helped rid London of the footpads and highwaymen and kept up the spirits of the hanged!

This ends the walk; so, like Wentworth's Miss Eversley, go through the underpass to the Marble Arch Underground Station.

11

CHELSEA WALK

BACKGROUND

Chelsea, on the north bank of the Thames south of Hyde Park, was first mentioned when Offa, King of the Mercians, held a Synod there in 787 AD.

During the Middle Ages there were also various mentions of Chelsea, but it did not come into its own until 1520, when Sir Thomas More, who was Henry III's chancellor, built his country house there.

Chelsea soon became known as a "Village of Palaces." Henry VIII, the Duke of Norfolk, and the Earl of Shrewsbury all had splendid houses there.

Elizabeth I lived in Chelsea as a child.

Many writers and artists, including Swift, Addison, Carlyle, Whistler, and Sargent, made their homes in Chelsea. It became renowned as a gathering place for intellectuals.

In more recent times, Chelsea has been called London's Bohemia, reflecting the continuing reputation as a home for artists, actors, and writers. The artsy Chelsea is the one you generally find in classic crime stories.

In the 1930s, Sinister, the villain in Margery Allingham's *Mystery Mile* explained to his captive, Albert Campion, that he (Sinister) went where he liked and lived as he chose. He had a villa with a hanging garden on the Bosphorus, and the most delightful Queen Anne house in Chelsea, where he had moved from Mayfair when the fashion changed.

Agatha Christie, who collected houses the way other people collect her books, lived in Creswell Place in a small mews flat, and then, in 1948, she came to live off the King's Road in Swan Court.

The area has continued to move "up-scale." In the 1960s King's Road became the center for swingers. Today it is noted as the headquarters for the Sloane Rangers: Young, rich, assured, and bored, they include in their ranks the former Diana Spencer.

Chelsea is also one of London's most fashionable neighborhoods. John Le Carre's Smiley lived on Bayswater Street off King's Road with his aristocratic wife, Lady Ann.

LENGTH OF WALK: 5 miles

See the map on page 204 for the boundaries of this walk and pages 265–66 for a list of the authors, books, and detectives mentioned.

PLACES OF INTEREST

Royal Hospital, Royal Hospital Road. Military museum, chapel, great hall, and grounds are open to the public.

Chelsea Flower Show, Royal Hospital Grounds. Officially, the May Flower Show of the Royal Horticultural Society.

Chelsea Old Church (All Saints), Cheyne Walk.

Chelsea Physic Garden, Swan Walk. The second-oldest physic garden in the country.

PLACES TO EAT

Chelsea Potter, 119 King's Road. This pub retains some of its traditional Victorian decor and is hailed as "a trendy meeting place." 071-352-9479.

King's Head & Eight Bells, 50 Cheyne Walk. This pub is over 400 years old. 071-352-9157.

Front Page, 35 Old Church Street. This is the place for those who want a pub with a "club-room" atmosphere. 071-352-2908.

CHELSEA WALK

Begin this walk at the Sloane Square Underground Station, which was first opened in 1868. The waters of the River Westbourne, which run from the Serpentine to the Thames, are piped over the station.

When you leave the underground, you will find yourself in Sloane Square. It is named for the eighteenth-century Lord of the Manor, Sir Hans Sloane, whose art, antiquities, and natural history collections served as the nucleus for the founding of the British Museum.

On the east side of the square, next to the station on the right, is the Royal Court Theatre. It is known for having produced plays by the likes of Arthur Wing Pinero, George Bernard Shaw, Somerset Maugham, John Galsworthy, and John Osborne.

A memorial to the dead in both world wars stands in the center of the square.

On the west side of Sloane Square is Peter Jones Department Store. It was founded in 1877 by a young Welshman. The present building was built in 1936.

In *Jerusalem Inn* by Martha Grimes, Superintendent Jury admired an elegant Christmas display of the Three Wise Men at Peter Jones.

In *A Common Death* by Natasha Cooper, Willow King left the flat in Chapham and traveled to Sloane Square, changing identities in transit. Later, after her confrontation with Eustace Gripper, Willow retreated to the coffee shop on the fourth floor of Peter Jones to nurse her wounds.

On the underground train, Lark saw a woman carrying shopping bags from Harrods and Peter Jones. When the train pulled into Sloane Square Station, Ann and Lark's friend Milos was stabbed by a ferret-faced man in a brown pinstripe suit.

CHELSEA

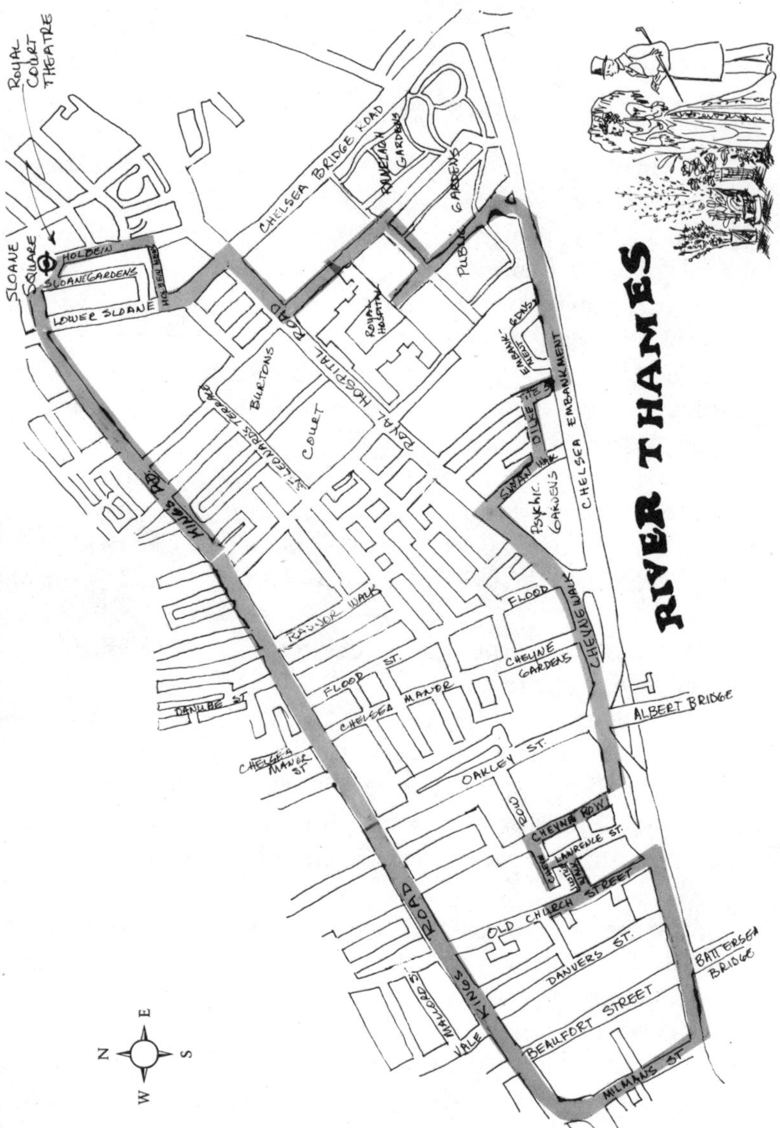

ROYAL COURT THEATRE
SLOANE SQUARE
HOLBEIN
SLOANE GARDENS
LOWER SLOANE
CHELSEA BRIDGE ROAD
RANELAGH GARDENS
PUBLIC GARDENS
ROYAL HOSPITAL
ROYAL HOSPITAL ROAD
BURTONS COURT
ST LEONARDS TERRACE
KINGS RD.
EMBANK GDNS
DILKE
SWAN WALK
CHELSEA EMBANKMENT
PSYCHIC GARDENS
RIVER THAMES
RADNOR WALK
FLOOD
FLOOD ST.
CHEYNE GARDENS
CHEYNE WALK
DANUBE ST
CHELSEA MANOR
CHELSEA MANOR ST
ALBERT BRIDGE
OAKLEY ST.
ROAD
CHEYNE ROW
LAWRENCE ST.
OLD CHURCH STREET
DANVERS ST.
KINGS ROAD
MALLORD ST
VALE
BEAUFORT STREET
BATTERSEA BRIDGE
MILMANS ST
N
E
S
W

The man squeezed out as the doors opened and was lost in the crowd. (*Skylark* by Sheila Simonson)

In *Bejeweled Death* by Marian Babson, Stacey, hoping to recover her missing tiara, set out for Sloane Square trying to locate Alistair Lord and the two young children.

Leave the station area and turn to your left. Descend along Sloane Gardens to Holbein Place; turn left and follow Holbein Place to Graham Terrace. Willow King was walking toward Graham Terrace, hoping to call on Mrs. Gripper, when she was confronted by a very angry Eustace Gripper who abused her verbally. (*A Common Death* by Natasha Cooper)

Continue on Holbein Place past Graham Terrace, turn right into Holbein Mews, and follow it to Lower Sloane Street, where you will turn left.

Stacey found a Birnbaum in the telephone directory with an address in Lower Sloane Street, but there was no military rank given. (*Bejewelled Death* by Marian Babson)

Follow Lower Sloane Street to Royal Hospital Road. Turn right into Royal Hospital Road. On the left you will see the Old Burial Ground. Dr. Charles Burney, father of novelist Fanny Burney and member of Dr. Johnson's literary circle, is buried here.

At Franklin's Row, turn left to enter the Royal Hospital Grounds. The Royal Hospital was founded by Charles II and designed by Christopher Wren as a home for old soldiers (often referred to as the Chelsea Pensioners). It is the most famous of Chelsea's monuments. It was begun in 1682 and is still in business.

At the second gate, turn right into Light Horse Court and go straight ahead through the arch leading into the colonnade. Go straight ahead into the middle of the central court (Figure Court). About 400 pensioners live here. The pensioners are famous for their knee-length coats of scarlet in summer and navy blue in winter.

The bronze statue by Grinling Gibbons in the center of the court depicts Charles II in the dress of a Roman Emperor. Above the colonnade there is an inscription in Latin that recounts that the hospital is for the support and relief of maimed and superannuated soldiers and that it was founded by Charles II, enlarged by James II, and completed, in 1692, by William III.

In the opposite direction, there is a good view across the hospital grounds to the old Battersea Power Station on the south bank of the River Thames. With its four white towers sticking up in the air like legs, it resembles a cow that has flipped onto its back. That is why it is often fondly referred to as "the old dead cow." No longer in use, the power station is being converted into a leisure center. (In Patricia Moyes's *Who Is Simon Warwick?*, Inspector Reynolds tracked a murder suspect by seeking signatures on a petition to preserve the power station.)

In front of the flagpole turn left along the terrace and pass through an arch into Light Horse Court. Turn right out of the Court and go through the gate ahead. Another gate immediately on the left leads into Ranelagh Gardens.

Ranelagh was the site of the Great Rotunda (demolished in 1805), the late eighteenth century's favorite pleasure garden. People would promenade around and around the circular area below tiers of boxes where others sat eating, drinking, listening to an orchestra, and watching. Dr. Johnson loved it, and Horace Walpole, the father of the Gothic novel, went there daily.

In *The Expedition of Humphrey Clinker* by Tobias Smollett, Matthew Bramble and his family visited Ranelagh.

In *The Secret of Chimneys* by Agatha Christie, the socialite Virginia Revel played tennis in Ranelagh Gardens.

Walk on past the entrance to Ranelagh Gardens and turn right in front of the hospital into the public park area. This is where the Chelsea Flower Show is held each year in May.

Turn left down the central walk past the Chillianwallah Memorial. (The Battle of Chillianwallah in 1849 was the hardest battle ever fought by the British in India—nearly 3,000 British troops were killed or wounded.)

In the Victorian whodunit *Murder at Plum's* by Amy Meyers, Colonel M. Worthington would time his arrival at Plum's for precisely seven o'clock. He had done so for fifteen years, since his retirement from the 24th Foot. To anyone unfortunate enough to have to listen, he would explain "That's how we did things at Chillianwallah." He seldom mentioned anything else, only the glorious doings of the 24th Foot and the perils of Chillianwallah.

Leave the park and turn right onto the Chelsea Embankment. Built in 1872, it extends over a mile from Chelsea Bridge to Battersea Bridge. From here you can look out over the river and see the old power station and Chelsea Bridge. Continue on the right along the Embankment, past Embankment Gardens.

In *Behold, a Mystery!* by Joan Smith, Felix Chapman gave Jessica Greenwood his friend's Chelsea Embankment address.

In *Tourists Are for Trapping* by Marian Babson, Penny, the office girl-of-all-work, confesses to her boss, Douglas Perkins, that in the afternoon she often takes his cat, Pandora, down to Embankment Gardens where she can play: "She rides on my shoulder until I tell her she can get down, and then she stays with me. She never runs away. . . ."

Turn right into Tite Street. No. 34 was once the residence of Oscar Wilde. He lived there at the height of his early popularity and was still living there when he was arrested for homosexuality, which was a crime in the nineteenth century. The American-born painter John Singer Sargent had his studio in Tite Street, as did Augustus John.

Tite Street was known for a number of specially built studio houses, among them the Tower House, which seems a likely model for the Chelsea home of Troy and Roderick Alleyn in Ngaio Marsh's novels.

In Marsh's *Black As He's Painted,* this house was described as being in a cul-de-sac with a garden and a detached studio built for a Victorian academician.

Turn left off Tite Street into Dilke Street. No. 7, on the left with a lantern above the door, is the home of the London Sketch Club, an artist's club. It was founded in 1898 by *Punch* cartoonist Phil May.

At the end of Dilke Street turn right into Swan Walk. This street runs along the east side of the Chelsea Physic Garden, established by the Apothocaries Society in 1673. Sir Hans Sloane gave the society the land, with the understanding that 2,000 specimens of plants grown there, well dried and preserved, should be sent yearly to the Royal Society in batches of fifty. The request is still being honored.

Some of the first cotton seed planted in America was exported from the Chelsea Physic Garden in 1732.

This garden was the scene of the crime in Harry Keating's

short story "Mrs. Craggs Gives a Dose of Physic." A Cockney cleaning woman, Mrs. Craggs, saved the life of the curator who had been poisoned by dosing him with lobelia, a common plant from the garden.

Swan Walk brings you again to Royal Hospital Road where you will turn left. Just before the end of the road to your right is Flood Street. This is where former prime minister Margaret Thatcher once lived. Detective Mason, in Lionell Davidson's *The Chelsea Murders,* considered the neighborhood to be an area of troublemakers of all kinds–judges, bankers, and politicians. The houses were "plumply prosperous." There was a "copper" outside the Thatcher house, but that was nothing to note.

Flood Street leads to Flood Walk, the location of Pamela Branch's truly funny mystery *The Wooden Overcoat.*

Flood Street also leads to Swan Court, where Agatha Christie lived at No. 48.

At the end of Royal Hospital Road, as it curves into the Chelsea Embankment, go to the right into Cheyne Walk just before the strip of grass that separates it from the Embankment. Cheyne Walk is a long terrace running along the Chelsea waterfront. Before 1874, when the embankment was built, the river came up to the edge of Cheyne Walk. Walk on the right side of the street, the side with the houses.

Sir Thomas More built a house in Cheyne Walk which may have been the model for his *Utopia.* Later Henry VIII built a palatial manor house there. Elizabeth I also lived there. Like More, the King found Chelsea a convenient place to access by water from Westminster.

The lovely eighteenth-century riverside houses along Cheyne Walk have been occupied over the years by a number of well-known people–from Henry James, author of the chillingly unsettling *The Turn of the Screw,* to poet Hilaire Belloc to T. S. Eliot, author of *Murder in the Cathedral.*

Detective Mason, the "ambitious lad" in *The Chelsea Murders* by Lionel Davidson, decided to have a look down by the river at the site of the third murder. He cut through to Cheyne Walk. "This is the life," he thought, as he strolled past the huge gated mansions pockmarked with plaques indicating their illustrious residents. Detective Mason rattled them off: George Eliot, Rossetti, Swinburne, Whistler—all the lads. Suddenly, he realized that the Chelsea murder victims were ordinary people who shared the initials of these Chelsea greats.

In *Bertie and the Tinman* by Peter Lovesey, the Prince of Wales (Bertie) and his sidekick, Charlie Buckfast, were set upon as they drove to the London house of the Dowager Duchess of Montrose on Cheyne Walk. Both men were thrown into the water. The Prince of Wales managed to swim ashore and appeared soaking wet at the Duchess's home, but Buckfast's body was later picked up in Battersea Reach.

In *The Unpleasantness at the Bellona Club,* Dorothy L. Sayers placed the studio home of potter Marjorie Phelps on the river in Chelsea. Much later, in *Busman's Honeymoon,* the Dowager Duchess took Peter and Harriet to dine with her brother, Paul Delagardie, who lived in Cheyne Walk.

Lord Robert (Bunchy) Gospell lived (and was murdered) at No. 200 Cheyne Walk in Ngaio Marsh's *Death in a White Tie*.

Glamourous leading lady Destiny Meade, who played Shakespeare's Dark Lady for Peregrin Jay in Marsh's *Killer Dolphin,* also lived on Cheyne Walk in an apartment Superintendent Roderick Alleyn found sumptuous to a degree and in maddeningly good taste.

A narrow lane leads off to the right on No. 24 Cheyne Walk. A plaque on the lane's right wall says that Henry VIII's Chelsea Manor House, built in 1536, stood here. It was later the home of Sir Hans Sloane and was demolished in 1753 after Sloane's death. All that survives today are part of the garden along with the mulberry trees said to have been planted by Queen Elizabeth I.

Cheyne Walk merges with the Chelsea Embankment just before Albert Bridge. Continue along past Cheyne Mews, and cross Oakley Street. Take the first turn on the right into Cheyne Row. No. 10 on the right has a plaque to Margaret Damer Dawson, the founder of the women's police force. She was its first chief officer.

No. 24 Cheyne Row was the home of Thomas Carlyle, one of the most influential intellectual figures of the nineteenth century. Carlyle's house is now a National Trust museum.

In *Skylark* by Sheila Simonson, Lark sized up the discreet brick building, tucked opposite a posh terrace of pseudo-Victorian houses, at the high-priced end of the Fulham Road: "Some architect of the Prince Charles school had made up his mind to clone Thomas Carlisle's [sic] neighborhood in Cheyne Walk."

At the end of Cheyne Row turn left into Upper Cheyne Row and then left again into Lawrence Street. On the right, a plaque marks the location of the famous Chelsea Porcelain Works. For almost forty years, until the factory moved to Derby in 1784, porcelain was produced here.

Near the location of the porcelain works was the large house where novelist Tobias Smollett lived for twelve years. He is the author of *The Adventures of Peregrine Pickle, The Expedition of Humphrey Clinker,* and a raft of others.

Further along Lawrence Street on the left, there are two houses, Duke's House and Monmouth House, which share a common porch. It is probably what is left of a large residence called Monmouth House, which stood at the northern end of Lawrence Street. The house belonged to the Duke of Monmouth, Charles II's illegitimate son. The duke was beheaded in 1685 after leading an unsuccessful rebellion against his uncle, James II.

Turn right into Justice Walk and then left into Old Church Street. Old Church Street was Chelsea's main street until 1830 when the King's Road became a public thoroughfare. Until then it had been a private road used exclusively by the royal family as they traveled to and from their country houses.

At the southern end of Old Church Street stands Chelsea Old Church. There are documents to indicate that a Norman church stood on this site in 1157, but the church was not named All Saints until 1290. A monument to Sir Thomas More is in the sanctuary of the church, and his statue stands out front. His first wife's tomb is there, and he planned for it to be his and his second wife's tomb as well. But that was not to be.

After his execution in 1535, his head was buried in Canterbury but no one knows the whereabouts of his body. Also in the More chapel is the badly damaged tomb of the Duchess of Northumberland, matriarch of an illustrious family. She was the mother of Guildford, the husband of the ill-fated Lady Jane Grey, and of Robert Dudley, Earl of Leicester, Elizabeth I's friend and, perhaps, lover. The duchess was the grandmother of the courtier-poet, soldier, and Renaissance man Sir Philip Sidney.

Henry VIII married his third wife, Jane Seymour, in the Old Church in 1536, and Sir Hans Sloane was buried in its churchyard in 1753. An urn beneath a stone canopy marks his grave at the eastern end of the churchyard.

The church was badly damaged by bombs in 1941, and five firewatchers were killed.

Turn right at the church and walk along Cheyne Walk past Roper's Garden. The garden, with the statue called *Awakening,* was created on a bombsite. The land once belonged to Will Roper. It was given to him by his father-in-law, Sir Thomas More.

Cross Danvers Street. The boarded-up building on the right is Crosby Hall. It was part of a medieval wool merchant's house which was brought to this site from the City to save it from demolition. Crosby Hall occupies land that once was Sir Thomas More's garden.

Cross Beaufort Street where More's house, which was demolished in 1740, was located. Continue along Cheyne Walk. Ahead you will see the new residential development built on the former wharves and railway sidings at Lots Road. The site of the third murder in Lionel Davidson's *The Chelsea Murders* was along the river there.

Detective Mason, trying to figure out whether or not Greer's presence in the vicinity of the river fit the time of the murder, remembered that Greer had hailed a taxi at the corner of Beaufort Street. (*The Chelsea Murders* by Lionel Davidson)

Continue along Cheyne Walk. On the right, at No. 93, there is a plaque marking the residence of Mrs. Gaskell. She was a friend and biographer of Charlotte Brontë.

Whistler lived at No. 98 and painted the famous portrait of his mother there. Hilaire Belloc lived at No. 104. Belloc was the brother of crime novelist Mrs. Belloc Lowdes and a close friend of Father Brown's creator, G. K. Chesterton.

Turn right into Milman's Street and follow it through to the King's Road, where you cross the street and turn right onto the King's Road.

The long trek along the King's Road will bring you back to the Sloane Square Underground Station. Along the way there are several more mystery references.

To the left off the King's Road, the Vale leads to Mallord Street where A. A. Milne, creator of Winnie-the-Pooh and author of *The Red House Mystery,* lived, first at No. 11 and later at No. 13.

When his tour bus let him off in the King's Road, Douglas Perkins was glad to see that he was opposite a supermarket, as he had necessary shopping to see to. (*Tourists Are For Trapping* by Marion Babson)

Continue along the King's Road past Chelsea Manor and Danube Street. This will bring you to Jubilee Place to the left. Jubilee Place was the "scene of Miss Manningham-Worsley's exit" in Davidson's *The Chelsea Murders.*

Cross the street and walk past the library on the right-hand side of the street. The library is part of the Old Town Hall. The Chelsea Antiques Fair is held in the Old Town Hall every March and September.

Continue on the King's Road until you come to the Chelsea Potter Pub at Radnor Walk.

In *The Chelsea Murders,* Mooney was getting a beer in the Chelsea Potter. She was there because Frank regularly used the Potters, as it was called. You may decide that the Chelsea Potter is an ideal place for refreshments as you near the end of the walk.

After the Potters, continue past Smith Street to the right. It leads to St. Leonard's Terrace where Bram Stoker, the author of *Dracula,* lived at No. 4 Durham Place.

Continue straight ahead up the King's Road to the Sloane Square Underground Station where this walk ends.

12

BELGRAVIA/ PIMLICO WALK

BACKGROUND

This walk covers the neighborhoods known as Belgravia and Pimlico.

Belgravia takes its name from the small village of Belgrave on the outskirts of Leicester where the Grosvenor family had an estate.

In medieval times Belgravia was known as Five Fields because it was cut into five sections of intersecting footpaths. The area was rife with highwaymen. Here a wooden bridge called the Bloody Bridge crossed the Westbourne. It was so called because of the number of violent robberies that took place there. The area remained a haunt of highwaymen until well into the eighteenth century. Because Five Fields was fairly remote from London, it was also often the setting for duels.

When George III moved to Buckingham House in 1726, a row of "fair houses" was built in what is now Grosvenor Place. The present Belgravia was laid out by the builder Thomas Cubitt in 1825 and became one of the most fashionable neighborhoods in the West End. Cubitt and his successors built simple, terraced houses and garden squares that have worn well, although it is the smaller houses and the mews that are most sought after today. Although the Victorians came to think that Belgravia looked monotonous, with its thousands of shining cream or white stucco or brick houses, it is still a very desirable area. The village-like neighborhoods are extremely quiet during the day. Belgravia is a beautiful part of London for an early morning walk or a late stroll on a long summer evening.

Walking through this neighborhood of very important people, companies, and embassies, you can think about the ironic words of mystery writer C. P. Snow. In his last book, a detective story called *A Coat of Varnish,* Lord Snow insisted that Belgravia's civilization was only skin deep, "a coat of varnish." Snow's real subject was the end of the empire and civilization itself, for which he used Belgravia as the symbol.

Pimlico, Belgravia's neighbor to the south, is a cheaper, shabbier version of Belgravia. It was bombed heavily in World War II (the Germans were aiming at Victoria Station), but its Victorian atmosphere lingers in its rows of identical tall houses with solid, columned porticos. Once cream or white like their neighbors to the north, many have been repainted in rainbow colors that range from dark chocolate to pink and bright yellow. Instead of specialty shops catering to the wealthy, Pimlico has a variety of odd little shops offering an assortment of bargains. There are small cafes of just about every description, and a multitude of bed-and-breakfast hotels that are patronized by the hordes of backpacking tourists who descend on the neighborhood from Victoria Station.

At Pimlico's southern boundary along the Thames, once an area of docks and warehouses, there are blocks of modern high-rise housing that seem quite alien to the essential character of either Pimlico or Belgravia.

The origin of the name Pimlico is not known. It may have come from a long-forgotten local drink, or from the Pamlico Indian tribe that exported timber to England in the seventeenth century, or perhaps it was named for Ben Pimlico, a sixteenth-century publican.

LENGTH OF WALK: 3 miles

See the map on page 216 for the boundaries of this walk and pages 266–67 for a list of the authors, books, and detectives mentioned.

PLACES OF INTEREST

Belgrave Square

Foreign embassies, including, counterclockwise from the northwest corner: Syria, Portugal, Ghana, Austria, Germany, Spain, Saudi Arabia, Trinidad, Turkey, Malaysia, and Mexico.

Eaton Square

St. Peter's Church.

Embassies: Belgium and Bolivia.

Chester Square

St. Michael's Church.

Gerald Road Police Station.

Tate Gallery, Milbank. British painting since 1500, foreign painting, and modern sculpture. Special collections of Constable, Blake, Turner, Pre-Raphaelite. Admission charge for special exhibits.

PLACES TO EAT

Ebury Court Hotel, 26 Ebury Street. An alcoved restaurant can be found in this old-fashioned hotel. There is an English atmosphere with English food—roasts, grills, steak and kidney pie, and sherry trifle. Reservations are needed. 071-730-8147.

Tate Gallery, Milbank. The Tate has two places to eat on its lower ground floor. The restaurant (licensed) has murals by Rex Whistler and is elegant and expensive. Reservations are needed. 071-834-6754. The Refreshment Room (cafeteria) is open 10:30 AM to 5:30 PM.

Duke of Wellington, 63 Eaton Terrace. This cozy neighborhood pub with bookpaneled walls is decorated with brasses and military prints and serves good curry, cottage pie, and quiche, as well as real ale. 071-730-3103.

BELGRAVIA/PIMLICO

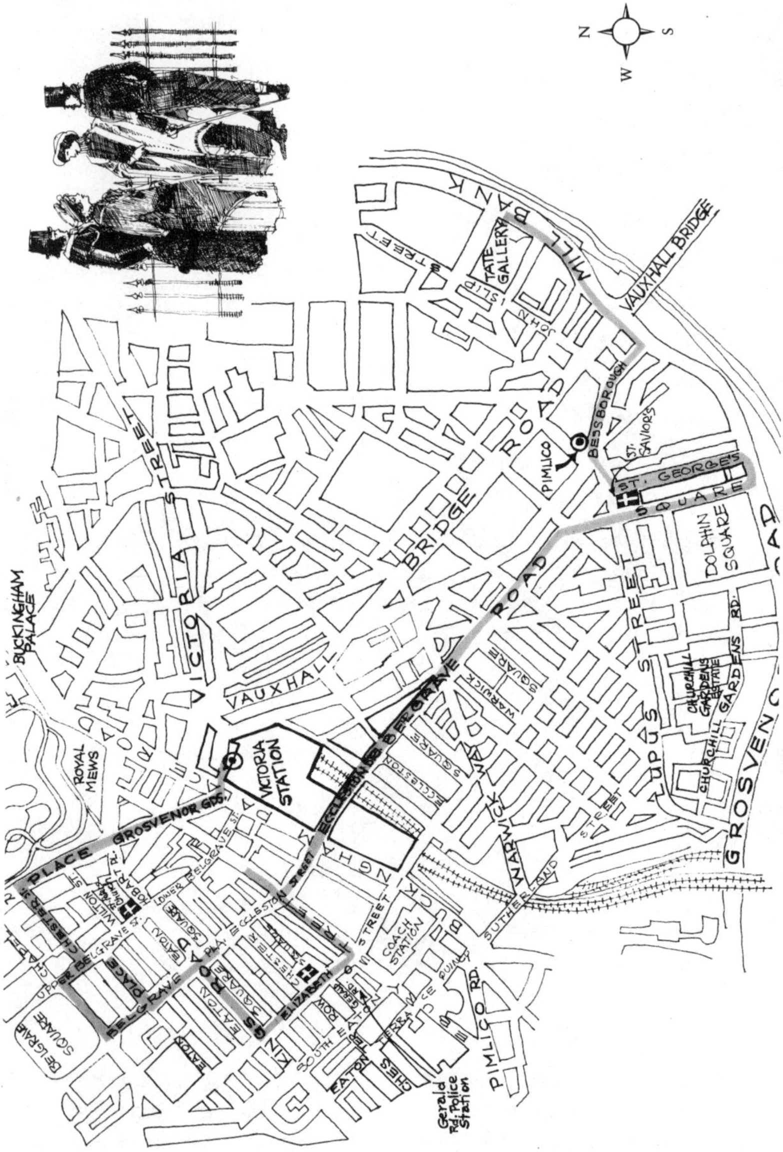

BELGRAVIA/PIMLICO WALK

BELGRAVIA

This residential walk is especially pleasant on a sunny day. Begin by taking the Grosvenor Gardens exit from Victoria Underground Station and turning left to walk along Grosvenor Gardens. You will pass by a tiny, fenced park that contains a mounted statue of Marshal Foch, who led the Allied armies in World War I.

Cross Hobart Place to Grosvenor Place, which stretches all the way along the back wall of Buckingham Palace's extensive grounds. It was inside these grounds that Aidan Mackey set the beginning of his delightful story *Mr. Chesterton Comes to Tea.* It is based on G. K. Chesterton's drawings for the children of literary editor Archibald Marshall. In Mackey's adventure, the king, who was tired of being good and opening public buildings, one night set out in search of adventure. He used a forgotten door to slip out of the palace near Constitution Hill where he caught a hansom cab.

Cross Wilton Street and continue until you reach Chester Street. Turn left and go down Chester to Upper Belgrave Street. You will begin to pass the typically elegant Belgravian terraces of townhouses.

In *A Scandal in Belgravia* by Robert Barnard, Peter Proctor pointed out that the tidy, affluent Belgravia of the 1990s is a far cry from the tattered, down-at-the-heels elegance found there in the 1950s.

Turn right and walk straight into Belgravia Square, an enormous park covering ten acres. It is often called the most notable square in all London.

A century ago, this square, now the home of a variety of foreign embassies whose gaily colored flags will test your international savoir faire, was the home of three dukes, thirteen peers, including baronets, and as many MPs. The surrounding terraces now house a variety of institutions, societies, colleges, and professional associations, and a few remaining private homes.

In Robert Barnard's *A Scandal in Belgravia,* Peter Proctor

hunted out Lady Thorrington's house at No. 49 Belgrave Square.

No. 21 Belgrave Terrace was the residence of Patricia Moyes's fabulously wealthy Lord Charlton in *Who Is Simon Warwick?* The mystery began on a rainy November night when Lord Charlton summoned his solicitor, Ambrose Quince, to tell him to search for Charlton's missing nephew, Simon Warwick.

In Leela Cutter's *Death of the Party,* Julia and Max drove to Belgrave Square in his Jaguar and parked across the street from the Hoggwell house.

Belgrave Square was the location of Marsden House, where, in Ngaio Marsh's *Death in a White Tie,* the debutante ball for Lady Carrados's daughter Bridget was held.

Turn to your left and walk across the southern side of Belgrave Square. Go past the statue of the South American liberator Simon Bolivar at the southwestern corner at Belgrave Place. Turn left and walk down Belgrave Place past Belgrave Mews to Eaton Place.

Upstairs, Downstairs, written by sometime-mystery writer Mollie Hardwick, has an Eaton Place setting.

There are also a number of fictional mystery addresses in Eaton Place, so turn to your left and walk along the square taking a look at the houses there.

In Ngaio Marsh's *A Wreath for Rivera,* No. 3 Duke's Gate, Eaton Place, was the townhouse of eccentric Lord Pastern, who insisted on playing the drums in Breezy Bellair's band and secretly wrote a lovelorn advice column. In contrast to his eccentric manners, the front of his house, with a fanlight and beautifully designed doors, had "an air of reticence." His lordship's band practiced in the dining room beyond the drawing room on the first floor.

In *Cool Repentance* by Antonia Fraser, actress Christabel Herrick took her scandalous young lover, Barry Blagge, to her flat in Eaton Place.

Arnold Vereker, who was murdered in Georgette Heyer's *Death in the Stocks,* had a "consciously opulent" mansion in Eaton Place.

Walk back to Belgrave Place and turn left to walk south toward Eaton Square, a parkway made up of two long, narrow green strips divided by the roaring traffic of the King's Road.

Peter Potter, wondering where the supermarkets were for Belgravia, decided that perhaps they were on the King's Road. (*A Scandal in Belgravia* by Robert Barnard)

At the northeast corner stands the colonnaded front of St. Peter's Eaton Square, scene of many society weddings.

Although most are divided into flats, the houses along Eaton Square remain quite fashionable. In a fussy, feminine drawing room here, Cordelia Gray returned a lost cat and met actress Clarissa Lyle. (*The Skull Beneath the Skin* by P. D. James)

In Anne Perry's *Farriers' Lane,* Inspector Pitt called on Mrs. Liversey in her home at No. 5 Eaton Square.

No. 36 Eaton Square was the home of a rich, upwardly mobile Labor MP, Tom Thirkell, in C. P. Snow's *A Coat of Varnish*.

Wealthy Graham Bendix had his townhouse in Eaton Square in Anthony Berkeley's *The Poisoned Chocolates Case*. It was the murder of Bendix's wife that Roger Sheringham had the Crimes Circle undertake to solve for Scotland Yard.

Eaton Square was also where Lady Nest and Geoffrey Poulton lived in Georgette Heyer's *Duplicate Death*. Lady Nest had been a "Bright Young Thing" in the 1920s.

After dropping Emma at her house, Willow King drove through Eaton Square where she saw lights in the Biggleigh-Clark's second-floor flat. (*Bloody Roses* by Natasha Cooper)

Turn right and walk through Eaton Square along the King's Road. (Farther west, beyond Sloane Square, the King's Road becomes the village "high street" of Chelsea.)

Turn left when you reach Elizabeth Street and walk across the southwestern side of Eaton Square.

In *A Coat of Varnish,* it was between Eaton Square and Chester Square that C. P. Snow placed his imaginary Aylesworth Square, which lay just east of Elizabeth Street. Lord Snow described Aylesworth Square as symbolic of all Belgravia, a part of the "most homogeneous residential district in any capital city in the world and in a quiet and seemly fashion, the most soothing to the eye." Snow wrote that "although the mansions now had basement flats and little domestic help, they were still big and gracious. Built around a fenced garden, they had tiny patio gardens in back, which opened into mews" (just as the houses do in Eaton Square).

Snow's mystery opened on a hot summer night when Humphrey Leigh, a retired civil servant, set out to pay a visit to old Lady Ashbrook, his neighbor in the square. Leigh, a rather Jamesian detached observer of society, thought it ironic that Elizabeth Street, now a posh shopping quarter, was once Eliza Street, where prostitutes worked the river traffic. Snow's Aylesworth Square had its own parish church, much like St. Michael's Church at the corner of Elizabeth Street and Chester Row. Lady Ashbrook's funeral was later held there.

Later on, Leigh and a Jewish-American friend went to a pub between Eaton Square and Buckingham Palace Road. Because the two men were interested in the habits of English natives, they met for a ritual Saturday drink there in the quiet, comfortable surroundings of stained glass and varnished wood. One summer Saturday, a bunch of rowdies stormed in from a cricket match and terrorized everyone until the police got there from the Gerald Road Police Station south off Elizabeth Street. (For atmosphere, drop into the Duke of Wellington on Eaton Terrace, two blocks to your right along King's Road, running parallel to Elizabeth Street.)

Continue along Elizabeth Street past Eaton Mews to Chester Row. Charles Dickens lived at 1 Chester Row in 1846, the year that he founded and began to edit the *Daily News*.

Chester Row leads to your left into Chester Square. It was in this vicinity that the House of the Sacred Flame was found in Ngaio Marsh's *Death in Ecstasy*. It stood off Chester Terrace at the end of a cul-de-sac called Knocklatcher's Row. In the March tradition, both locations were fictional.

Continue to walk south along Elizabeth Street past Gerald Row with its police station, St. Michael's Church, and Ebury Mews, until you come to Ebury Street. Turn left on Ebury Street and walk northeast until you have crossed Eccleston

Street. The Ebury Court Hotel is in the middle of the next block on the north side of the street.

There are a number of cafes and restaurants around here, but the Ebury Court Hotel at 26 Ebury Street is small and cozy in a very English way, and has a good restaurant serving excellent British food. If you didn't know that she stayed at Bertram's Hotel in Mayfair, you would expect to see Agatha Christie's Miss Marple sitting in the lounge.

The Ebury Court has both the atmosphere and geography to have appeared in two Father Brown stories in G. K. Chesterton's *The Innocence of Father Brown.* It could be the place in "The Blue Cross" where Father Brown and the French master thief Flambeau (disguised as another Roman Catholic priest) had breakfast, and Father Brown put salt in the sugar and threw coffee at the wall. The two then caught a bus that they took all the way north to Hampstead Heath, pursued by the French detective, Valentin.

The Ebury Court Hotel could also be Chesterton's Vernon Hotel, situated at the corner of the square in Belgravia, where the annual dinner of the exclusive Twelve True Fishermen men's club was held. In the story "The Queer Feet," Father Brown was called to administer extreme unction to a dying waiter and stopped Flambeau from stealing the club's silver fish service. Father Brown realized someone wearing evening clothes was pretending to be both a waiter and a gentleman. When Father Brown explained the trick to the club members, they hastily decided to wear green evening clothes to prevent such an embarrassing episode from happening again.

The bandleader Breezy Bellairs, in Ngaio Marsh's *A Wreath for Rivera,* lived on Pikestaff Row near Ebury Street, and the two acolytes of the House of the Sacred Flame shared a flat at 17 Ebury Mews in *Death in Ecstasy.*

Turn right at the Ebury Court Hotel and walk back along Ebury Street to Eccleston Street. Then turn left again and follow Eccleston Street over Victoria Railroad Station on Eccleston Bridge. This street becomes Belgrave Road at Buckingham Palace Road, the boundary between Belgravia and Pimlico, which you are now entering.

PIMLICO

In the area just north of Victoria Station, Ann Radcliffe lived at 5 Stafford Row, which used to be located where Bressenden Place joined Buckingham Palace Road. Her Gothic novels combined horror, sensibility, and the picturesque in a manner that made her a forerunner of such modern mystery writers as Ruth Rendell, whose macabre stories Antonia Fraser's Jemima Shore adores.

The fictional Amber Street in Pimlico, where Danny Miller lived, was also around here. He was a gangster in Josephine Tey's *The Man in the Queue* who was called to Scotland Yard to talk to Inspector Grant.

To the west, Buckingham Palace Road runs into Pimlico Road. The drummer in Breezy Bellairs's band lived there in Marsh's *A Wreath for Rivera.*

It was on fictional Parrot Street that Albert Campion nearly walked into thin air in Margery Allingham's *Flowers for the Judge.*

In the *English School Murder* by Ruth Dudley Edwards, Amiss, Milton, and Ellis agreed to meet in a pub in Pimlico, off the beaten path.

In Jack M. Bickham's *Breakfast at Wimbledon,* Brad Smith moved from his rooms in the Cumberland Hotel to the Victoria in Belgrave Road.

Continue on Belgrave Road, crossing Hugh Street. The next street will bring you into Eccleston Square, which will be to your right. This is a large, attractive square containing a fenced garden with grass, flowers, and tall trees; it is surrounded by colonnaded townhouses. Winston Churchill lived for a time at No. 9. A number of the houses, like the cream-colored Elizabeth Hotel, are bed-and-breakfast places or have been broken up into flats. Both Eccleston Square's appearance and its geography make it a good substitute for P. D. James's fictional Caldecote Square.

In James's *Innocent Blood,* sociology professor Maurice Palfrey was married to Lady Helena, an earl's daughter, who had been raised in a Palladian mansion in Wiltshire. Lady Helena had decided views on what kind of London residence was appropriate. According to her, "Hampstead was too trendy, Mayfair too expensive, Bayswater too vulgar, Belgravia too smart." Fortunately they found a house in fictional Caldecote Terrace, on the fringes of Pimlico, southeast of Victoria Station and Eccleston Bridge.

Like Antonia Fraser, P. D. James is fascinated by architecture, so she described the perfectly decorated Palfrey house in great detail. Through the eyes of Palfrey's adopted daughter, Philippa, you see its restored elegance, with twin panels of Burne-Jones stained glass in the front door and a delicate stairway banister in pale polished mahogany that curved up to the landing. The dining room had French doors that led by wrought-iron steps, into a small walled garden with roses and white-painted tubs of geraniums, where the Palfreys had coffee on summer nights. Philippa Palfrey had her own long, low room on the top floor, sparsely furnished in pale, modern wood, with a view over the treetops.

Several of the houses in Eccleston Square could be converted into the Palfrey house, given enough money and taste.

Now walk around the square and choose one of the bed-and-breakfast places that could be the shabby, stuccoed Hotel Casablanca, which catered to weekly groups of Spanish tourists. The avenging Mr. Scase, on the trail of Philippa Palfrey's biological mother, rented a room at the Hotel Casablanca so that he could sit with his binoculars and watch the Palfrey house at No. 68.

Return to Belgrave Road at the northeast corner of Eccleston Square and, turning right, follow Belgrave Road, crossing Warwick Way and, farther south and to your right, Warwick Square. As you walk through Pimlico toward the river, you will cross intersections with Gloucester Street, Denbigh Street, Charlwood Street, and, farther along, Moreton Street. You will pass by rows and rows and rows of Victorian housing, some gentrified, some completely derelict. The streets, with their assortment of shops and cafes reflect Pimlico's polyglot population.

Finally, you will reach Lupus Street, a major crossroads across Pimlico's southern end. To the west (or right), where Belgrave Road and Lupus Street meet, you will find yourself at St. George's Square.

Long and narrow, a square in name only, St. George's Square leads to Grosvenor Road and the Thames. The square was laid out in the 1850s. No. 97A (a fictitious address near the Thames end of the square on your left, as you face south on Lupus Street) was Miss Climpson's flat, rented for her by Lord Peter Wimsey. In Dorothy L. Sayers's *Unnatural Death,* Lord Peter mischievously took Charles Parker there, acting as if they were going to see his latest mistress. Sayers commented that the house, designed for a Victorian family with fatigue-proof servants, had been dissected by the late 1920s into half a dozen inconvenient bandboxes and let out as flats.

After ringing the bell, Lord Peter and Parker mounted six flights of steep stairs to meet the head of the Cattery. Miss Alexandra Katherine Climpson, a thin, middle-aged woman with a sharp sallow face and a very vivacious manner, wore a neat dark coat and skirt, a high-necked blouse, and a long gold neckchain with a variety of small ornaments. Miss Climpson was Dorothy Sayers's answer to Agatha Christie's Miss Marple and Patricia Wentworth's Miss Silver. In a letter to Christie about their joint project for the BBC, Sayers described such female detectives as "Dear Old Tabbies," a compliment, of course, because Sayers adored cats. Given Miss Climpson's devoted high-churchmanship, it adds just the proper realistic Sayers touch to note that St. Savior's, the church at the head of St. George's Square on Lupus Street, follows only the most Anglo-Catholic of practices.

Off to the west, along the Thames toward Chelsea, stretches the modern high-rise development called Chuchill Gardens Estate. It makes an appropriate stand-in for the disputed Powers Estate owned by confused Sister Miriam in Antonia Fraser's *Quiet as a Nun.*

This area was once the site of the kind of warehouses from which Fu Manchu, crated like furniture, once again escaped in Sax Rohmer's *The Trail of Fu Manchu.*

Walk past the Pimlico Underground Station, turn right on Bessburough Street, and follow it to Vauxhall Bridge Road. Cross Vauxhall Bridge Road to Milbank, which runs beside the

Thames River. Continue on Milbank past Ponsonby Place and Atterbury Street. On your left is the Tate Gallery, with its famous collections of modern painting and sculpture.

The Tate was built in 1897 on the site of the eighteen-acre brick fortress of the Milbank Penitentiary, which was demolished in 1890.

In *The Sign of Four,* Sherlock Holmes and Watson landed by the penitentiary after crossing the Thames River.

This neighborhood where the Tate is now is near the one that Inspector Pitt knew as the dreadful, brothel-ridden slum called Devil's Acre, "under the shadow of Westminster" in Anne Perry's *The Devil's Acre.*

The glories of the Tate Gallery have blotted out older, dreadful connotations and replaced them with the glories of the creative arts.

The Tate houses the national collection of British and foreign modern art. Its holdings include famous examples of the "Golden Age" of British painting, including Reynolds, Gainsborough, Romney, Lawrence, George Stubbs, Constable, and Blake, as well as an incredible collection by J. M. W. Turner. There are also representative contemporary works displayed here.

After a day of sightseeing, Ann, Jay, and Lark spent only enough time at the Tate to drink in the Turners and leave the rest for later. (*Skylark* by Sheila Simonson)

In Jessica Mann's *Grave Goods,* Tamara Hoyland was taken to the Rex Whistler Room by an art dealer before going to look at an alleged Giotto in Pimlico. The two ended up in a mad chase after the Horn Treasure, which was the regalia of Emperor Charlemagne.

In Antonia Fraser's *A Splash of Red,* the painter Kevin John Athlone had a painting hung in the Tate. He was one of the lovers of Jemima Shore's friend, Chloe. Chloe owned his canvas called "A Splash of Red," and the similarity between the paintings was noticed by Jemima's pal "Pompey" from Scotland Yard.

On the lower level of the gallery, you can find refreshment

at either the Refreshment Room cafeteria or the expensive Rex Whistler Restaurant, noted for its murals, wine list, and excellent food.

Amiss had been instructed to take his group to "punters" to the Tate Gallery for lunch, but he needed Rich to fill in the details. (*English School Murders* by Ruth Dudley Edwards)

After you are finished enjoying the Tate, exit to Milbank, where Lester Furnival lived with here husband Richard in Charles Williams's *All Hallows' Eve.*

Turn to your right and walk across Vauxhall Bridge Road. Turn right into Bessborough Street, which you will follow back to the Pimlico Underground Station to end this walk.

13

HAMPSTEAD VILLAGE/HIGHGATE VILLAGE WALK

BACKGROUND

Lying on high, open ground to the northwest of London, the village of Hampstead has the clean, refreshing feel of the rural English countryside. Its winding, hilly streets with their jumble of attractive eighteenth- and nineteenth-century houses present reason enough for a ramble through the area.

Although the village of Hampstead has been around just about forever, there is little that is left from ancient times; in fact, only two barrows remain to mark the presence of the prehistoric tribes that once shared the dense forest and the hill with deer, boars, and wild cattle. Although the barrow on Primrose Hill has been flattened, the one on Parliament Hill, where legend says Queen Boudicca (Boadiceia) was buried in AD 62, remains. (The barrow was opened in 1894 and no trace of Boudicca was found.)

Traces of both Romans and Saxons have been found in Hampstead, which probably got its name from a Saxon farmer who had cleared part of the forest as his homestead.

Hampstead, which was first mentioned in 987 in a charter from King Edgar, celebrated its millennium in 1987.

The area developed slowly from its ancient beginnings. In medieval times, the village was just a clutch of buildings on the road from London to St. Albans. It received little notice from London to the south, until the great plague struck and Londoners fled their disease-ridden homes and invaded the area to the north.

In 1666, the Great Fire rid London of the plague, but left the city a smoldering ruin. Again Londoners turned to Hampstead, this time for timber to rebuild their charred city and, in the process, all but stripped Hampstead's forests.

The eighteenth century was a golden time when Hampstead developed as a spa, complete with health-giving water from the chalybeate springs. Fashionable London flocked here to drink the waters that bubbled from the earth. Flask Walk and Well Walk both date from those days. The Hampstead spring water "of the same nature and equal in virtue with Tunbridge Wells" was available to all takers for merely three pence a flask. Because the waters had such a nasty taste, a chaser was needed, which is why Hampstead is also known for its many pubs.

By Georgian times Hampstead had developed into an exclusive suburb, furnishing, on a maze of picturesque and immaculate lanes, hideaway homes for the rich and famous, as well as an abundance of shops, tearooms, and cafes.

At 400 feet above sea level, Hampstead is London's highest village; higher than St. Paul's Cathedral, local people will quickly tell you. From these northern heights, the great panoramic view across the Heath toward the City of London is breathtaking.

The Heath and adjoining Parliament Hill dominate the Hampstead area. A chain of warning beacons blazed from the top of Parliament Hill in 1588, when the Spanish Armada came into sight.

During the day Hampstead Heath is a prime place for kite flying, sunning, and walking, but when night falls it is empty and forbidding. In times past, highwaymen lurked in the deep shadows of the Heath. In fact, the pistols of one of the most feared of the breed, the notorious Dick Turpin, are on display in the Spaniards Inn on Spaniards Road.

Readers of mystery and detective stories find Hampstead,

the Heath, and the neighboring village of Highgate especially interesting because they serve as settings for some of the best-known tales of detection and intrigue.

Walter Hartright, the young artist in Wilkie Collins's *The Woman in White,* left his mother's cottage in Hampstead one evening when "the quiet twilight was still trembling on the topmost ridges of the heath." He turned his steps toward London. "The moon was full and broad in the dark blue starless sky; and the broken ground of heath looked wild enough in the mysterious light to be hundreds of miles from the great city that lay beneath it." The idea of descending into the city repelled Hartright, so he determined to walk home by the most roundabout way that he could, to follow the white, winding paths across the lonely heath. He was on the Finchley Road when "every drop of blood in [his] body was brought to a stop by a touch of a hand laid lightly and suddenly on [his] shoulder." And so the tale unfolds, the sense of the mysterious created so irrevocably by the eerie loneliness of the setting.

The poet Alfred Noyes vividly recreated the Heath's highwayman period in a wildly romantic poem called "The Highwayman," which has for its setting Hampstead's Spaniards Inn. In the poem, Noyes tells the tale of the ill-fated love "Bess, the landlord's black-eyed daughter" has for the rakish highwayman in velvet and lace who is shot down "like a dog in the moonlight" by the king's men. It is easy to visualize Noyes's entire scenario as you stand at nightfall in the Inn's yard gazing into the darkness that shrouds Hampstead Heath.

Charles Dickens, creator of so many memorable characters, not least among them "Sergeant Bucket of the Detective," loved all of Hampstead and would walk there almost daily.

Crime novels often have a vague association with Hampstead. This character or that will go to Hampstead, be murdered in Hampstead, or even live in Hampstead, as does Nell Bray, who was relaxing at home in Hampstead when Emmeline Pankhurst arrived. (*Sister Beneath the Sheet* by Gillian Linscott)

In Glady's Mitchell's *Watson's Choice,* Chief Detective Inspector Robert Gaven escorted his fiancee, Laura Menzies, and her boss, Dame Beatrice Bradley, to a masquerade party on the

Heath. Inevitably, in the course of the evening, a murder was committed.

Kate Kennedy, preparing for her move to a rural cottage, ferried her worldly goods to the attic of Bill's house in Hampstead. (*Midnight Is a Lonely Place* by Barbara Erskine)

William Thomas DeWarre, Ellis Martin's fiance, lived in Hampstead but was coming to Wildesham the next day to talk with Ross. (*The Killing of Ellis Martin* by Lucretia Grindle)

In Lynda La Plante's *Prime Suspect 3,* policemen Alan Thorpe and Kenny Lloyd spent an evening looking for a house that was located "somewhere just off the Heath." In the course of their search, they drove up and around through Highgate and circled along the northeast fringe of Hampstead Heath.

In *The Men in Her Death* by Anne Morice, it was assumed that the girl Sandy had been abducted from her flat "in respectable, residential Hampstead."

Hampstead has a long association with literature of all kinds, as well as with the arts and politics. In the 1900s, it was the *Monmartre* of England. It has since been the seat of the artistic avant-garde, politicians, eccentrics, and radicals.

Keats, Constable, George Orwell, D. H. Lawrence, R. L. Stevenson, E. C. Bentley, and Edgar Wallace, as well as Frederick Forsyth, John Le Carre, Sigmund Freud, Boy George, Jeremy Irons, and Glenda Jackson, have all called Hampstead home.

This area, which includes the villages of Hampstead and Highgate and the great Heath they border, is rich in history, mystery, and adventure. Suburban Georgian elegance vies with rural charm for the attention of the traveler. On a visit to Hampstead and Highgate you will encounter evidence of art, intellect, and money, as well as the haunts of highwaymen and vampires. The walks offered here are designed to be partially sampled, enjoyed in segments over several days, or undertaken as a one-day excursion that will leave you footsore but triumphant.

LENGTH OF WALK: Each walk is 4-plus miles

See the maps on page 232 and 239 for the boundaries of this walk and pages 267–68 for a list of the authors, books, and detectives mentioned.

PLACES OF INTEREST

Keats' House, Keats Grove. Where Keats lived when he wrote "Ode to a Nightingale" and "Ode on a Grecian Urn." Open afternoons. Free.

Fenton House, Windmill Hill. Built in 1693. Features a collection of early keyboard instruments, including the harpsichord that Handel played. Admission charge.

The Freud Museum, 20 Maresfield Gardens. House to which Freud came after he fled Vienna. Features video footage of Freud and recordings of his voice. Admission charge.

Kenwood House, Hampstead Lane. Designed by the Adam brothers for Lord Mansfield. Features magnificent library and art collection. Free.

St. John's Church, Church Row. Fourteenth-century church, rebuilt 1744–47. John Constable is buried in churchyard.

The Heath, A great place to walk, but not a place to venture after sunset.

St. Michael's Highgate, Highgate West Hill. Coleridge buried beneath the center aisle.

Highgate Cemetery, Swains Lane, Highgate.

PLACES TO EAT

Jack Straw's Inn, Northend Way. 071-435-8885.

The Spaniard's Inn, Spaniard's Road. 081-455-3276.

Flask Pub, 77 West Hill, Highgate. This pub dates from 1663. 081-340-3969.

HAMPSTEAD WALK

To reach Hampstead from central London, take the Northern Line underground train marked Edgware. For Highgate, take the Northern Line underground train marked High Barnett. The No. 210 bus runs across Hampstead Heath from Golders Green to Highgate. (Golders Green is on the same fork of the Northern Line as Hampstead.)

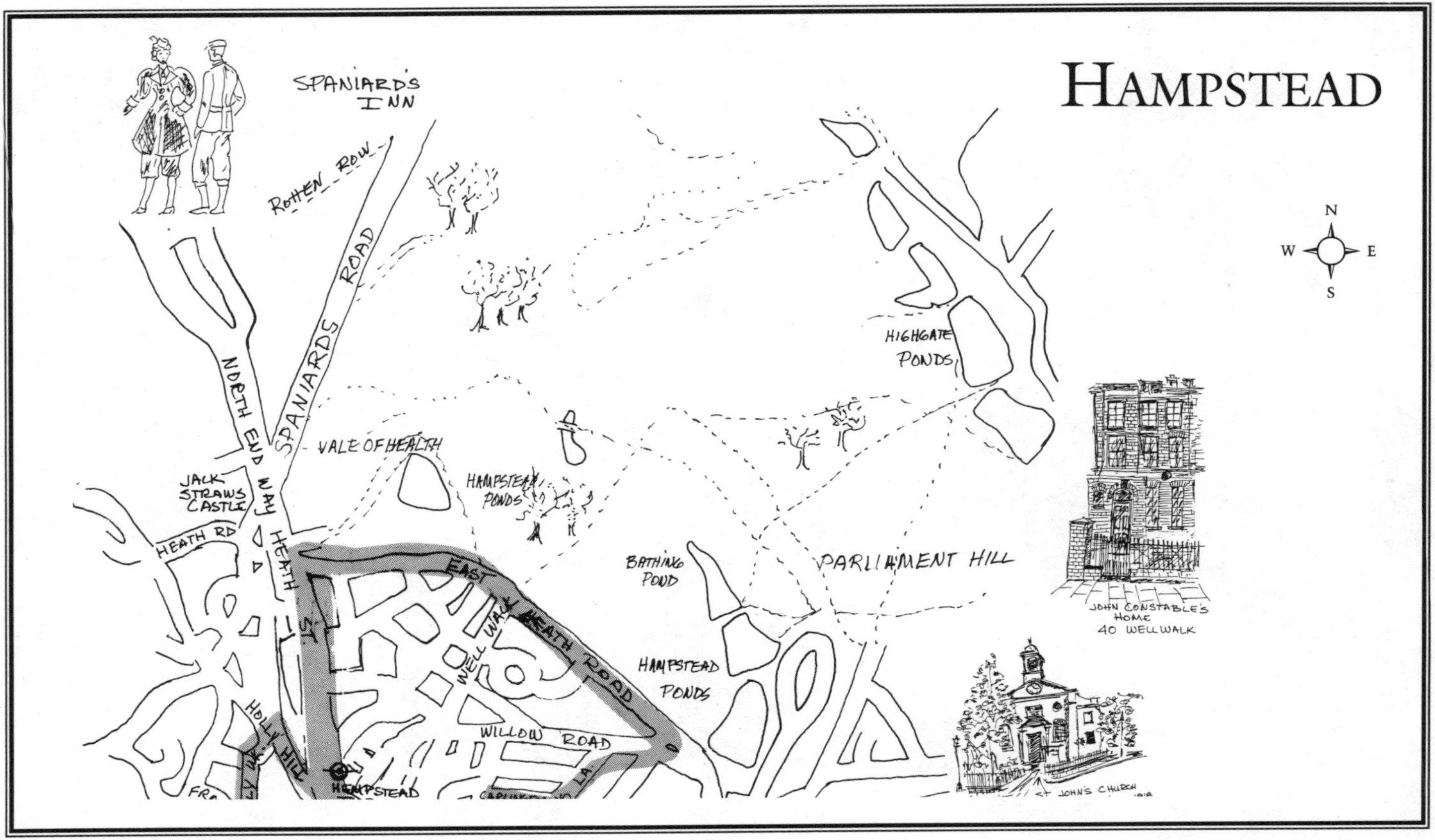
HAMPSTEAD
N
W
E
S
SPANIARD'S INN
ROTTEN ROW
SPANIARDS ROAD
NORTH END WAY
VALE OF HEALTH
JACK STRAWS CASTLE
HEATH RD
HEATH
ST.
HAMPSTEAD PONDS
HIGHGATE PONDS
BATHING POND
PARLIAMENT HILL
EAST HEATH ROAD
WELL WALK
WILLOW ROAD
HAMPSTEAD PONDS
HOLLY HILL
HAMPSTEAD
LA
JOHN CONSTABLE'S HOME
40 WELL WALK
ST JOHN'S CHURCH

Begin this walk at the Hampstead Tube Station. The station, which was opened in 1907, is the deepest in London—192 feet below street level. During World War II, it functioned as an air-raid shelter. Passengers arriving by a late train often had to step over rows of people sleeping on the platform.

Hampstead and Highgate are both extremely hilly. This walk should be undertaken only if you are up to hill walking, or if you have time to do this walk in small segments. To begin with, you will be walking downhill.

Two streets Y-out from the station, Heath Street to the right and Hampstead High Street to the left. You want the High Street, so bear tightly to the left.

In Deborah Crombie's *All Shall Be Well,* Duncan Kincaid, feeling depressed, emerged from "the bowels of the Hampstead tube station and blinked in the brilliant light." He turned the corner onto the High Street and the colors hit him like a physical force.

Hampstead's High Street still has much of the homeliness of a small-town high street. A miscellany of shops, pubs, and small cafes, as well as assorted street vendors, line the way as you begin your walk. Don't be surprised if the temptation to wander and to shop is irresistible. The ambiance you find here makes it extremely difficult to grasp that the heart of London lies only four miles away.

Follow Kincaid's route along the High Street, walking on the left-hand side of the road. Halfway down the High, you will pass the pub where Kincaid liked to stop for a pint and a pie. He favored the King George, but the ones you will pass are the William IV and the King of Bohemia.

Soon the High will turn into Rosslyn Hill. As for Duncan Kincaid, by the time he reached Rosslyn Hill he was feeling better. Seeing the flowerseller at the corner of Pilgrim's Lane brought his friend Jasmine to mind. Perhaps partially from guilt, Kincaid bought her a bouquet of freesias. (A plaque on the shop at the corner of Willoughby Road pays tribute to Maggie, the last of a family of flowersellers who, for nearly a century, sold flowers from this spot. Perhaps Crombie was thinking of Maggie when she moved the flowerseller down the street to Pilgrim's Lane.)

Follow Rosslyne Hill to Pilgrim's Lane, where the Hampstead Police Station, an evocative building designed by J. Dixon Butler, loomed over Kincaid at the turn into Pilgrim's Lane.

(If you wish to visit Keats's house, continue along Rosslyn Hill to Downshire Hill, and turn left on Downshire to Keats' Grove. After you have walked along Keats' Grove for a short distance, you will find Keats's house on the right-hand side, next to the library. When you have completed your visit to Keats's house return to Pilgrim's Lane and continue your walk.)

Turn left into Pilgrims Lane (right if you are returning from Keats's house). A short distance along, you will come to Carlinford Road. Turn left into Carlinford to find the building where both Duncan and Jasmine lived. (*All Shall Be Well* by Deborah Crombie)

Later, after the murder, when Duncan was trying to drive the kinks out of his mind, he changed into jeans and an anorak, and struck out across East Heath Road and headed north.

After finding a building that resembled the block of flats where Jasmine and Kincaid lived, return to Pilgrim's Lane and turn left. Follow Pilgrim's Lane to Willow Road and turn right to cross East Heath Road and enter the Heath near the Mixed Bathing Pond as Kincaid did. (If a walk across the Heath sounds like too much to undertake, choose instead to go left on East Heath Road and walk along the edge of the Heath to Heath Street, where you will turn right to Jack Straw's Castle.)

Max Genader's small, tastefully furnished flat overlooking Hampstead Heath in Leela Cutter's humor-filled *Death of the Party* was most likely located along here.

Follow the path as it winds westward. As Kincaid headed across the Heath, he took the path that crossed the viaduct pond and stopped there to admire the view. When he started walking again, he bent his head into the wind and began the long uphill climb to the top of the Heath.

Kincaid's path dead-ended at Heath Street just across from Jack Straw's Castle. To the left is Whitestone Pond, where Percy Bysshe Shelley and his friend Leigh Hunt sailed paper boats to the delight of children playing nearby.

In G. K. Chesterton's short story "The Blue Cross," when

French policeman Valentin and his squad of accompanying policemen arrived in Hampstead in pursuit of the arch criminal Flambeau, they hurried through the narrow, shut-in streets to the Heath.

A flagstaff at Whitestone Pond marks the highest point in Hampstead. From here on a clear day you can catch a view of ten counties.

Cross Heath Street to Jack Straw's Castle on your left. From this point, Valentin went out onto the Heath where he spied two figures dressed in clerical garb making their way along the "green contour of a hill." The two were deep in conversation as they went to the "wilder and more silent heights of the Heath."

Jack Straw's is a famous old coaching inn. The original building was named for one of the leaders of the 1381 Peasants' Revolt, and the inn was first mentioned in public records in 1712.

Charles Dickens, who often mentions the Heath in his books, used to walk miles from his rooms in Doughty Street to dine on chops at Jack Straw's. The inn was also a favorite of Robert Louis Stevenson, Wilkie Collins, and William Makepeace Thackery. Washington Irving immortalized it in his *Tales of a Traveller*.

The original inn was severely damaged by World War II bombs, but Jack Straw's was rebuilt in 1964. The mantle-tree over the kitchen fireplace is said to be made from the gallows on which a highwayman called Jackson was hanged.

In *The Highwayman and Mr. Dickens* by William J. Palmer, Palmer, in the persona of Wilkie Collins, observes that Jack Straw's Castle at the top of Hampstead Heath is a respectable inn and public house. He is comparing it with the Spaniard's Inn, named for an infamous pirate and highwayman, and located along Spaniard's Road on the way to Highgate.

When Sergeant Gemma James and her small son came to Hampstead to help Kincaid go through Jasmine's belongings in *All Shall Be Well,* he promised to take them to lunch in a pub and then for a walk on the Heath. Perhaps you would like to follow suit and, after appropriate refreshments at Jack Straw's, take time to explore the Heath.

In *A Masculine Ending* by Joan Smith, Dr. Loretta Lawson, who had unwillingly been swept into the investigation of the murder of an Oxford don, spent her Sunday afternoon walking on Hampstead Heath.

The area across from Jack Straw's and to the left is called the Vale of Health. It is a curiously named valley below the Spaniard's Road. Originally it was a pestilential swamp called Hatches Bottom, where a parish poorhouse was located. The swamp was drained in 1800, and the name was changed to the Vale of Health.

The poet James Leigh Hunt lived here and was often visited by his friends John Keats and Percy Bysshe Shelley. D. H. Lawrence and Edgar Wallace also lived in the Vale at a later time. Wallace, master of the locked-room mystery, was so widely read in the late 1920s that, at the time, every fourth book purchased in Britain was written by him.

Dick Turpin's ghost is reputed to haunt the Heath in the vicinity of the Vale of Health. According to witnesses, when the ghost appears, it is wearing a tricorn hat, is dressed all in black, and sits astride a great black horse. (*Haunted London* by Peter Underwood)

Follow in Duncan Kincaid's footsteps by leaving Jack Straw's and taking Heath Street south to where it curves just beyond the underground station and into Church Row. Turn right into Church Row and follow it to St. John's Churchyard.

Church Row is lined on both sides with houses, most of which date from the early eighteenth century. Many of the original wrought-iron railings, gates, lamp brackets, and fanlights have somehow survived.

The street has had among its residents the actor George du Maurier at No. 27, and the writer H. G. Wells at No. 17.

In Wilkie Collins's *The Woman In White,* the young artist Walter Hartright, after leaving his mother's cottage, walked along Church Row to St. John's Church where Constable is buried.

Crombie's Kincaid also entered Church Row, the spire of St. John's drawing him like true north does the needle of a compass. He entered the churchyard through the massive wrought-iron gates. He turned left into the dim greenness of the burial ground, halting at John Constable's grave near the outer boundary wall.

St. John's, Hampstead's parish church, is located at the far end of Church Row. The present church was built in 1745 on the site of a medieval building. It was enlarged in the nineteenth century and reoriented, making in one of the few churches in the country to have its altar at the west end.

The wrought-iron gates to the churchyard are called the Handel Gates, because in 1747 they were brought from Canons Park, Edgware, where Handel was organist.

As Kincaid left the churchyard, he heard the strains of evensong coming from the church and on impulse he went in.

Take time to explore the church as well as the churchyard, where in one corner you will find the grave of John Constable. The actress, Kay Kendall, as well as George and Gerald du Maurier, are also buried here.

Leave the churchyard and cross Church Row to Holly Walk. In one of the old houses near the parish church, the ghost of a child can be heard crying and running as she tries to escape her killer.

Take Holly Walk to Holly Place, which was developed about the time of the Battle of Waterloo (1815). The Church of St. Mary, located in Holly Place, was one of the first Roman Catholic churches built in London. The World War II French hero, General Charles de Gaulle, worshipped there.

Hampstead's first police station was in the building called the Watch House at No. 9 Holly Place.

Walk past Hollyberry Lane to Mount Vernon and turn right on Mount Vernon. (A left turn on Mount Vernon would bring you to Frognall, where, at No. 99, Charles de Gaulle took temporary refuge during World War II.)

Continue on Mount Vernon, noting Abernethy House. It is where Robert Louis Stevenson once lodged. Stevenson was especially interested in the idea of human beings having both a good and an evil nature. Although he worked with this idea in several of his books, it emerged as a full-blown theme in his horror-thriller *The Strange Case of Dr. Jekyl and Mr. Hyde.*

Turn right off Mount Vernon into Holly Hill and follow Holly Hill to the Hampstead Underground Station at the top of the High Street. End this portion of the walk at the underground station.

HIGHGATE

BACKGROUND

Highgate, which at one time belonged almost entirely to the Bishop of London, was just a tiny village in the thirteenth century. In the fourteenth century, the then bishop allowed a road to be built over the great hill because the old road that went around it was becoming impassable in the winter. Tollgates were set up along the road, the highest one giving the village its name.

Highgate's Ye Old Gate House Inn dates back to the fourteenth century. The ancient hostelry was built next to the former tollgate on Highgate Hill, on the very edge of the estate of the Bishop of London who had granted the original license to the inn.

As is the case with most places of its years, the inn as a long and varied history. For one instance, there is a dummy cupboard from which Dick Turpin is said to have escaped.

Many names of note are associated with the old inn. Henning drew the very first cartoon for *Punch* at Ye Olde Gate House, and Lord Byron, Charles Dickens, and George du Maurier were regular visitors.

Quite obviously, an inn so old must have a ghost. She is a widow called Mother Marnes, who was murdered in the inn for her money. Her ghost haunts the gallery, which is the oldest part of the building. Mother Marnes is not often seen, because she only appears when there are no children or animals in the building.

Near the inn is Highgate School. It is located where, in 1565, Sir Roger Cholmey founded a free school. (The poet, Samuel Taylor Coleridge, was buried in Highgate School until 1961, when he was moved to St. Michael's Church where he is entombed in the aisle.)

HIGHGATE

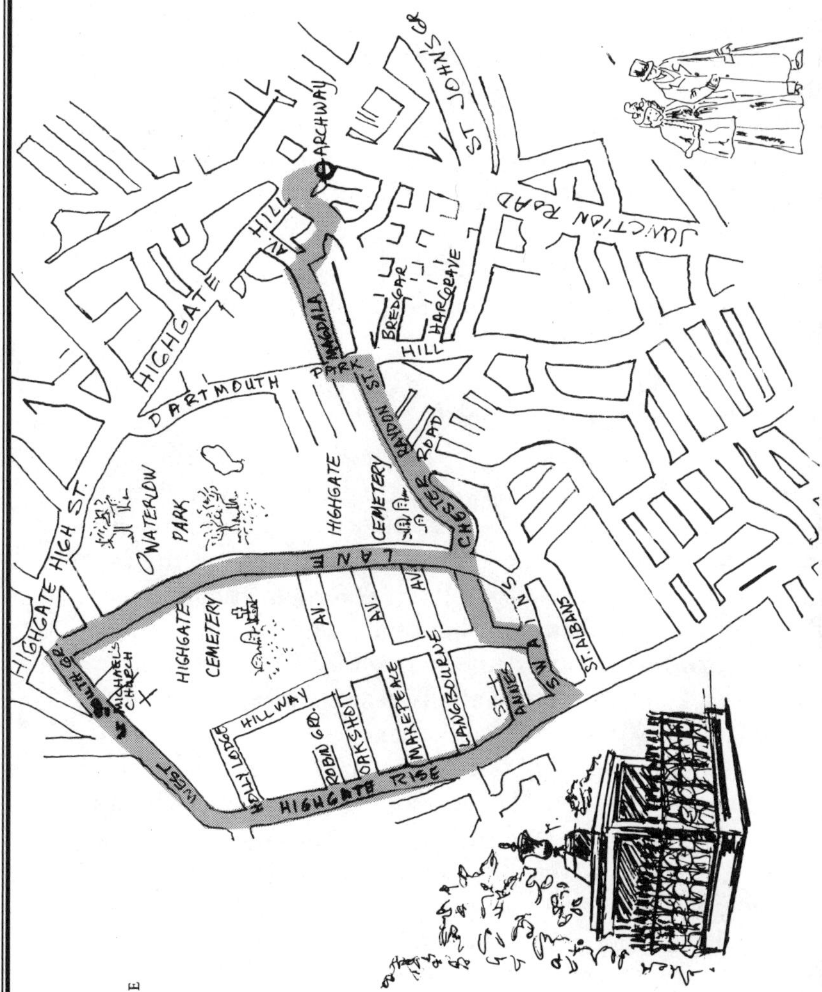

ARCHWAY
ST JOHN'S
JUNCTION ROAD
HIGHGATE
HILL
AV.
MAGDALA
BREDGAR
HARGRAVE
HILL
DARTMOUTH
PARK
RAYDON
ST
ROAD
CHESTER
HIGHGATE HIGH ST.
WATERLOW
PARK
HIGHGATE
CEMETERY
LANE
AV.
AV.
AV
S
W
A
I
N
S
ST. ALBANS
HIGHGATE
HIGHGATE
CEMETERY
MICHAEL'S
CHURCH
HILLWAY
ROBIN GR.
OAKSHOTT
MAKEPEACE
LANGBOURNE
ST.
ANNES
HOLLY LODGE
HIGHGATE RISE
WEST
N
E
S
W

HIGHGATE WALK

Begin the Highgate Walk at the Archway Underground Station or by walking across Hampstead Heath by way of the path to the north of Parliament Hill.

Leave the underground station and turn left to walk up Highgate Hill. The magistrate, Samuel Digby, whom Julian Kestrel hoped to enlist as an ally in a murder investigation, lived in a stately red-brick home on Highgate Hill. The house had a big brass door knocker in the form of the head of a smiling, satisfied lion. (*A Broken Vessel* by Kate Ross)

Walk along Highgate Hill as far as the Whittington Stone pub where, according to legend, Richard Whittington—the Dick Whittington of cat fame—heard the message pealed by Bow Bells as he rested:

> Turn again Whittington,
> Thrice Lord Mayor of London Town.

Turn left into Magdala Avenue and go to the end. Now turn left on Dartmouth Park, then right into Raydon Street. Follow Raydon to Chester Street, and turn right into the intersection with Swain's Lane. (The Gothic enclave on the left is called Holly Village. It was built in 1865 by the philanthropist Baroness Burdett-Coutts for her estate workers.)

In *Highgate Rise* by Anne Perry, Obadiah Parkinson was treated by Dr. Shaw after Parkinson was hit on the head and robbed in Swan's Lane (Swain's Lane).

Turn right up the hill until you come to the twin entrances to Highgate Cemetery. The Cemetery of St. James at Highgate lies on the southern slope of Highgate Hill.

The cemetery covers fifty acres on both sides of the road. The original twenty-acre section was consecrated in 1839. The landscape gardener, David Ramsay, designed serpentine roads and footpaths leading upward through the burial area to the buildings and terrace just beneath St. Michael's church. These buildings are approached through an arch flanked by Egyptian columns and obelisks, beyond which is the Egyptian Avenue.

In Barbara Hambly's *Those Who Hunt the Night*, Asher went to Highgate Cemetery by day to further investigate the grave of Lotta, the murdered vampire. It was an easy matter to enter through the "narrow avenue of tombs behind the Egyptian gate. . . ."

In 1857, the eastern section of the cemetery, an additional thirty acres, was opened across Swain's Lane.

The western cemetery is the earliest and the most interesting because of the Gothic atmosphere created by the Victorian monuments, but the eastern section contains the graves of a number of well-known people, including Karl Marx and George Eliot.

When you leave the cemetery, continue north on Swain's Lane to South Grove. Turn left on South Grove and follow it to where it joins with West Hill and the Grove. (To the right you will see the Flask pub named after the flasks of Hampstead water which were sold there in Hampstead's golden spa era.) Built in 1767, it is a pretty pub with a cozy bar and an open fire. The basement was another of Dick Turpin's hideaways. The artist Hogarth often frequented the bar.

The Grove Ys to the left of the northern fork of West Hill. In Anne Perry's *Highgate Rise*, when Pitt questioned Miss Lutterworth about the fire in which Clemency Shaw died, all Miss Lutterworth could tell him was that Mr. Arroway and the Misses Barking ". . .went up to the Grove in Highgate itself."

The Grove is Highgate's finest street. The nearest houses are the oldest; they date from the 1680s. For nine years No. 3 was the home of the poet Samuel Taylor Coleridge. An aura of mystery surrounds much of his work, especially *The Rime of the Ancient Mariner* and the haunting *Christabel,* as well as the opium-inspired *Kubla Khan*.

To your left as you stand at the juncture of West Hill and the Grove is the Old Hall and St. Michael's Church. They occupy the site where Arundel House once stood. The essayist, philosopher, and Renaissance man Sir Francis Bacon died in Arundel House in 1626 after catching a chill while carrying out an early experiment in refrigeration. He wanted to see if meat could be preserved by freezing, so he was out in the cold stuffing a chicken with snow when he was taken ill. Some say that today this spot is haunted, not by the ghost of Bacon but by that of a partially plucked chicken. (*Haunted London* by Peter Underwood)

If you wish to visit Coleridge's grave, go into St. Michael's Church. The poet is buried in the center aisle.

The point where the vampire Ysidro and Asher went over the wall into (and out of) the cemetery, is just beyond the church. (*Those Who Hunt the Night* by Barbara Hambly)

When Ysidro and Asher came out of the cemetery, the fog hung heavy. Asher heard the clock on St. Michael's Church chime three-quarters past eleven. Highgate Hill was deserted, as were the suburban streets below it, ". . .the shops and houses little more than dark bulks in the drifting fog through which the gaslights made weak yellow blobs." (*Those Who Hunt the Night* by Barbara Hambly)

The walk continues down West Hill left to Highgate Road (Rise), where most of the action in Anne Perry's book of that name took place. Late in the novel, Pitt learned of a duel at sunrise—with swords—that was scheduled to be held in a field between Highgate Road and the cemetery. Determined to put a stop to it, he set off through the field, "Highgate Road to his left and the wall of the magnificent cemetery to his right."

The house where Clemency Shaw died in the fire would have been along this way. Water to fight the blaze was brought from Highgate Ponds to the Heath.

Continue south to Highgate Road (Rise) past Robin Grove, Oakeshott, Makepeace, and Langbourne; turn left into St. Anne's Close. Here you will find St. Anne's Church, where Clemency Shaw's funeral was to be held at two o'clock on Thursday. (*Highgate Rise* by Anne Perry)

Leave St. Anne's and return to Highgate Road. At Swain's Lane, turn left and follow it to Hillway, then turn left again.

In *Highgate Rise,* Hillway was a path called Bromwich Walk, which Murdo said led from the parsonage to St. Anne's Church to the south, parallel with the Rise, and ended in Highgate proper.

Later in *Highgate Rise,* Flora asked Constable Murdo to meet her at the parsonage end of Bromwich Walk so they might walk up Bromwich Walk to Highgate and find a lemonade stall where they could refresh themselves.

Turn right into Bromwich Avenue. It will bring you to Swain's Lane farther north. Cross Swain's Lane into Chester Road. On Chester, bear to the left into Raydon Street. Walk along Raydon until you reach Dartmouth Park where you will turn left. Take Dartmouth Park to Magdala and turn right. Continue on Magdala to Highgate Hill where you turn right again and return to the Archway Underground Station and the end of this walk.

SPECIAL HELPS

Authors, Books, and Sleuths by Walk

CITY WALK: Authors and Books

Aird, Catherine, *A Going Concern* (1993); *In Harm's Way* (1984)
Babson, Marion, *Tourists Are for Trapping* (1989)
Bentley, E. C., *Trent's Last Case* (1941)
Berkeley, Anthony, *The Poisoned Chocolates Case* (1929)
Carr, John Dickson, *The Mad Hatter Mystery* (1950)
Chesterton. G. K., *The Ball and the Cross* (1911)
Christie, Agatha, *The Golden Ball* (1971); *The Mystery of the Blue Train* (1928); *The Secret Adversary* (1922); *The Secret of Chimneys* (1925)
Collins, Wilkie, *The Moonstone* (1868)
Cooper, Natasha, *A Common Death* (1990); *Bloody Roses* (1992)
Doyle, Sir Arthur Conan, "A Case of Identity" (1900); "The Dancing Men" (1900); "The Mazarin Stone" (1900); "The Three Garridebs" (1900)
Francis, Dick, *Banker* (1982); *Odds Against* (1965)
Grimes, Martha, *The Dirty Duck* (1984)
Harding, Paul, *By Murder's Bright Light* (1994)
Harrison, Ray, *Deathwatch* (1985)
Heyer, Georgette, *Death in the Stocks* (1952)
Keating, H. R. F., *Inspector Ghote Hunts the Peacock* (1968)
Marsh, Ngaio, *A Surfeit of Lampreys* (1941); *A Wreath for Rivera* (1960)
Mason, A. E. W., *The House in Lordship Lane* (1946)
Mitchell, Gladys, *Watson's Choice* (1975)
Orczy, Baroness, *Lady Molly of Scotland Yard* (1926)
Ripley, Mike, "Brotherly Love" (1989); *Angel Touch* (1989)
Rohmer, Sax, *The Trail of Fu Manchu* (1934)

Sayers, Dorothy L., *Murder Must Advertise* (1933); *Whose Body?* (1923)
Symons, Julian, *The Blackheath Poisonings* (1978)
Tey, Josephine, *The Daughter of Time* (1951)
Wallace, Edgar, *The Crimson Circle* (1953)
Williams, Charles, *All Hallows' Eve* (1948); *War in Heaven* (1949)
Yorke, Margaret, *Cast for Death* (1976)

CITY WALK: Sleuths

Roderick Alleyn Marsh
Fitzroy Maclean Angel Ripley
Brother Athelstan Harding
Superintendent Battle Christie
Tommy Beresford Christie
Dame Beatrice Bradley Mitchell
Sergeant Brag Harrison
Father Brown Chesterton
Tuppence Cowley Christie
Sergeant Cuff Collins
Tim Ekaterin Francis
Dr. Gideon Fell Carr
Inspector Ghote Keating
Inspector Alan Grant Tey
Patrick Grant Yorke
Sid Halley Francis
Inspector Hannasyde Heyer
M. Hannaud Mason
Sheridan Haynes Symons
Sherlock Holmes Doyle
Superintendent Jury Grimes
Willow King Cooper
Lady Molly Orczy
Constable Morton Harrison
Inspector Parr Wallace
Douglas Perkins Babson
Hercule Poirot Christie
Roger Sheringham Berkeley
Detective Inspector C. D. Sloan Aird
Sir Denis Nayland Smith Rohmer

Philip Trent Bentley
Lord Peter Wimsey Sayers

INNS OF COURT/FLEET STREET WALK: Authors and Books

Allingham, Margery, *Flowers for the Judge* (1969); *Police at the Funeral* (1932); *Tiger in the Smoke* (1969)
Babson, Marion, *The Lord Mayor of Death* (1977); *Tourists Are for Trapping* (1989)
Bentley, E. C., *Trent's Last Case* (1941)
Brand, Christianna, *Fog of Doubt* (1953)
Byrne, Murial St. Clare, ed., *The Lisle Letters* (1981)
Carr, John Dickson, *The Bride of Newgate* (1950)
Caudwell, Sarah, *Thus Was Adonis Murdered* (1981)
Chesterton, G. K., "The Purple Wig" (1911); *The Man Who Was Thursday* (1908)
Collins, Wilkie, *The Moonstone* (1868); *The Woman in White* (1900)
Cooper, Natasha, *Bitter Herbs* (1993)
Creasey, John, *Leave It to the Toff* (1963)
Dickens, Charles, *Bleak House* (1853)
Doyle, Sir Arthur Conan, "The Speckled Band" (1912)
Francis, Dick, *Forfeit* (1968)
Gilbert, Michael, *Death Has Deep Roots* (1978); *Smallbone Deceased* (1950)
Grimes, Martha, *The Anodyne Necklace* (1983)
Hambley, Barbara, *Those Who Hunt the Night* (1988)
Harding, Paul, *By Murder's Bright Light* (1994)
Hare, Cyril, *Tragedy at Law* (1980)
Heyer, Georgette, *Death in the Stocks* (1952); *Duplicate Death* (1951)
James, P. D., *An Unsuitable Job for a Woman* (1972); *The Skull Beneath the Skin* (1972); *Unnatural Causes* (1967)
Marsh, Ngaio, *A Surfeit of Lampreys* (1941); *Black As He's Painted* (1974); *Killer Dolphin* (1966); *Light Thickens* (1982)
Moody, Susan, *Death Takes a Hand* (1993)
Mortimer, John, "Rumpole and the Man of God" (1979)
Moyes, Patricia, *Who Is Simon Warwick?* (1978)
Peters, Ellis, *City of Gold and Shadows* (1974)

Sayers, Dorothy L., "The Piscatorial Farce of the Stolen Stomach" (1942); *Busman's Honeymoon* (1937); *Clouds of Witness* (1926); *Murder Must Advertise* (1933); *Strong Poison* (1930); *The Unpleasantness at the Bellona Club* (1928); *Unnatural Death* (1927); *Whose Body?* (1923)
Smith, Joan (English), *A Masculine Ending* (1987)
Stuart, Ian, *A Growing Concern* (1985)
Symons, Julian, *A Three Pipe Problem* (1975); *The Blackheath Poisonings* (1978)

INNS OF COURT/FLEET STREET WALK: Sleuths

Roderick Alleyn Marsh
Professor James Asher Hambly
Brother Athelstan Harding
Father Brown Chesterton
Albert Campion Allingham
Inspector Cockrill Brand
Sergeant Cuff Collins
Superintendent Adam Dalgleish James
George Felse Peters
Cordelia Gray James
David Grierson Stuart
Inspector Hannasyde Heyer
Sheridan Haynes Symons
Inspector Hazelrigg Gilbert
Sherlock Holmes Doyle
Superintendent Jury Grimes
Willow King Cooper
Loretta Lawson Smith (English)
Sir Henry Merrivale Carr
Inspector Parr Wallace
Douglas Perkins Babson
Rumpole Mortimer
Cassandra Swann Moody
Hilary Tamar Caudwell
Dr. Thorndyke Freeman
Henry Tibbett Moyes
The Toff Creasey
Philip Trent Bentley
James Tyrone Francis

Dr. Watson Doyle
Lord Peter Wimsey Sayers

COVENT GARDEN/THE STRAND WALK: Authors and Books

Anthony, Evelyn, *The Defector* (1981)
Babson, Marion, *In the Teeth of Adversity* (1990); *Tourists Are for Trapping* (1989)
Barnard, Robert, *A Scandal in Belgravia* (1991)
Bentley, E. C., *Trent's Last Case* (1941)
Berkeley, Anthony, *The Poisoned Chocolates Case* (1929)
Bickham, Jack M., *Breakfast at Wimbledon* (1991)
Blake, Nicholas, *End of Chapter* (1957)
Buchan, John, *The Thirty-Nine Steps* (1919)
Carr, John Dickson, *The Bide of Newgate* (1950)
Chesterton, G. K., "In Defense of Detective Stories" (1911); *The Man Who Was Thursday* (1908); "The Man in the Passage" (1910)
Christie, Agatha, *The Big Four* (1927); *Witness for the Prosecution* (play, 1954); *The Mystery of the Blue Train* (1928); *The Mousetrap* (play, 1952)
Creasey, John, *The Masters of Bow Street* (1974)
Crispin, Edmund, *Frequent Hearses* (1950); *Swan Song* (1947)
Dickens, Charles, *Bleak House* (1853)
Doyle, Sir Arthur Conan, "A Scandal in Bohemia" (1900); "The Adventure of the Bruce-Partington Plans" (1900); "The Man with the Twisted Lip" (1900); *The Sign of Four* (1890)
Fraser, Antonia, *A Splash of Red* (1981)
George, Elizabeth, *Missing Joseph* (1992)
Grindle, Lucretia, *The Killing of Ellis Martin* (1993)
Hall, Robert Lee, *Benjamin Franklin and a Case of Christmas Murder* (1991)
Heyer, Georgette, *Death in the Stocks* (1952); *Regency Buck* (1951)
James, P. D., *An Unsuitable Job for a Woman* (1972)
Kelly, Susan B., *Times of Hope* (1990)
Linscott, Gillian, *Sister Beneath the Sheet* (1991)
Marric, J. J. (John Creasey), *Gideon's Wrath* (1967)
Marsh, Ngaio, *A Surfeit of Lampreys* (1941); *Death in Ecstasy* (1976); *Light Thickens* (1982)
Metzger, Barbara, *A Suspicious Affair* (1994)

Meyers, Amy, *Murder at Plum's* (1989)
Moyes, Patricia, *Who Is Simon Warwick?* (1978)
Parker, Robert B., *The Judas Goat* (1978)
Perry, Anne, *Resurrection Row* (1981)
Rendell, Ruth, *The Veiled One* (1988)
Sayers, Dorothy L., *Busman's Honeymoon* (play, 1937); *Love All* (1940); *Murder Must Advertise* (1933); *Strong Poison* (1930); *The Unpleasantness at the Bellona Club* (1928); *Whose Body?* (1923)
Symons, Julian, *The Blackheath Poisonings* (1978)
Tey, Josephine, *The Daughter of Time* (1953); *The Man in the Queue* (1953)
Underwood, Peter, *Haunted London* (1973)
Williams, Charles, *All Hallows' Eve* (1948)
Yorke, Margaret, *Cast for Death* (1976)

COVENT GARDEN/THE STRAND WALK: Sleuths

Roderick Alleyn Marsh
Tommy Beresford Christie
Nell Bray Linscott
Father Brown Chesterton
Tuppence Cowley Christie
Auguste Didier Meyers
Mr. Jeremiah Dimm Metzger
Dr. Gideon Fell Carr
Gervase Fen Crispin
Benjaman Franklin Hall
Gideon Marric
Davina Graham Anthony
Inspector Alan Grant Tey
Patrick Grant Yorke
Cordelia Gray James
Inspector Hannasyde Heyer
Richard Hannay Buchan
Sheridan Haynes Symons
Sherlock Holmes Doyle
Alison Hope Kelly
Sir Henry Merrivale Carr
Douglas Perkins Babson
Charlotte and Thomas Pitt Perry

Hercule Poirot Christie
Peter Proctor Barnard
Chief Inspector Ross Grindle
Deborah St. James George
Roger Sheringham Berkeley
Jemima Shore Fraser
Brad Smith Bickman
Mr. Snerd Crispin
Spenser Parker
Nigel Strangeways Blake
Henry Tibbett Moyes
Philip Trent Bentley
Dr. Watson Doyle
Chief Inspector Wexford Rendell
Lord Peter Wimsey Sayers

BLOOMSBURY WALK: Authors and Books

Barnard, Robert, *A Scandal in Belgravia* (1991); *Posthumous Papers* (1992)
Bentley, E. C., *Trent's Last Case* (1941)
Blake, Nicholas, *End of Chapter* (1957)
Carr, John Dickson, *The Mad Hatter Mystery* (1950)
Chesterton, G. K., "The Diabolist" (1911); *The Man Who Was Thursday* (1908)
Crispin, Edmund, *Frequent Hearses* (1950)
Edwards, Ruth Dudley, *English School Murder* (1990)
Francis, Dick, *Forfeit* (1968)
Fraser, Antonia, *A Splash of Red* (1981); *Quiet as a Nun* (1977)
Gash, Jonathan, *The Very Last Gambado* (1990)
Hambly, Barbara, *Those Who Hunt the Night* (1988)
Hope, Sir Anthony, *The Prisoner of Zenda* (1898)
Innes, Michael, *From London Far* (1946)
James, P. D., *Innocent Blood* (1980)
Mann, Jessica, *Funeral Sites* (1982)
Morgan, Janet, *Agatha Christie* (1984)
Moyes, Patricia, *Who Is Simon Warwick?* (1978)
Parker, Robert B., *The Judas Goat* (1978)
Perry, Anne, *Callander Square* (1980); *Traitors Gate* (1995)
Rendell, Ruth, *From Doom with Death* (1965)
Ross, Kate, *A Broken Vessel* (1994)

Sayers, Dorothy L., "The Vindictive Story of Footsteps that Ran" (1972); *Busman's Honeymoon* (play) (1937); *Gaudy Night* (1936); *Love All* (1940); *Murder Must Advertise* (1933); *Strong Poison* (1930); *The Documents in the Case* (1930); *Unnatural Death* (1927); *Whose Body?* (1923)
Simonson, Sheila, *Skylark* (1992)
Symons, Julian, *The Blackheath Poisonings* (1978)
Tey, Josephine, *The Daughter of Time* (1951)
Truman, Margaret, *Murder in the Smithsonian* (1983)
Underwood, Peter, *Haunted London* (1973)
Wentworth, Patricia, *The Case Is Closed* (1937)
Yorke, Margaret, *Cast for Death* (1976)

BLOOMSBURY WALK: Sleuths

Robert Amiss Edwards
Professor James Asher Hambly
Father Brown Chesterton
Superintendent Adam Dalgleish James
Lark Dodge Simonson
Dr. Gideon Fell Carr
Gervase Fen Crispin
Inspector Alan Grant Tey
Patrick Grant Yorke
Sheridan Haynes Symons
Greg Hocking Barnard
Sherlock Holmes Doyle
Tamara Hoyland Mann
Julian Kestrel Ross
Lovejoy Gash
Heather McBean Truman
Meredith Innes
Charlotte and Thomas Pitt Perry
Peter Proctor Barnard
Jemima Shore Fraser
Miss Maud Silver Wentworth
Spenser Parker
Nigel Strangeways Blake
Henry Tibbett Moyes
Philip Trent Bentley

James Tyrone Francis
Harriet Vane Sayers
Chief Inspector Wexford Rendell
Lord Peter Wimsey Sayers

SOHO WALK: Authors and Books

Allingham, Margery, *Black Plumes* (1940); *Tether's End* (1969); *Tiger in the Smoke* (1969)
Brett, Simon, *Not Dead, Only Resting* (1984)
Buchan, John, *The Three Hostages* (1924)
Byrne, Murial St. Clare, *Busman's Honeymoon* (play, 1937)
Chesterton, G. K., *The Man Who Was Thursday* (1908)
Christie, Agatha, *The Big Four* (1927); *The Secret Adversary* (1922); *The Seven Dials Mystery* (1929)
Cooper, Natasha, *A Common Death* (1990); *Bitter Herbs* (1993); *Poison Flowers* (1991)
Creasey, John, *The Masters of Bow Street* (1974); *The Toff and the Deadly Parson* (1944)
Crispin, Edmund, *Frequent Hearses* (1950); *Swan Song* (1947)
Doyle, Sir Arthur Conan, *A Study in Scarlet* (1900)
Grimes, Martha, *The Dirty Duck* (1984)
Hambly, Barbara, *Those Who Hunt the Night* (1988)
Hanff, Helene, *Eighty-Four Charing Cross Road* (1970)
Heyer, Georgette, *Death in the Stocks* (1952)
Innes, Michael, *From London Far* (1946)
James, P. D., *An Unsuitable Job for a Woman* (1972); *The Skull Beneath the Skin* (1982); *Unnatural Causes* (1967)
LeCarre, John, *Tinker, Tailor, Soldier, Spy* (1974)
MacInnes, Helen, *Cloak of Darkness* (1982)
Marric, J. J. (John Creasey), *Gideon's Wrath* (1967)
Marsh, Ngaio, *A Surfeit of Lampreys* (1941); *Artists in Crime* (1938); *Death in Ecstasy* (1976)
Meyers, Amy, *Murder at Plum's* (1989)
Mitchell, Gladys, *Watson's Choice* (1975)
More, Sir Thomas, *Historie of Richard III* (1548)
Morice, Anne, *The Men in her Death* (1981)
Parker, Robert B., *The Judas Goat* (1978)
Perry, Anne, *Bluegate Fields* (1984); *Resurrection Row* (1981); *The Devil's Acre* (1985)
Ripley, Mike, *Angel Touch* (1989)

Rohmer, Sax, *The Trail of Fu Manchu* (1934)
Ross, Kate, *A Broken Vessel* (1994)
Sayers, Dorothy L., "The Haunted Policeman" (1952); *Busman's Honeymoon* (play, 1937); *Clouds of Witness* (1926); *Murder Must Advertise* (1933); *The Unpleasantness at the Bellona Club* (1928); *Unnatural Death* (1927); *Whose Body?* (1923)
Simonson, Sheila, *Skylark* (1992)
Simpson, Helen, *Enter Sir John* (1928)
Stewart, Mary, *The Gabriel Hounds* (1967)
Symons, Julian, *A Three Pipe Problem* (1975); *Mortal Consequences* (1972); *The Blackheath Poisonings* (1978)
Tey, Josephine, *The Daughter of Time* (1951); *The Man in the Queue* (1953)
Wallace, Edgar, *The Crimson Circle* (1953)
Yorke, Margaret, *Cast for Death* (1976)

SOHO WALK: Sleuths

Roderick Alleyn Marsh
Fitzroy Maclean Angel Ripley
Professor James Asher Hambly
Superintendent Battle Christie
Tommy Beresford Christie
Dame Beatrice Bradley Mitchell
Father Brown Chesterton
Albert Campion Allingham
Tuppence Cowley Christie
Tessa Crighton Morice
Auguste Didier Meyers
Lark Dodge Simonson
George Felse Peters
Gervase Fen Crispin
Gideon Marric
Inspector Gideon Creasey
Inspector Alan Grant Tey
Patrick Grant Yorke
Cordelia Gray James
Inspector Hannasyde Heyer
Richard Hannay Buchan
Sheridan Haynes Symons
Superintendent Jury Grimes
Julian Kestrel Ross

Willow King Cooper
Meredith Innes
Charles Paris Brett
Inspector Parr Wallace
Charlotte and Thomas Pitt Perry
Hercule Poirot Christie
Robert Renwick MacInnes
Roger Sheringham Berkeley
George Smiley Le Carre
Sir Denis Nayland Smith Rohmer
Spenser Parker
The Toff Creasey
Dr. Watson Doyle
Lord Peter Wimsey Sayers

MAYFAIR/OXFORD STREET WALK: Authors and Books

Allingham, Margery, *Black Plumes* (1940); *Police at the Funeral* (1932)
Babson, Marion, *Tourists Are for Trapping* (1989)
Barnard, Robert, *A Scandal in Belgravia* (1991)
Berkeley, Anthony, *The Piccadilly Murder* (1930); *The Poisoned Chocolates Case* (1929)
Blake, Nicholas, *Minute for Murder* (1977)
Brightwell, Emily, *Mrs. Jeffries on the Ball* (1994)
Buchan, John, *The Three Hostages* (1924)
Butler, Gwendoline, *Coffin on Murder Street* (1991)
Carr, John Dickson, *The Skeleton in the Clock* (1948)
Chan, C. M., "Murder at Christmas" (1990)
Christie, Agatha, "The Case of the Middle-Aged Wife" (1934); *At Bertram's Hotel* (1965); *Mr. Parker Pyne, Detective* (1934); *The Golden Ball* (1934); *The Mystery of the Blue Train* (1928); *The Secrety Adversary* (1922); *The Secret of Chimneys* (1925)
Creasey, John, *The Baron and the Missing Old Masters* (1969); *The Toff and the Deadly Parson* (1944)
Crispin, Edmund, *Frequent Hearses* (1950)
Doyle, Sir Arthur Conan, "The Adventures of the Bruce-Partington Plans" (1900); "The Adventure of the Illustrious Client" (1900)
Edwards, Ruth Dudley, *English School Murder* (1990)
Francis, Dick, *Forfeit* (1968)
Fraser, Antonia, *Cool Repentance* (1982); *Quiet as a Nun* (1977)

Gilbert, Michael, *Death Has Deep Roots* (1978)
Grimes, Martha, *I Am the Only Running Footman* (1986); *The Dirty Duck* (1984)
Hambly, Barbara, *Those Who Hunt the Night* (1988)
Heyer, Georgette, *Regency Buck* (1966)
James, P. D., *An Unsuitable Job for a Woman* (1972)
Keating, H. R. F., *Inspector Ghote Hunts the Peacock* (1968)
Mann, Jessica, *Funeral Sites* (1982); *Grave Goods* (1985)
Marsh, Ngaio, *A Surfeit of Lampreys* (1941); *A Wreath for Rivera* (1949); *Death in a White Tie* (1938); *Death in Ecstasy* (1936)
Meyers, Amy, *Murder at Plum's* (1989)
Morice, Anne, *The Men in Her Death* (1981)
Mortimer, John, *Rumpole of the Bailey* (1978)
Moyes, Patricia, *Who Is Simon Warwick?* (1978)
Orczy, Baroness, *Lady Molly of Scotland Yard* (1926)
Parker, Robert B., *The Judas Goat* (1978)
Rohmer, Sax, *The Trail of Fu Manchu* (1934)
Ross, Kate, *A Broken Vessel* (1994)
Sayers, Dorothy L., "The Article in Question" (1952); *Busman's Honeymoon* (play, 1937); *Clouds of Witness* (1926); *The Documents in the Case* (1930); *The Unpleasantness at the Belonna Club* (1928); *Unnatural Death* (1927); *Whose Body?* (1923)
Scholefield, Alan, *Threats and Menaces* (1993)
Simonson, Sheila, *Skylark* (1992)
Smith, Joan (Canadian), *Behold, A Mystery!* (1994)
Symons, Julian, *A Three Pipe Problem* (1975); *The Blackheath Poisonings* (1978)
Tey, Josephine, *The Daughter of Time* (1951)
Theroux, Paul, "Half Moon Street" (1984)
Underwood, Peter, *Haunted London* (1973)
Wallace, Edgar, *The Crimson Circle* (1953)
Walpole, Horace, *The Castle of Otranto* (1908)
Wentworth, Patricia, *Spotlight* (1975)
Winn, Dilys, ed., *Murder Ink* (1984)
Yorke, Margaret, *Find Me a Villian* (1986)

MAYFAIR/OXFORD STREET WALK: Sleuths

Roderick Alleyn Marsh
Robert Amiss Edwards
Ashenden Maugham

Professor James Asher Hambly
The Baron Creasey
Albert Campion Allingham
John Coffin Butler
Tessa Crighton Morice
Auguste Didier Meyers
Lark Dodge Simonson
Gervase Fen Crispin
Inspector Ghote Keating
Inspector Alan Grant Tey
Patrick Grant Yorke
Cordelia Gray James
Jessica Greenwood Smith (Canadian)
Inspector Hannasyde Heyer
M. Hannaud Mason
Richard Hannay Buchan
Sheridan Haynes Symons
Inspector Hazelrigg Gilbert
Sherlock Holmes Doyle
Tamara Hoyland Mann
Mrs. Jeffries Brightwell
Superintendent Jury Grimes
Julian Kestrel Ross
Detective Superintendent George Macrae Scholefield
Miss Jane Marple Christie
Sir Henry Merrivale Carr
Lady Molly Orczy
Inspector Parr Wallace
Douglas Perkins Babson
Peter Proctor Barnard
Rumpole Mortimer
Jemima Shore Fraser
Roger Sheringham Berkeley
Leo Silver Scholefield
Miss Maud Silver Wentworth
Spenser Parker
Nigel Strangeways Blake
The Toff Creasey
Philip Trent Bentley
James Tyrone Francis
Lord Peter Wimsey Sayers

ST. JAMES WALK: Authors and Books

Allingham, Margery, *Black Plumes* (1940)
Brand, Christianna, *Fog of Doubt* (1953)
Buchan, John, *The Thirty-Nine Steps* (1919); *The Three Hostages* (1903)
Carr, John Dickson, *The Bride of Newgate* (1950); *The Skeleton in the Clock* (1948)
Christie, Agatha, *At Bertram's Hotel* (1965); *The Golden Ball* (1934); *The Mousetrap* (play, 1949); *The Mystery of the Blue Train* (1928); *The Secrety Adversary* (1922); *The Secret of Chimneys* (1925); *The Seven Dials Mysters* (1929)
Cooper, Natasha, *A Common Death* (1990); *Poison Flowers* (1991)
Edwards, Ruth Dudley, *English School Murder* (1990)
Fraser, Antonia, *A Splash of Red* (1981)
Greene, Graham, *The Human Factor* (1978)
Heyer, Georgette, *Death in the Stocks* (1952); *Duplicate Death* (1951); *Regency Buck* (1966)
Innes, Michael, *From London Far* (1946)
Mann, Jessica, *Funeral Sites* (1982)
Marsh, Ngaio, *A Wreath for Rivera* (1949); *Black As He's Painted* (1974)
Metzger, Barbara, *A Suspicious Affair* (1994)
Meyers, Amy, *Murder at Plum's* (1989)
Milne, A. A. "Buckingham Palace" (1926); *The Red House Mystery* (1922)
Morgan, Janet, *Agatha Christie* (1984)
Parker, Robert B., *The Judas Goat* (1978)
Sayers, Dorothy L., *Busman's Honeymoon* (play, 1937); *Clouds of Witness* (1927); *Gaudy Night* (1936); *Have His Carcase* (1932); *Love All* (1940); *Murder Must Advertise* (1933); *The Unpleasantness at the Bellona Club* (1928); *Unnatural Death* (1927); *Whose Body?* (1923)
Symons, Julian, *Mortal Consequences* (1972); *The Blackheath Poisonings* (1978)
Truman, Margeret, *Murder on Embassy Row* (1984)
Yorke, Margaret, *Cast for Death* (1976); *Find Me a Villian* (1986)

ST. JAMES WALK: Sleuths

Roderick Alleyn Marsh
Robert Amiss Edwards

Superintendent Battle Christie
Tommy Beresford Christie
Inspector Butler Greene
Albert Campion Allington
Inspector Cockrill Brand
Tuppence Cowley Christie
Auguste Didier Meyers
Mr. Jeremiah Dimm Metzger
Detective-Inspector Farrell Christie
Patrick Grant Yorke
Inspector Hannasyde Heyer
Richard Hannay Buchan
Sheridan Haynes Symons
Sherlock Holmes Doyle
Tamara Hoyland Mann
Willow King Cooper
Miss Marple Christie
Heather McBean Truman
Meredith Innes
Sir Henry Merrivale Carr
Hercule Poirot Christie
Raffles Hornung
Jemima Shore Fraser
Spenser Parker
Lord Peter Wimsey Sayers

MARYLEBONE/REGENT'S PARK WALK: Authors and Books

Allingham, Margery, *Tether's End* (1969)
Babson, Marian, *Bejewelled Death* (1981); *The Twelve Deaths of Christmas* (1977)
Blake, Nicholas, *Minute for Murder* (1977)
Brand, Christianna, *Fog of Doubt* (1953)
Brett, Simon, *Not Dead, Only Resting* (1984)
Buchan, John, *The Thirty-Nine Steps* (1919); *The Three Hostages* (1934)
Byrne, Murial St. Clare, *Busman's Honeymoon* (play, 1937)
Charteris, Leslie, "The Beauty Specialist" (1936)
Chesterton, G. K., *The Man Who Was Thursday* (1908)
Christie, Agatha, *At Bertram's Hotel* (1965); *The Secret of Chimneys* (1925)

Collins, Wilkie, *The Moonstone* (1868)
Detection Club, "Behind the Screen" (radio serial, 1930); "The Scoop" (radio serial, 1932); *Crime on the Coast* (1932); *The Floating Admiral* (1932)
Doyle, Sir Auther Conan, "A Scandal in Bohemia" (1900); "The Adventure of the Illustrious Client" (1900); "The Final Problem" (1900); "The Mazarin Stone" (1900); "The Valley of Fear" (1900)
Edwards, Ruth Dudley, *Egnlish School Murder* (1990)
Francis, Dick, *Forfeit* (1968)
Fraser, Antonia, *A Splash of Red* (1981); *Jemima Shore Investigates* (1983)
Gash, Jonathan, *The Very Last Gambado* (1991)
Granger, Ann, *Say It with Poison* (1991)
Hambly, Barbara, *Those Who Hunt the Night* (1988)
Hervey, Evelyn (H. R. F. Keating), *The Man of Gold* (1985)
Heyer, Georgette, *Regency Buck* (1966)
James, Henry, *The Turn of the Screw* (1898)
James, P. D., *Innocent Blood* (1980); *The Skull Beneath the Skin* (1982)
Keating, H. R. F., *Inspector Ghote Hunts the Peacock* (1968)
Marsh, Ngaio, *Death in a White Tie* (1938)
Mason, A. E. W., *The House in Lordship Lane* (1946)
Morice, Anne, *The Men in Her Death* (1981)
Orczy, Baroness, *Lady Molly of Scotland Yard* (1926); "The Woman in the Big Hat" (1908)
Parker, Robert B., *The Judas Goat* (1978)
Sayers, Dorothy L., *Busman's Honeymoon* (play, 1937); *The Unpleasantness at the Bellona Club* (1928); *Whose Body?* (1923)
Smith, Joan (English), *A Masculine Ending* (1987)
Symons, Julian, "'Twixt the Cup and the Lip" (1963); *A Three Pipe Problem* (1975)
Tey, Josephine, *The Man in the Queue* (1953)
Wallace, Edgar, *The Crimson Circle* (1953)

MARYLEBONE/REGENT'S PARK WALK: Sleuths

Roderick Alleyn Marsh
Robert Amiss Edwards
Professor James Asher Hambly
Superintendent Battle Christie

Father Brown Chesterton
Albert Campion Allingham
Inspector Cockrill Brand
Tessa Crighton Morice
Sergeant Cuff Collins
Inspector Ghote Keating
Inspector Alan Grant Tey
Cordelia Gray James
M. Hannaud Mason
Richard Hannay Buchan
Sheridan Haynes Symons
Sherlock Holmes Doyle
Detective Superintendent Knowles Babson
Lady Molly Orczy
Loretta Lawson Smith (English)
Lovejoy Gash
Chief Inspector Markby Granger
Miss Marple Christie
Meredith Mitchell Granger
Charles Paris Brett
Inspector Parr Wallace
Jemima Shore Fraser
Spenser Parker
Nigel Strangeways Blake
Simon Templar Charteris
James Tyrone Francis
Miss Unwin Hervey
Dr. Watson Doyle
Lord Peter Wimsey Sayers

WESTMINSTER WALK: Authors and Books

Allingham, Margery, *Black Plumes* (1940); *Tether's End* (1969)
Bentley, E. C., *Trent's Last Case* (1941)
Berkeley, Anthony, *The Piccadilly Murder* (1930); *The Poisoned Chocolates Case* (1929)
Blake, Nicholas, *Minute for Murder* (1977)
Buchan, John, *The Thirty-Nine Steps* (1919)
Carr, John Dickson, *Fire Burn!* (1957); *The Mad Hatter Mystery* (1950); *The Skeleton in the Clock* (1948)
Caudwell, Sarah, *Thus Was Adonis Murdered* (1981)

Chesterton, G. K., "The Eye of Apollo" (1911); *The Man Who Was Thursday* (1908)
Christie, Agatha, *At Bertram's Hotel* (1965); *The Big Four* (1927); *The Secret Adversary* (1922); *The Secret of Chimneys* (1925)
Cooper, Natasha, *Bitter Herbs* (1993)
Creasey, John, *The Masters of Bow Street* (1974)
Crispin, Edmund, *Frequent Hearses* (1950)
Doyle, Sir Arthur Conan, "His Last Bow" (1900); "The Adventure of the Bruce-Partington Plans" (1900); "The Noble Bachelor" (1900); "The Priory School" (1900); "The Second Stain" (1900); *The Hound of Baskervilles* (1930)
Fraser, Antonia, *A Splash of Red* (1981)
James, Henry, *The Turn of the Screw* (1898)
James, P. D., *An Unsuitable Job for a Woman* (1972)
Linscott, Gillian, *Sister Beneath the Sheet* (1991)
Mann, Jessica, *Funeral Sites* (1982)
Marsh, Ngaio, *A Surfeit of Lampreys* (1941); *A Wreath for Rivera* (1949); *Black As He's Painted* (1974)
Orczy, Baroness, *Lady Molly of Scotland Yard* (1926)
Palmer, Willialm J., *The Highwayman and Mr. Dickens* (1992)
Parker, Robert B., *The Judas Goat* (1978)
Perry, Anne, *Resurrection Row* (1981)
Rohmer, Sax, *The Trail of Fu Manchu* (1934)
Sayers, Dorothy L., *Busman's Honeymoon* (play, 1937); *Clouds of Witness* (1926); *Gaudy Night* (1936); *Murder Must Advertise* (1933); *The Documents in the Case* (1930); *Thrones, Dominations* (unpublished); *Whose Body?* (1923)
Simonson, Sheila, *Skylark* (1992)
Snow, C. P., "Corridors of Power" (1964)
Symons, Julian, *A Three Pipe Problem* (1975); *Mortal Consequences* (1972)
Tey, Josephine, *The Daughter of Time* (1951)
Thomson, Basil, *The Story of Scotland Yard* (1936)
Wallace, Edgar, *The Crimson Circle* (1953)
Williams, Charles, *All Hallows' Eve* (1948)
Winn, Dilys, ed., *Murderess Ink* (1979)
Yorke, Margaret, *Cast for Death* (1976)

WESTMINSTER WALK: Sleuths

Roderick Alleyn Marsh
Superintendent Battle Christie

Tommy Beresford Christie
Nell Bray Linscott
Father Brown Chesterton
Albert Campion Allingham
Tuppence Cowley Christie
Superintendent Adam Dalgleish James
Charles Dickens Palmer
Lark Dodge Simonson
Dr. Gideon Fell Carr
Gervase Fen Crispin
Inspector Alan Grant Tey
Patrick Grant Yorke
Cordelia Gray James
Richard Hannay Buchan
Sheridan Haynes Symons
Chief Inspector Hazelrigg Gilbert
Sherlock Holmes Doyle
Tamara Hoyland Mann
Willow King Cooper
Lady Molly Orczy
Sir Henry Merrivale Dickson (Carr)
Inspector Parr Wallace
Charlotte and Thomas Pitt Perry
Hercule Poirot Christie
Roger Sheringham Berkeley
Jemima Shore Fraser
Sir Denis Nayland Smith Rohmer
Spenser Parker
Nigel Strangeways Blake
Hilary Tamar Caudwell
The Toff Creasey
Philip Trent Bentley
Dr. Watson Doyle
Lord Peter Wimsey Sayers

BROMPTON/HYDE PARK WALK: Authors and Books

Anthony, Evelyn, *Avenue of the Dead* (1982)
Barnard, Robert, *A Scandal in Belgravia* (1991)
Brightwell, Emily, *Mrs. Jeffries on the Ball* (1994)
Chesterton, G. K., *The Man Who Was Thursday* (1908)
Christie, Agatha, *The Big Four* (1927)

Cooper, Natasha, *Poison Flowers* (1991)
Creasey, John, *The Masters of Bow Street* (1974)
Francis, Dick, *Odds Against* (1965)
Fraser, Antonia, *A Splash of Red* (1981)
Heyer, Georgette, *An Infamous Army* (1953); *Behold, Here's Poison* (1971); *Death in the Stocks* (1952); *Regency Buck* (1966)
Household, Geoffrey, *Hostage: London* (1977)
James, P. D., *Innocent Blood* (1980)
Mann, Jessica, *Funeral Sites* (1982)
Marsh, Ngaio, *A Surfeit of Lampreys* (1941); *Black As He's Painted* (1974); *Death in Ecstasy* (1936)
Moody, Susan, *Death Takes a Hand* (1993)
Morice, Anne, *The Men in Her Death* (1981)
Orczy, Baroness, *Lady Molly of Scotland Yard* (1926)
Parker, Robert B., *The Judas Goat* (1978)
Perry, Anne, *The Hyde Park Headsman* (1994)
Sayers, Dorothy L., *Murder Must Advertise* (1933)
Scholefield, Alan, *Threats and Menaces* (1993)
Simonson, Sheila, *Skylark* (1992)
Stallwood, Veronica, *Death and the Oxford Box* (1993)
Symons, Julian, *A Three Pipe Problem* (1975); *The Blackheath Poisonings* (1978)
Tey, Josephine, *The Daughter of Time* (1951); *The Man in the Queue* (1953)
Wentworth, Patricia, *The Case of William Smith* (1948)
Yorke, Margaret, *Cast for Death* (1976)

BROMPTON/HYDE PARK WALK: Sleuths

Roderick Alleyn Marsh
Father Brown Chesterton
Tessa Crighton Morice
Lark Dodge Simonson
Davina Graham Anthony
Inspector Alan Grant Tey
Patrick Grant Yorke
Sid Halley Francis
Inspector Hannasyde Heyer
Sheridan Haynes Symons
Tamara Hoyland Mann

Kate Ivory Stallwood
Mrs. Jeffries Brightwell
Willow King Cooper
Lady Molly Orczy
Detective-Superintendent George Macrae Scholefield
Charlotte and Thomas Pitt Perry
Hercule Poirot Christie
Peter Proctor Barnard
Jemima Shore Fraser
Miss Maud Silver Wentworth
Spenser Parker
Cassandra Swann Moody
Lord Peter Wimsey Sayers

CHELSEA WALK: Authors and Books

Allingham, Margery, *Mystery Mile* (1929)
Babson, Marian, *Bejewelled Death* (1981); *Tourists Are for Trapping* (1989)
Branch, Pamela, *The Wooden Overcoat* (1934)
Christie, Agatha, *The Secret of Chimneys* (1925)
Cooper, Natasha, *A Common Death* (1990)
Davidson, Lionel, *The Chelsea Murders* (1978)
Eliot, T. S., *Murder in the Cathedral* (1935)
Grimes, Martha, *Jerusalem Inn* (1984)
James, Henry, *The Turn of the Screw* (1898)
Keating, H. R. F., "Mrs Craggs Gives a Dose of Physic" (1967)
Lovesey, Peter, *Bertie and the Tinman* (1988)
Marsh, Ngaio, *Black As He's Painted* (1974); *Death in a White Tie* (1938); *Killer Dolphin* (1966)
Meyers, Amy, *Murder at Plum's* (1989)
Milne, A. A., *The Red House Mystery* (1969)
Moyes, Patricia, *Who Is Simon Warwick?* (1978)
Sayers, Dorothy L., *Busman's Honeymoon* (play, 1937); *The Unpleasantness at the Bellona Club* (1928)
Simonson, Sheila, *Skylark* (1992)
Smith, Joan (Canadian), *Behold, A Mystery!* (1994)
Smollett, Tobias, *The Adventures of Peregrine Pickle* (1751); *The Expedition of Humphrey Clinker* (1771)
Stoker, Bram, *Dracula* (1897)

CHELSEA WALK: Sleuths

Roderick Alleyn Marsh
Albert Campion Allingham
Auguste Didier Meyers
Lark Dodge Simonson
Inspector Ghote Keating
Jessica Greenwood Smith (Canadian)
Superintendent Jury Grimes
Willow King Cooper
Miss Jane Marple Christie
Detective Mason Davidson
Stacey Orpington Babson
Douglas Perkins Babson
Henry Tibbett Moyes
Lord Peter Wimsey Sayers

BELGRAVIA/PIMLICO WALK: Authors and Books

Allingham, Margery, *Flowers for the Judge* (1969)
Barnard, Robert, *A Scandal in Belgravia* (1991)
Berkeley, Anthony, *The Poisoned Chocolates Case* (1929)
Bickham, Jack M., *Breakfast at Wimbledon* (1991)
Chesterton, G. K., "The Blue Cross" (1911); "The Queer Feet" (1911); *The Innocence of Father Brown* (1911)
Cooper, Natasha, *Bloody Roses* (1992)
Cutter, Leela, *Death of the Party* (1985)
Doyle, Sir Arthur Conan, *The Sign of Four* (1890)
Edwards, Ruth Dudley, *English School Murder* (1990)
Fraser, Antonia, *A Splash of Red* (1981); *Cool Repentance* (1982); *Quiet as a Nun* (1977)
Heyer, Georgette, *Death in the Stocks* (1952); *Duplicate Death* (1951)
James, P. D., *Innocent Blood* (1980); *The Skull Beneath the Skin* (1982)
Mackey, Aidan, *Mr. Chesterton Comes to Tea* (1978)
Mann, Jessica, *Grave Goods* (1985)
Marsh, Ngaio, *A Wreath for Rivera* (1949); *Death in a White Tie* (1938); *Death in Ecstasy* (1936)
Moyes, Patricia, *Who Is Simon Warwick?* (1978)
Perry, Anne, *Farrier's Lane* (1993); *The Devil's Acre* (1985)

Rohmer, Sax, *The Trail of Fu Manchu* (1934)
Sayers, Dorothy L., *Unnatural Death* (1927)
Simonson, Sheila, *Skylark* (1992)
Snow, C. P., *A Coat of Varnish* (1979)
Tey, Josephine, *The Man in the Queue* (1953)
Williams, Charles, *All Hallows' Eve* (1948)

BELGRAVIA/PIMLICO WALK: Sleuths

Roderick Alleyn Marsh
Robert Amiss Edwards
Father Brown Chesterton
Albert Campion Allingham
Lark Dodge Simonson
Inspector Alan Grant Tey
Cordelia Gray James
Inspector Hannasyde Heyer
Sherlock Holmes Doyle
Tamara Hoyland Mann
Willow King Cooper
Miss Marple Christie
Charlotte and Thomas Pitt Perry
Peter Proctor Barnard
Robert Sheringham Berkeley
Jemima Shore Fraser
George Smiley LeCarre
Brad Smith Bickham
Sir Denis Nayland Smith Rohmer
Henry Tibbett Moyes
Dr. Watson Doyle
Lord Peter Wimsey Sayers
Lettie Winterbottom Cutter

HAMPSTEAD/HIGHGATE WALK: Authors and Books

Chesterton, G. K., "The Blue Cross" (1911)
Collins, Wilkie, *The Woman in White* (1900)
Crombie, Deborah, *All Shall Be Well* (1994)
Cutter, Leela, *Death of the Party* (1985)
Erskine, Barbara, *Midnight Is a Lonely Place* (1994)

Grindle, Lucretia, *The Killing of Ellis Martin* (1993)
Hambly, Barbara, *Those Who Hunt the Night* (1988)
Irving, Washington, *Tales of a Traveller* (1824)
La Plante, Lynda, *Prime Suspect 3* (1994)
Linscott, Gillian, *Sister Beneath the Sheet* (1991)
Mitchell, Gladys, *Watson's Choice* (1975)
Morice, Anne, *The Men in Her Death* (1981)
Palmer, William J., *The Highwayman and Mr. Dickens* (1992)
Perry, Anne, *Highgate Rise* (1991)
Ross, Kate, *A Broken Vessel* (1994)
Smith, Joan (English), *A Masculine Ending* (1987)
Stevenson, Robert Louis, *The Strange Case of Dr. Jekyl and Mr. Hyde* (1886)
Underwood, Peter, *Haunted London* (1973)

HAMPSTEAD/HIGHGATE WALK: Sleuths

Professor James Asher Hambly
Dame Beatrice Bradley Mitchell
Nell Bray Linscott
Father Brown Chesterton
Sergeant Cuff Collins
Kate Kennedy Erskine
Julian Kestrel Ross
Duncan Kincaid Crombie
Loretta Lawson Smith (English)
Charlotte and Thomas Pitt Perry
Chief Inspector Ross Grindle
Lettie Winterbottom Cutter

BIBLIOGRAPHY

These are the books that were especially helpful in preparing this guide:

Cawelti, John G. *Adventure, Mystery and Romance*. Chicago: The University of Chicago Press, n.d.

Clark, Stephen P. *The Lord Peter Wimsey Companion*. New York: The Mysterious Press, 1985.

Crowl, Philip A. *The Intelligent Traveller's Guide to Historic Britain*. New York: Congdon & Weed, Inc., 1983.

Dale, Alzina Stone. *Maker and Craftsman*. Grand Rapids, MI: William B. Eerdmans, 1987.

______. *The Outline of Sanity*. Grand Rapids, MI: William B. Eerdmans, 1982.

Francis, Dick. *The Sport of Queens*. London: Pan Books, 1974.

Han, Robert W., ed. *Sincerely, Tony/Faithfully, Vincent, The Correspondence of Anthony Boucher and Vincent Starrett*. Privately printed, 1975.

Haycraft, Howard, ed. *The Art of the Mystery Story*. New York: Grosset & Dunlap, 1946

______. *Murder for Pleasure*. New York: Carroll & Graff Publishers, Inc., 1984.

Hodge, Jane Aiken. *The Private World of Georgette Heyer*. London: The Bodley Head, 1984.

Honeycombe, Gordon. *The Murders of the Black Museum 1870–1970*. Special rev. ed. London: Arrow Books, 1984.

Keating, H. R. F., ed. *Agatha Christie, First Lady of Crime*. New York: Holt, Rinehart, and Winston, 1977.

Lejeune, Anthony. *The Gentlemen's Clubs of London.* New York: Dorset Press, 1984.

Marsh, Ngaio. *Black and Honeydew, An Autobiography.* London: Collins, 1966.

Morgan, Janet. *Agatha Christie.* London: Collins, 1984.

Morley, Frank. *Literary Britain.* New York: Dorset Press, 1983.

Penzler, Otto, ed. *The Great Detectives.* New York: Penquin Books, 1979.

Sanders, Ann. *The Art and Architecture of London.* Oxford: Phaidon Press, 1984.

Sayers, Dorothy L., and Muriel St. Clare Byrne. *Love All.* Alzina Stone Dale, ed. Kent, OH: Kent State University Press, 1984.

Symons, Julian. *Great Detectives.* New York: Harry N. Abrams, Inc., Publishers, 1981.

______. *Mortal Consequences.* New York: Schocken Books, 1973.

______. *The Tell-Tale Heart, The Life and Works of Edgar Allen Poe.* Middlesex: Penquin Books, 1978.

Winks, Robin W. *Modus Operandi, An Excursion into Detective Fiction.* Boston: David R. Godine, Publisher, n.d.

Winn, Dilys, ed. *Murder Ink.* New York: Workman Publishing, 1977.

______, ed. *Murderess Ink.* New York: Bell Publishing, 1981.

INDEX